A GRIM ALMANAC OF

OXFORDSHIRE

A GRIM ALMANAC OF

OXFORDSHIRE

NICOLA SLY

First published 2013

The History Press
The Mill, Brimscombe Port
Stroud, Gloucestershire, GL5 2QG
www.thehistorypress.co.uk

Reprinted 2017

British Library Cataloguing in Publication Data.
A catalogue record for this book is available from the British Library.

ISBN 978 0 7524 6581 4

Typesetting and origination by The History Press
Printed in Great Britain by TJ International Ltd, Padstow, Cornwall

CONTENTS

ALSO BY
THE AUTHOR

INTRODUCTION &
ACKNOWLEDGEMENTS

Beneath Oxfordshire's apparent cultured and peaceful façade lurks a historical catalogue of dark deeds and shocking scenarios which, on occasions, seem to beggar belief. However, all the stories within are true and are sourced entirely from the contemporary newspapers listed in the bibliography at the rear of the book. Much as today, not everything was reported accurately and there were frequent discrepancies between publications, with differing dates and variations in names and spelling – in addition, the county boundaries of Oxfordshire and Berkshire historically seem very fluid, so even the location of events sometimes seems to change at will, depending on which newspaper reports them.

As always, there are a number of people to whom I owe a debt of gratitude for their assistance. The *Oxford Mail* kindly gave me permission to use one of their archive pictures as an illustration. On a personal level, I couldn't have written this book without the support of my husband, Richard, and I would also like to thank Matilda Richards, my editor at The History Press, for her help and encouragement in bringing this book to print.

Every effort has been made to clear copyright; however, my apologies to anyone I may have inadvertently missed. I can assure you it was not deliberate but an oversight on my part.

Nicola Sly, 2013

JANUARY

The Lock, Abingdon. (Author's collection)

1 JANUARY

1895 Coroner Henry F. Galpin held an inquest into the death of Marston farmer James Aries.

On 30 December 1894, the farmer's neighbours heard him shouting. Richard Smith sent his workman to see what Aries wanted, and Charles Culley found sixty-one-year-old Aries lying in his porch, a revolver about a yard away. 'Is it done accidental or no?' Culley asked, and Aries replied, 'No.' He gave the same response when Smith asked him that question.

Aries was taken to hospital, where surgeons found a single gunshot wound in his chest. They determined that the revolver must have been held very close to Aries' body when it was fired.

Once in hospital, Aries was adamant that the shooting was an accident. He had purchased the gun three months earlier for protection against burglars and now, according to Aries, 'The thing wouldn't go off and I was looking at it and it shot me.'

Aries' adopted son, Frank Haynes, told the inquest that his father was 'jolly' shortly before shooting himself and added that there was nothing about his affairs to suggest that he might be contemplating suicide. Aries had told him that his gun was malfunctioning and that 'a man who knows about such things' said that it just needed more regular use.

When Aries died from internal bleeding, it was left to the inquest jury to decide between suicide and accidental death – they chose the latter option.

2 JANUARY

1894 Coroner Mr Robinson held an inquest at the vicarage, Beckley, into the death of Revd George Theophilus Cooke.

The vicar had been feeling a little under the weather and his doctor prescribed a tonic for neuralgia and rheumatism. On 30 December, Cooke's sister, Caroline, collected a fresh bottle of the tonic, purchasing a large bottle of carbolic acid for domestic cleaning at the same time. She left the carbolic acid on the piano in the drawing room and placed her brother's medicine on a table outside his bedroom.

That evening, seventy-four-year-old Cooke, who had no sense of smell, came to his sister's room complaining about the taste of the tonic and saying that it burned his mouth. When Caroline investigated, she found that he had taken the carbolic acid from the drawing room and, in spite of the fact that it was clearly labelled 'Poison', had drunk a teaspoonful under the mistaken impression it was his tonic. Although every effort was made to induce Cooke to vomit with mustard, salt water and ipecacuanha, he died within fifteen minutes.

The inquest jury returned a verdict of 'death from accidental poisoning.'

3 JANUARY

1853 After heavy rains, a railway tunnel near Wolvercote had collapsed and was under repair, limiting the amount of traffic that the line could cope with. At Oxford Station, a passenger train waited to depart but was prohibited from leaving the station until the 5.20 p.m. coal train arrived.

A telegraph was received to say that the coal train had left Islip and, shortly afterwards, a ballast train belonging to the contractors working on the tunnel pulled into the station. The driver of the passenger train wrongly assumed that this was the coal train and set off, disregarding all the signals against him.

Guard Joseph Kinch realised his driver's mistake and waved his flag and the station porter blew his whistle, but the driver and stoker didn't notice them. At a bridge just outside Oxford, the wrong signal was unaccountably displayed, showing a green light for the driver to proceed.

The passenger train, carrying twenty-one passengers, and the coal train collided head-on less than a mile from the station, killing six people outright. Two more died within days and many were badly injured.

An inquest was opened and adjourned, since Kinch, who was a key witness, was not well enough to appear. The proceedings eventually concluded on 16 January with a verdict of manslaughter against Kinch, on the grounds that he bore the ultimate responsibility for starting the train. He was promptly arrested but acquitted at his trial at the Oxford Assizes on 3 March.

4 JANUARY

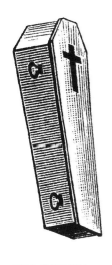

1899 A letter was read out at the regular meeting of the Chipping Norton Board of Guardians concerning a complaint made to Messrs H. and C. Burden about a defective coffin.

Burden's supplied all of the coffins used for parish funerals and, at a recent pauper's funeral at Milton-under-Wychwood, the mourners complained that the body was clearly visible inside the coffin and that the stink emanating from within was unacceptable.

In response to the complaint by the Board of Guardians, Messrs Burden wrote that, like all of their coffins, this one was made from sound elm boards, well and properly put together and well pitched inside. If the corpse was visible, it was because the lid wasn't properly screwed down, and since this occurred at the Workhouse, Burden's felt that they couldn't be held responsible.

It was established that, after death, the corpse became so swollen with gas that it no longer fitted the purpose-made coffin and, fearing that it might explode, the Workhouse staff were keen to get it buried as soon as possible.

5 JANUARY

1900 Thirty-two-year-old Edwin James Harris appeared before magistrates at the Oxford City Court, charged with assaulting and threatening his wife with violence on 29 December.

Harris's wife and daughter both testified that Harris punched his wife in the forehead and then picked up a carving knife, with which he threatened to cut her throat. However, when Harris himself entered the witness box, he swore 'before God his maker' that his wife and daughter had sworn falsely against him, adding that he might at times have 'kicked up a bit of a row' but had never laid a finger on his wife.

In spite of his protests, the Bench found him guilty of aggravated assault, fining him £1, with 9s costs or one month's hard labour in default. Mrs Harris promptly applied for a separation order, which the magistrates granted, ordering Harris to pay 8s a week maintenance.

6 JANUARY

1899 An inquest was held at the Radcliffe Infirmary by coroner Mr H.F. Galpin into the death of forty-three-year-old Fred Shurmer, who died following an accident on Boxing Day 1898.

Henry Miller was driving a four-wheeled coach carrying a party of people to Headington and stopped to adjust the bridle. As he was climbing back onto the coach, the horse moved suddenly and Miller was knocked over. Finding the reins loose, the horse bolted, the passengers screaming in terror as the coach raced out of control through the streets. When it reached Magdalen Bridge, Shurmer bravely leaped out in front of the runaway horse and tried to grab the bridle.

Magdalen College and bridge, 1950s. (Author's collection)

Although nobody actually saw what happened, passers-by found Shurmer semi-conscious on the pavement and called a doctor, who transferred him to hospital, where he was initially treated for a broken ankle. By the time that doctors realised that Shurmer had internal injuries it was too late and he died from a four-inch rupture to his bladder.

At the inquest, the coroner stated that the police had been unable to find anyone who had actually witnessed what happened on the bridge, so there was only the deceased's account to his wife that he had tried to stop the coach and that nobody was to blame for his accident. The jury accepted this and returned a verdict of 'accidental death'.

7 JANUARY

1920 Fourteen-year-old Thomas Edward Newton was shooting sparrows in the garden of his parents' cottage in Wantage when he accidentally fired his rifle through a window. The bullet hit his mother in the chest, fatally wounding her.

In returning a verdict of accidental death on forty-one-year-old Mary Newton, the inquest jury asked the police to take action against the showman from the fair who sold the rifle to Thomas, and also against the person who supplied the boy with cartridges.

8 JANUARY

1933   After a severe gale, Ernest Bruce came across a fallen tree partially blocking a road near Oxford. Bruce's first thought was to warn other motorists and he ran back along the road to stop approaching traffic. The first vehicle to come along was a motorcycle, ridden by twenty-year-old James Charles Walters of Benson, near Wallingford, with James's brother, seventeen-year-old Lawrence as a pillion passenger.

Hearing the motorcycle, Bruce stepped into the road and waved his arms for it to stop. However, Walters ignored his signal and swerved round him, continuing at speed until he hit the tree. Both he and his brother were swept off the bike by a branch, dying almost immediately.

At the inquest, the jury returned two verdicts of accidental death, commending Bruce for trying to alert others to the danger.

9 JANUARY

1861   Twenty-four-year-old servant Henrietta Clarke died in Henley-upon-Thames Workhouse. She weighed only 50lb and was extremely emaciated, as well as being dirty and having gangrene in four of her toes, due to frostbite. An inquest returned a verdict of manslaughter against her employer, Robert Durno Mitchell.

Henrietta had worked for the Mitchell family since August of the previous year. Their house in Henley was hidden behind high walls and the gate was usually kept locked, so very few people actually saw Henrietta, who was said to have been in perfect health when she started her new job. However, those who did see her told the inquest that she always seemed ravenously hungry.

Chimneysweep Henry Palmer once gave Henrietta a piece of soot-covered bread from his pocket. Palmer stated that he would not have eaten the bread himself, since it was so dirty, but Henrietta bolted it as if she were starving. The people who delivered milk to the house stated that they never saw Henrietta, as they placed the milk on the top of the high wall and she took it down from inside. They related that she often gave them money to buy her a penny loaf, which they did.

A doctor was called to attend to Henrietta on 4 January and, in front of Mrs Mitchell, she told him that she always had plenty of food to eat. Henrietta was taken to the Workhouse Infirmary, where she ate ravenously, but the food came too late and she died five days after admission.

Mitchell was charged with feloniously killing Henrietta Clarke and tried at the Oxford Assizes on 4 March 1861. Mitchell's family and other servants all stated that Henrietta was well-treated and given plenty of food. Mitchell's defence counsel pointed out that Henrietta made no complaint to anyone, adding that she was free to come and go as she pleased. Although she had asked the people who delivered milk to fetch her food, she had never once complained to them about being starved.

By profession, Mitchell was a retired naval surgeon and when the jury at his trial found him not guilty, he was discharged to vigorous booing and hissing from the courtroom.

10 JANUARY

1928   An inquest was held into the death of ten-month-old John Bowen of Oxford.

Baby John was sitting on his father's knee being fed, when the glass feeding bottle slipped from Mr Bowen's hand and shattered on the floor. As it fell, Bowen tried to catch it and, in doing so, tipped the baby out of his lap. John fell onto the broken glass, severely cutting his head, and bled to death before a doctor could reach him. The inquest jury returned a verdict of 'accidental death'.

11 JANUARY

1886   An inquest was held at Shipton-on-Cherwell into the death of eight-year-old Arthur Henry Abbott. On the previous day, Arthur and five of his friends were sliding on ice on the village pond when someone mentioned that the Oxford Canal was frozen over. Excitedly, the boys rushed to a section of the canal near the churchyard to see.

The ice near the banks appeared thick enough to support their weight and Arthur decided that he was going to walk across from one side to the other. Unfortunately, the ice in the middle of the canal was much thinner that that at the edges and it gave way, plunging the little boy into the freezing cold water.

Arthur managed to hang onto the edge of the ice for five minutes until help arrived. Two men from the village went out onto the ice with horse halters, venturing as close to Arthur as they dared. They threw the halters to Arthur but he was too cold and exhausted to grab them and soon sank. His body was recovered within fifteen minutes but it proved impossible to resuscitate him.

The inquest jury returned a verdict of 'accidentally drowned'.

12 JANUARY

1805   An inquest held in Tetsworth into the death of Ruth Lee found that she had died 'by visitation of God'.

Nobody had been permitted to enter Ruth's house for many years and when neighbours noticed that she was no longer out and about in the village as she normally was, they investigated and found her dead in her bedroom.

Reports in the contemporary newspapers state: 'She had not suffered any person to enter into her apartment for a number of years; nor had a broom or any other article been used to clean it.' A number of shillings and sixpences were found on her bedside table, having been completely covered by several years' accumulation of dust. Ruth also had plenty of new bed linen but apparently preferred to sleep on the sacking of her bedstead, without even the comfort of a mattress.

13 JANUARY

1880   John 'Jacky' Cluff of North Street, Banbury, was a month short of his second birthday and, during the day, he attended nursery school, where Mrs Neighbour, also of North Street, looked after fifteen toddlers in her home.

At two o'clock in the afternoon, Mrs Neighbour briefly left the children unattended while she went to hang out some washing in her garden. When she returned, a child was missing and, on questioning the other children, she was told 'Jacky's gone'.

Mrs Neighbour assumed that John had wandered home but when there was no sign of him there, a search of the neighbourhood was quickly organised.

It wasn't until much later that somebody suggested checking Mrs Neighbour's well. The well was in a pantry off the kitchen and was usually kept covered by a wooden lid. Mrs Neighbour remembered using the well shortly before John disappeared but was sure that she had covered it and closed the pantry door after her. Nevertheless, John's body was discovered floating on the surface of the water and, on reflection, Mrs Neighbour recalled leaving the pantry door unfastened and the well only partially covered.

At the inquest, the jury charitably returned a verdict of 'accidental death', although they added that they believed that Mrs Neighbour was at fault. Coroner Mr A. Weston was clearly not happy but, unable to change the verdict, he settled for reprimanding Mrs Neighbour. If she had these children in her house, warned Weston, she had a duty to look after them and it seemed improper – if not illegal – to have a dangerous well like this with so many toddlers around. If she continued her school, she must see that the well was made safe or that a pump was installed.

14 JANUARY

1891   Coroner Mr E.L. Hussey held an inquest at the Radcliffe Infirmary into the death of seventeen-year-old William John Ing.

Ing worked at Thame Grammar School and one of his responsibilities was attending to the baths. A new boiler had been installed in September 1870 and, on 10 January, gardener James Rush lit the fire, making sure that water had been pumped into the boiler first.

Rush fed the fire until lunchtime, when he left Ing in charge. At four o'clock, Rush checked the fire and found that Ing had created a tremendous blaze in the boiler's firebox, far fiercer than was necessary to heat the water.

'The water wasn't heating and I thought it would make it hot,' Ing explained when Rush questioned him. Rush left Ing pumping water into the boiler and had just gone into the yard when there was an explosion. Ing disappeared in a cloud of smoke and steam and Rush could only locate him by his repeated exclamations of 'Oh dear! Oh dear!'

Taken to hospital, Ing's injuries initially seemed superficial, the most serious being a deep cut on his left arm. However, he quickly began to show symptoms of internal bleeding and died from a lacerated liver on 11 January.

At the inquest, boiler expert John Horton stated that the most likely cause of the explosion was that the supply pipe was frozen. The boiler had not been used for two days prior to the catastrophe and, according to Horton, the recent frosts were the severest he had ever known and resulted in him being called out to mend hundreds of split pipes since Christmas. On hearing that, the inquest jury returned a verdict of 'accidental death'.

15 JANUARY

1877   Thirteen-year-old Annie Coombes (aka Annie Dipper) worked for the Viner family of Witney as a maidservant. Caleb Viner's wife was a very religious woman and, while she and their four children were at

The Memorial, Witney, 1950s. (Author's collection)

chapel, Caleb took liberties with Annie, who, knowing no better, made no complaint about his actions.

However, after Caleb's assault on 15 January, Annie went to her mother and stepfather. Mr and Mrs Dipper confronted Mrs Viner with Annie's allegations against her husband, at which Mrs Viner threatened that, if Annie left her job, she would prosecute her for leaving without notice.

Inexplicably, the Dipper's left their daughter at Witney and went home to Standlake. Five days later, Mr and Mrs Viner and Mrs Viner's sister visited the Dippers at home to ask them not to prosecute. Mr Viner was keen to make amends for his wrongdoing and it was suggested that he might financially compensate Annie. The sum of £40 was agreed on, with Viner giving the Dippers £1 there and then 'on account'. However, although he also wrote off £4 that the Dippers owed him, Viner made no more payments and was summoned.

He appeared at the Oxford Assizes, charged with three counts of ravishing Annie on 10, 12 and 15 January. Although a doctor testified that Annie was no longer a virgin, he found no marks of violence when he examined her. Thus, according to Viner's defence counsel, the allegations of rape were an improbability, designed to discredit and exhort money from his client and as a way of ensuring that the Dippers weren't prosecuted for Annie leaving her situation without notice. The jury concurred and Viner was acquitted.

16 JANUARY

1881 Coroner Mr E.L. Hussey held an inquest into the death of thirty-four-year-old Eliza Pavior, who worked as the cook for Revd George Lynch Kemp at the vicarage of St Frideswide's Church in Osney. There was no question about the cause of Eliza's death – she died on 15 January after a boiler in the vicarage kitchen exploded and literally blew her brains from her head. However, the jury needed to consider whether the boiler was properly installed and in good working order and whether anyone was to blame for Miss Pavior's demise.

It was shown that the boiler pipes had frozen and there was no supply of cold water. Once the fires were lit, the boiler built up a head of steam for which there was no escape. Blaming the severe weather for the tragedy, the inquest jury returned a verdict of 'accidental death'.

17 JANUARY

1938 Aircraftsman Second Class Walter George Goodhand of Hull died after falling out of an aeroplane at Upper Heyford.

The plane, flown by Pilot Officer C.T. Norman, was engaged in Lewis gun practice and Goodhand fell out as it turned at a height of 250ft. He landed in a hedge on the boundary of the airfield and died instantly.

Norman was initially unaware of the accident and an inquest later concluded that the plane may have hit an 'air bump' as Goodhand leaned out.

18 JANUARY

1754 John Spurritt (or Spurrier) and his wife kept The Holt Hotel at Hopcroft's Holt in the parish of Steeple Aston.

Trade was poor and the couple dispensed with their servants in favour of casual labour. On 18 January, two of these servants left in the evening and, when they returned the following morning, they found that the hotel had not opened up for the day. The couple knocked and shouted for some time before checking the back door of the pub, which was unlocked. The Spurritts' bed had not been slept in and several boxes in their bed chamber had been ransacked. Mr Spurritt was eventually found dead in a pool of blood in the kitchen, while his wife sat senseless in a chair by the fireplace, her head bruised and one arm broken. She died three days later, without having regained consciousness.

The pub had obviously been robbed of its recent takings and, as far as anyone could ascertain, there were two brown waistcoats and two linen handkerchiefs missing. Mr Spurritt had six wounds on his head and one finger almost severed. It was apparent that he had been badly beaten and, close to his body lay a broken mug, a candlestick and a heavy ash club, which appeared to have been freshly cut and was thought to be the murder weapon.

The coroner's inquest returned verdicts of 'wilful murder by person or persons unknown' and, although the police had several suspects, the murder was apparently never solved.

The hotel, which was also regularly visited by the notorious seventeenth-century highwayman Claude Duval, is said to be among the most haunted hotels in the country, with the ghosts of Duval and the Spurritts making regular appearances.

19 JANUARY

1827 Thirty-seven-year-old James Payne of Abingdon died. He was buried on 25 January in the Baptist burial ground and once his coffin had been lowered into the open grave, the minister and mourners went into the Meeting House to conclude the funeral ceremony.

Abingdon, 1950s. (Author's collection)

As the sexton stood at the graveside, he noticed the coffin moving. He called over undertaker Mr Petty for a second opinion and both men clearly saw movement from within the grave. Gradually more and more people came to look and all were in agreement that the movement was not an illusion and that Payne's corpse had miraculously come back to life.

Eventually, the coffin was carried to the rectory, where Mr Petty unscrewed the lid. Payne was clearly dead, although to everyone's surprise there had been no apparent deterioration or discolouration of his body. With Payne's coffin removed from the open grave, the reason for its movement became apparent. There was another coffin already buried in the grave and the weight of the new coffin and body was causing it to crumble, giving the appearance that Payne's coffin was moving.

20 JANUARY

1899 Labourer James Bushnell appeared at Oxford City Court charged with an aggravated assault on two of his sons.

On 5 January, neighbours were drawn to Bushnell's house by the sound of children screaming. Through the window, they saw him thrashing nine-year-old John and thirteen-year-old Frederick with a stick and heard the boys begging him to stop.

The police were called and, finding Bushnell drunk, arrested him for the safety of the children. John had a bad cut on the left-hand side of his head, while Frederick had a large swelling.

When Bushnell appeared before magistrates, John did not understand the concept of swearing an oath and was not allowed to testify, although the police pointed out that, on the day in question, the boy told them that he had hurt his head falling over.

Frederick told the Bench that their father had not beaten them for more than six months and only usually beat them when they deserved it. He freely admitted to stealing and to obtaining goods from shops by false pretences, saying that he was usually punished by being sent to bed. The hiding on 5 January was provoked by the disappearance of nearly half a pound of best butter from a cupboard – Bushnell thought that the boys had eaten it and didn't believe them when they swore that they hadn't. Frederick closed his evidence by telling the magistrates that he believed that his father had hit them 'accidentally', while he was 'beery'.

Bushnell himself insisted that he never intended to hit the boys on their heads, saying that he planned only to spank their bottoms. Magistrates agreed that Frederick in particular was incorrigible but felt that the punishment meted out by his father was not acceptable chastisement. Since Bushnell had already spent time in prison awaiting his court appearance, the magistrates fined him 10s, with 12s 6d costs, or fourteen days' imprisonment with hard labour in default. He was additionally bound over in the sum of £5 to keep the peace for six months.

21 JANUARY

1899 Eighteen-year-old travelling hawker John Buckland appeared at the Bullingdon Petty Sessions charged with an indecent assault on twenty-year-old Mary Francis.

Mary stated that, on 15 January, she was walking from Wolvercote to Oxford when she met Buckland, who crossed the road and grabbed the back of her dress. Mary told him to 'leave go', which he did, and Mary ran off as fast as she could but Buckland chased her, throwing her down on the road and indecently assaulting her.

Mary screamed and Buckland ran away. Mary then continued her journey to a Salvation Army meeting but made no complaint of any assault. In fact it wasn't until the following day that she spoke to the Wolvercote police constable about Buckland. PC Godden took her to the field where Buckland's father's caravan was located and Mary positively identified John Buckland as her assailant.

There were numerous people in the area at the time of the alleged assault, all of whom saw different things. Buckland's brother, Andrew, insisted that his brother was with him at the time of the assault. Some ponies belonging to the family had escaped into the garden of a man named Joseph Rowland and the brothers had been trying to recapture them. Rowland corroborated Andrew Buckland's testimony, stating that John was in his garden throughout the entire period during which Miss Francis was allegedly assaulted. Rowland saw Mary pass his house and, just minutes later, saw Buckland walking with his brother in the opposite direction towards his caravan.

The magistrates found it unusual that Mary had waited until the following morning before reporting the assault and also that she said nothing about it to anybody for four-and-a half hours. They also found it strange that, in describing her assailant, she neglected to make any mention of Buckland's thick black moustache and, on one occasion, she even identified Andrew Buckland as her attacker. Mary's evidence did not add up and the magistrates eventually dismissed the case against Buckland on the grounds that no court would ever convict him.

22 JANUARY

1849 Seventeen-year-old Charles Elliott was part of a shooting party near Bicester. He successfully fired his single-barrelled gun three times but then aimed at a blackbird and pulled the trigger. There was a loud bang and Elliott fell backwards. The other shooters rushed to him to find that his gun had exploded, part of it taking out one of his eyes and penetrating deep into his brain.

Elliott lingered for almost four hours before finally dying from his injuries and an inquest held by coroner Mr W. Brunner later recorded a verdict of 'accidental death'. The gun had recently been repaired by clock and watchmaker John Baxter and the jury expressed an opinion that cheap guns should not be so readily available and that they should not be repaired by those ill-qualified to do so.

23 JANUARY

1836 An inquest was held into the death of twenty-one-year-old Susan Garrett, who worked as an under ladies maid in the household of the Earl of Jersey.

For some months, Susan's fellow servants had suspected that she was pregnant, although Susan vehemently denied it. The family and their servants were in residence at their country home, Middleton Hall in Oxford, when valet Edward Goulde noticed a maid's cap floating in a large cistern, which supplied water to the entire mansion. There appeared to be a track on the floor leading to the cistern and handprints on the sides.

Goulde followed the track back to Susan Garrett's room. Susan had retired early complaining of a headache so, when there was no reply to his knocks on the door, Goulde alerted the other maids, who went into Susan's room, finding it awash with blood. The cistern was searched and Susan's body was recovered, along with that of a newborn baby boy.

The bodies were removed from the water and laid in an adjoining room, where a surgeon attempted resuscitation for some time before pronouncing Susan and the baby dead. The inquest jury found that Susan drowned herself in a state of temporary mental derangement. They were unable to determine whether her baby was born alive.

24 JANUARY

1899 Richard and Mary Ann Eltham appeared at Abingdon magistrates' court charged with neglecting their grandchild.

The case was brought by the National Society for the Prevention of Cruelty to Children, whose inspector informed the Bench that the five-year-old girl had been admitted to the Workhouse for her own protection. Her grandparents were both addicted to drink and their house was extremely dirty.

The child suffered from abscesses on her head, caused by infected insect bites. When she was removed from her grandparents' care on 12 January, her scalp was encrusted with a thick layer of dirt and dried pus and, twelve days later, the Workhouse attendants were still trying to remove it.

The child's mother admitted that her parents were addicted to drink but swore that, when she saw her daughter at Christmas, she was 'nice and clean', whereas the NSPCC inspector testified that the child was extremely dirty, ridden with vermin and covered in flea bites.

The magistrates chose to believe the inspector and sentenced both defendants to one month's imprisonment with hard labour.

25 JANUARY

1937 Three fully grown Russian wolves broke out of Oxford Zoo by gnawing their way through the reinforced wire netting of their enclosure. With lambing taking place, there were obvious concerns for the safety of farm animals.

The first escapee was shot by a police inspector in the garden of an empty house on the northern by-pass road. The second was shot at Hampton Poyle, where a farmer caught it worrying sheep.

The final fugitive was seen swimming across a canal and was eventually run to ground and shot at Cuttlestowe on 28 January. During its brief period of freedom, it had killed thirteen sheep.

26 JANUARY

1880 University coroner Mr F.P. Morrell held an inquest at Oxford into the death of nineteen-year-old Ernest Hughes Malcolm Irving Davies of Magdalen College, who died on 24 January.

Ernest was visited by his brother George, an undergraduate of Jesus College, Cambridge, and the two young men joined a party of students on a trip to Woodstock, where they planned to skate on Blenheim lake.

As they skated, George began to have serious doubts about the safety of the ice and, having failed to convince his brother of his fears, he withdrew to the bank. Shortly afterwards, the ice broke, sending Ernest and another student, Mr Watson, into the freezing lake.

Watson was closest to the bank and rescuers held out a large tree branch, which he managed to grasp and was pulled clear of the water. Ernest, however, was out of reach and after clinging to the edge of the ice

Magdalen College. (Author's collection)

Blenheim Park lake and bridge, 1904. (Author's collection)

for almost thirty minutes he was so cold and exhausted that he slipped under the water. It was more than an hour before his body was recovered.

The inquest jury returned a verdict of 'accidental death'.

27 JANUARY

1891 An inquest was held into the death of eleven-year-old Albert Lovegrove. On 26 January, instead of coming straight home from school for his lunch, Albert and two friends went to look at the frozen river at Christ Church Meadow. They couldn't resist walking on the ice, which immediately broke into large blocks that tilted like a see-saw, plunging all three boys into the water. Although two were rescued, Albert disappeared from view.

Hearing that his son was in the water, college servant Frederick Lovegrove raced to the scene. People were already prodding through the ice with poles and dragging the river but it was three-quarters of an hour before Albert's body was recovered. The inquest jury returned a verdict of 'accidental death'.

28 JANUARY

1846 An inquest was held at Abingdon into the death of Thomas Barnett, who died earlier that day.

The deceased had been employed by forty-six-year-old Thomas Fowler in his malthouse for almost two years, but Fowler came to doubt Barrett's honesty and dismissed him. On 22 January Barrett called on Fowler, demanding payment of 1s 6d, which he claimed was owed him in outstanding wages.

Fowler denied owing Barnett any money and Barnett assumed a fighting stance and threatened to break Fowler's head. Alarmed, Fowler picked up a malt shovel and hit Barnett over the head with it. Barnett crumpled to the ground and, on being assisted to his feet, was unable to stand unaided, dying five days later from a fractured skull.

The inquest jury returned a verdict of manslaughter against Fowler, a cripple, who was committed to Abingdon Gaol on the coroner's warrant. Tried at the Berkshire Assizes on 3 March, Fowler was acquitted on the grounds that he acted in self-defence and that Barrett had an unusually thin skull.

29 JANUARY

1900 Frederick William Cumberlidge, the landlord of The New Inn, St Aldate's, Oxford, heard a woman's desperate screams coming from a room occupied by former publican Alexander Sharpe Naylor and his wife Edith Hannah Naylor. When Cumberlidge went to investigate, Mrs Naylor begged, 'Pull him off me, he's killing me.'

The room was covered in blood. Mrs Naylor had a deep cut across the back of her neck, while her husband was close to death, having cut his throat with a sharpened table knife. He later died from his wounds.

Mrs Naylor had formerly worked at The New Inn as a barmaid and had been visiting since 19 January. She had written to her husband, asking him to come and stay at the inn with her and suggesting that they might get a pub together. Her letters to her husband included the words, 'I know how cross you are by your letter,' and 'If you cannot take my word about my staying only to help with the supper come and see. You can sleep with me.'

At the inquest, it was suggested that the Naylors had severe money troubles and that Alexander was a heavy drinker, who had suffered from *delirium tremens* in the past. It was also intimated that Mrs Naylor, who was much younger than her husband, was somewhat flirtatious with other men and that she often went out without him, causing him to become jealous. Mrs Naylor's statement was read, in which she said that her husband had been drinking brandy and whisky before cutting them both but that there had been no arguments or cross words between them.

Coroner Mr Galpin asked the jury if they wanted to adjourn the inquest in order for Mrs Naylor to have recovered sufficiently to attend. After a few minutes deliberation, the jury told him that all but one of their number were happy to give a verdict without hearing from Mrs Naylor.

'I will take upon myself to meet the convenience of the thirteen and to put the conscience of the fourteenth quite at rest,' said Galpin. 'I will take on myself the responsibility of not adjourning the inquest. What is your verdict?'

The jury agreed that Naylor committed suicide while in a state of temporary insanity.

30 JANUARY

1894 Shoemaker Edward Green appeared at the Oxford City Police Court charged with committing criminal assaults on his daughters Laura Florence and Harriet Louisa, aged thirteen and fifteen years old. There were multiple offences against both girls and Harriet had left home on account of her father's sexual assaults, which occurred so frequently that she couldn't possibly recall them all.

The majority of assaults on Laura were committed after the death of Green's wife in September. Harriet suspected the abuse after finding Laura and her father on the kitchen floor on 24 September 1893. However, since Laura and her father both insisted that they were searching for a dropped stud, she did nothing until she actually caught her father in Laura's bed, when she contacted the police.

Green denied any wrongdoing, saying that his children were making false allegations against him, but when Laura was examined by a doctor on 25 January, who found that she was no longer a virgin, he was charged with assault. Laura confirmed that her father had threatened to 'smash' her if she told anyone.

Tried at The Oxford Assizes, fifty-two-year-old Green was found guilty. According to the presiding judge, it was the worst case of its kind that he had ever dealt with and he sentenced Green to ten years' imprisonment with twelve months' hard labour.

31 JANUARY

1893 Thomas Ridge was unloading sacks of oilcake from a waggon and carrying them on his shoulder up a short ladder to the granary at his employer's farm at Standlake. As he unloaded his fifth sack, the ladder slipped and Ridge fell about 8ft to the ground.

Ridge complained of pain in his stomach, saying that he had fallen onto the edge of the entrance to the granary and that the sack, which weighed more than two hundredweight, had fallen on top of him. Dr Smallhorn determined that Ridge had a dislocated rib and advised him to rest, but his condition gradually worsened until the doctor ordered his admission to hospital on 2 February. He died four days later and the cause of his death was given as fractured ribs.

At Ridge's inquest, there were questions about whether he might have fallen out of bed while in hospital, since Smallhorn and his colleague were both certain that Ridge's ribs were only dislocated when he was admitted. However, the inquest jury believed that the injuries occurred as the result of his fall from the ladder and returned a verdict of 'accidental death'.

FEBRUARY

Old Charlbury. (Author's collection)

1 FEBRUARY

1891 Oliver Grubb Horn died from tetanus, arising from an accident on 19 January.

Horn was given the task of oiling the jack in the kitchen fireplace at Heythrop. In order to do this, he had to get inside the kitchen flue and to protect his clothes from soot he tied a large piece of matting around his waist.

Heythrop, 1900s. (Author's collection)

The mechanism by which the jack worked was contained in an iron box in the flue, roughly 10ft from the ground. As Horn was securing the box, he dropped a screw, which fell into the grate below. Horn called for help to find it and when nobody could locate it, he climbed down to the back of the range. As he bent over to look for the screw, the candle he was carrying came into contact with the matting he was wrapped in and it went up in flames. With difficulty, he was pulled from behind the range and a cloth thrown over him but the cloth itself caught fire.

Horn panicked and tried to run out of the kitchen until someone seized him and began to tear off the matting. By then Horn's clothes were also alight and it took some time to extinguish them and to dress his burns with linseed oil. His hair and whiskers were almost completely singed off and his arms, hands, throat and face were badly burned.

Horn initially made good progress until 30 January, when he began to display symptoms of tetanus. From then on, he went quickly downhill until his death.

Coroner Mr F. Westell held an inquest at which a verdict of 'accidental death' was recorded.

2 FEBRUARY

1849 There was a rat in the room occupied by Corpus Christi student Charles Blackstone. Traps failed to capture it and, after Blackstone saw the animal sitting and staring at him a couple of times, he hired a pistol, which he kept loaded under a pillow on his sofa, awaiting the opportunity to shoot it.

Corpus Christi College. (Author's collection)

Returning from a friend's rooms late at night, Blackstone lay on the sofa and dozed. Believing that he heard rats running around, he groped under the pillow for his pistol and, in withdrawing it, accidentally shot himself through the heart. The other students lodging in his house were quite used to him firing at the rat and therefore took no notice of the noise of the shot.

Coroner Mr G.V. Cox held an inquest, at which the jury determined that Blackmore 'caused his own death by accidentally discharging a loaded pistol, which he, as has been satisfactorily proved to the jury, was in the habit of incautiously handling in his room.'

3 FEBRUARY

1826 Richard Belcher was in charge of a horse towing a barge along the River Thames. When he reached Culham, there was a large, deep puddle on the towpath and Belcher climbed onto the horse's back to save getting his feet wet. He had only ridden a few yards when the horse slipped and plunged into the river.

Belcher, who couldn't swim, was terrified and maintained a tight grip on the horse's bridle. This caused the horse to swim round in circles and every time it attempted to scramble up the bank and get out of the water, Belcher checked it with the reins.

There were two men on the boat and they tried in vain to rescue Belcher and the horse, as did a passer-by, Joseph Gibbons. The horse continued swimming for about fifteen minutes before exhaustion set in and it drowned, turning on its side and floating to the surface.

Belcher was still sitting on the now dead horse and, with no resistance from the horse swimming, the current took it. Gibbons followed for almost half a mile. He had a pole in his hand with a hook on the end and made numerous attempts to snag the horse's bridle and stop its progress downstream. Eventually, the hook caught in Belcher's clothing and Gibbons was able to pull him ashore.

Finding that Belcher was dead, Gibbons left him on the river bank for some time while he continued to try and catch the horse. He eventually borrowed a punt from Culham and took Belcher to the nearest house, by which time it was far too late to try and resuscitate him.

Coroner Mr Cecil held an inquest the next day, at which the jury returned a verdict of 'accidentally drowned.' Cecil strongly censured Gibbons for leaving Belcher's body while he tried to recover the horse.

4 FEBRUARY

1900 At 1.15 a.m., PC Alfred Jones was patrolling the St Barnabas area of Oxford when he spotted smoke issuing from the bedroom of a residence on Wellington Street. The Superintendent of the Fire Brigade lived nearby and, having been alerted by the policeman, he telephoned the Fire Station, who sent a horse-drawn engine to the scene.

There was snow on the ground and the engine struggled on the slippery roads. Meanwhile, attempts were made to enter the house to rescue the sole occupant, an eighty-four-year-old police pensioner named President Ferrice 'George' Carr. However, the smoke was so dense that it proved impossible to reach him and, once the fire had been extinguished, his body was found in his sitting room, clad only in a nightshirt.

Carr had only one small burn on his body and was suffocated by the smoke rather than burned to death. His position in the living room was a mystery since, having got downstairs, it should have been easy for him to either walk out of the front door or climb out of the window. It was theorised that Carr either tried to save his pet – a caged dove – or that he went to look for the cashbox containing his savings.

Coroner Mr H.F. Galpin held an inquest on 6 February. It proved impossible to discover the cause of the fire but the coroner surmised that it was caused by Carr's paraffin lamp and the jury's verdict was that 'death arose from suffocation through the explosion of a paraffin lamp.'

5 FEBRUARY

1938 Sixteen-year-old Harold Matthews worked as a pantry boy at Wycliffe Hall, a theological training college in Oxford. Part of his duties involved taking telephone messages and, while cleaning the knives in the pantry on 5 February, he was called upstairs to answer the phone. He never returned.

The college and grounds were searched minutely, the search expanding to the streets and parks nearby. The next day, Harold's naked body was found on a flat roof, used by students as an open-air dormitory in the summer months.

A post-mortem examination determined that he had been strangled and student John Stanley Phillips quickly confessed to having strangled him.

Harold Matthews. (By kind permission of the *Oxford Mail* and the *Oxford Times*)

Phillips was an insular young man, who was described as intensely religious, reserved, and unsociable. Medical evidence suggested that he was suffering from schizophrenia and, at his trial at the Oxford Assizes for wilful murder, the jury found him guilty but insane. There was no indication that any prior relationship existed between the two young men but it seemed as though Matthews was merely unfortunate enough to encounter a man whose mental illness made it impossible for him to follow the doctrines of his own strictly-held religious beliefs.

Wycliffe Hall today. (© N. Sly)

6 FEBRUARY

1878 Twenty-two-year-old Elizabeth Sessions died before she could appear at the Oxford Assizes, charged with the wilful murder of her newborn baby.

Elizabeth worked as a servant at The Plough Inn at Little Bourton and, since July 1877, landlady Harriet Elkington had suspected that Elizabeth was pregnant, although she continually denied her mistress's suspicions.

On 17 January, PC David White called to see Mrs Elkington after closing time and was talking to her in the bar when her son came in and said that he could hear someone moving about. Mrs Elkington went to investigate and found Elizabeth creeping across the yard, carrying a cloth-covered chamber pot. Mrs Elkington demanded to know what was in the chamber pot but Elizabeth refused to say. Eventually PC White removed the cloth and discovered a baby, head down in a quantity of water.

Dr Hudson was summoned from Banbury and examined Elizabeth, who was still insisting that she had not given birth. Hudson's examination proved otherwise and, furthermore, the doctor was certain that her baby had met its death through drowning.

Coroner Mr C. Duffell Faulkner held an inquest, at which the jury returned a verdict of wilful murder against Elizabeth. She would normally have been taken to Oxford Gaol to await her trial at the next assizes but was too ill to be moved, eventually dying on 6 February from a combination of 'recent confinement, mental depression and a severe chill producing the pleurisy followed by rheumatism.'

7 FEBRUARY

1853 Coroner Mr W. Brunner held an inquest at Wootton into the mysterious death of twenty-five-year-old Ellen Willesden (Wilsdon/ Wilsden).

Ellen lived with her brother and acted as his housekeeper. Approximately two weeks before her death, she was taken ill with sickness and diarrhoea, which she attributed to having eaten too many lard cakes. Ellen had made the cakes herself, taking flour from a sack that was kept in the house and which contained a mixture of flour ground from old and new wheat. A servant girl suffered the same symptoms as Ellen but both quickly recovered.

On 1 February, Ellen made bread from the same flour and was again taken ill. This time, her bout of sickness and diarrhoea proved fatal and a post-mortem examination determined that she had taken arsenic. Others who had eaten the bread suffered no symptoms.

Sometime earlier, Mr Willesden had ordered a rick of wheat to be dressed with arsenic to kill rats and his shepherd had also used arsenic to make a dressing for sheep, which was once kept on the kitchen windowsill. The inquest jury could not determine how, why, when or where Ellen ingested the arsenic and recorded a verdict that 'the deceased died from the effects of poison but how administered there was no evidence to show.'

8 FEBRUARY

1857 An inquest concluded at Banbury on the death of four-year-old James Alfred Lancaster.

Coroner Mr T. Pain originally opened the inquest one week earlier but adjourned it in order to have the contents of the little boy's stomach analysed. James came from a large family, who were supposedly neglected by their parents. Given a stew made from tripe, swede, turnips, onions and carrots, within an hour James was dead and his five siblings were suffering from sickness and diarrhoea.

The analysis revealed no trace of poison and it was determined that James died from congestion of the lungs and brain. However, doctors were of the opinion that the child was so hungry that he had overeaten, gorging himself so voraciously that it killed him.

The inquest jury returned a verdict that 'the deceased child died from congestion of the lungs and brain and, from the evidence produced, it is the opinion of the jury that the parents of the deceased have neglected to perform their duties, in not providing those necessaries and comforts which the deceased and other members of the family had a right to demand.' In spite of their verdict, the jury fell short of an official censure and there is nothing to suggest that James's parents ever faced criminal charges in respect of their son's death.

9 FEBRUARY

1858 When Sarah Rivers married labourer Mr Welch, she already had a baby, who was not Welch's child.

The baby was not breast-fed and when her mother moved to East Lockinge with her new husband, there were no cows kept nearby. Unable to obtain fresh milk, Sarah fed three-month-old Alice on a mixture of boiled bread and sugar.

Alice died aged five months and a post-mortem examination conducted by Dr Clarke revealed that she was dreadfully emaciated and had died from starvation. At the inquest held by coroner Mr W.D. Wasbrough, the jury were told that, if a baby could not be breast-fed, the only suitable substitute was two parts cow's milk and one part water. Babies should not be fed any solid food and, in Clarke's opinion, Alice had died because of improper feeding.

The jury concluded that Sarah had shamefully neglected her child and was responsible for Alice's death. However, they accepted that she had not done so wilfully, with the intention of killing her daughter, and thus she escaped any criminal charges.

10 FEBRUARY

1355 Two university students, Walter Spryngeheuse and Roger de Chesterfield, were drinking in the Swindlestock (or Swyndlestock) Tavern and complained to landlord John Groidon about the quality of the drinks. An argument ensued, during which the students threw their drinks in Groidon's face and beat him up. The then Mayor of Oxford demanded that the Chancellor of the University arrest the two students but instead their fellow students came out in support and the Mayor was attacked.

It was the start of what became known as the St Scholastica Day Riot, the worst 'town and gown' riot in the city's history, with a protracted battle between the two that culminated in the deaths of sixty-three scholars and at least thirty townspeople (some sources estimate as many as sixty).

The University was said to have won the confrontation and every year on the anniversary of the start of the riot, the Mayor and town councillors marched bareheaded to the University and paid a fine of 1*d* for every dead scholar, a total of 5*s* 3*d*. This continued until 1825, when the Mayor refused to take part, but it wasn't until 1955 that the hatchet was formally buried – at a commemoration of the events of 1355, the Mayor was awarded an Honorary Degree and the Vice-Chancellor of the University was made an Honorary Freeman of the city.

11 FEBRUARY

1901 Richard Hopcroft faced a second trial at the Oxford Assizes for the wilful murder of his adoptive father.

On 16 November 1900, farmer Richard Savage and Hopcroft quarrelled at their farmhouse in Yarnton. So ferocious was the argument that their housekeeper went out rather than listen to them and, when she returned two hours later, she tripped over Savage's body in the kitchen.

Savage had a gunshot wound to his head and, earlier that afternoon, neighbours had seen Hopcroft leaving the house with a gun. Hopcroft later handed himself in at the County Police Station in Oxford, saying that he had accidentally caused Savage's death. However, an inquest jury returned a verdict of wilful murder against him and he was committed for trial at the next Oxford Assizes on 4 February.

In his defence, Hopcroft stated that he had loaded his gun in order to go out rabbit shooting. Savage tried to stop him from going and, during a struggle between them for possession of the gun, it went off. Asked why he didn't go for help, Hopcroft claimed to have been too frightened.

After deliberating for fifty minutes, the jury returned to announce that they were unable to agree on a verdict – even though there was evidence that Hopcroft had threatened to murder his father in the past, a small majority were of the opinion that the shooting was accidental. Mr Justice Wright had no alternative other than to dismiss the jury and order a retrial.

The retrial took place one week later and, after hearing the preliminary evidence, the counsel for the defence offered a guilty plea for the lesser offence of manslaughter. The prosecution accepted and Mr Justice Wright addressed Hopcroft before passing sentence, saying that he had apparently been in a highly murderous frame of mind and a danger to other people besides Savage. Since his crime was very little below the crime of murder, Wright sentenced Hopcroft to twenty-one years' penal servitude.

12 FEBRUARY

1890 Thirty-four-year-old William Christmas appeared at the Oxford Assizes charged with offences against a fourteen-year-old girl committed between October and November 1889. Initially, Christmas pleaded guilty but when it was pointed out to him that he could say in his own defence that he believed the girl to be sixteen, he withdrew his plea and pleaded not guilty.

Fourteen-year-old Abigail Biddle lived with her mother at Steeple Barton and Christmas was their lodger. There was only one bedroom in the house, which all three shared, and there was some argument in court about how many beds there were. The defendant said that there were two beds, one of which he slept in and one shared by Abigail and her mother, Eliza. However, Eliza insisted that all three shared the same bed.

Christmas maintained that Eliza Biddle had encouraged him to sleep with Abigail, assuring him that her daughter was sixteen, whereas Eliza was adamant that she had continuously told Christmas that he would 'get into trouble', since Abigail was so young. The alleged offence came to light when Christmas was heard to say that he was living with Abigail as man and wife. As a consequence, Christmas was arrested, although he refused to believe Abigail's true age until he was shown a copy of her birth certificate.

The case hinged on whether Christmas had reasonable grounds to suppose that Abigail was sixteen years old and the jury decided that he didn't, finding him guilty as charged. The judge deferred sentencing, finally telling Christmas that by law he could sentence him to up to two years' hard labour. However, the fact that Eliza Biddle had participated in Christmas's disgusting and immoral conduct towards her daughter surpassed his comprehension and he was therefore awarding a sentence of ten calendar months' hard labour.

13 FEBRUARY

1849 Borough Surveyor Mr Tew appeared before magistrates charged with assaulting Charles Cooper at Headington.

Cooper was one of several men employed to dig a drain and was hard at work when Tew arrived and began to abuse the men, saying that they were too slow and that they did less work than a bunch of washerwomen.

Old Headington, 1916. (Author's collection)

Cooper replied that it was a shame that they didn't receive washerwomen's wages, a remark which infuriated Tew. He told Cooper that he was fired and, when Cooper refused to leave the job, he dragged him out of the drain by his collar.

Several of Cooper's workmates spoke on his behalf, telling the magistrates that they were paid only 7s a week, with no food or drink allowed them while working. The magistrates cleared the court while they deliberated the case, returning to say that they found the assault proved and fining Tew 20s, including costs. They added that they were unanimous in their opinion that the men employed by Tew were 'ground down to their lowest point.'

Chief magistrate Dr Wynter stated that 7s was a starvation rate for a single man and that some of Tew's workmen were married with several children. It was hardly surprising, said Wynter, that men were goaded to violence when they met with such shameful behaviour as that displayed by Tew. Wynter found it inconceivable that Tew could expect a week's work for such a trifling sum and concluded by saying that it was the magistrates' opinion that he was not a fit person to fill the office of Borough Surveyor.

14 FEBRUARY

1830 A 'meteoric stone' fell to earth in a garden at Launton, near Bicester. The garden had been newly dug and the stone, which weighed about 2lb, narrowly missed a gardener and buried itself a foot deep in the soil. Its descent was preceded by three loud explosions that were heard up to four miles away and were likened to the discharge of a triple-barrelled gun.

The meteor looked like a large stone and was said to be magnetic and to contain large quantities of chromium and nickel. The fall of the meteor was thought to be the first such occurrence in Oxfordshire history.

15 FEBRUARY

1937 An inquest was held at Oxford into the death of four-year-old Michael James Richard Stroud of Shellingford. In preparation for an X-ray at the Radcliffe Infirmary, Oxford, Michael's arm was injected by house physician Dr T.W. Lloyd.

Lloyd drew liquid from an unlabelled brown bottle on a dressings tray but no sooner had he injected Michael than the child collapsed, dying within minutes. Unbeknown to the doctor, he had accidentally injected the child with methylated ether, normally used to clean the skin before puncturing it with a needle.

At the inquest, a remorseful Lloyd admitted that he had simply made a tragic mistake. The inquest jury returned a verdict of death by misadventure, expressing an opinion that Lloyd should have taken more care and that, in future, all bottles should be properly labelled.

16 FEBRUARY

1832 The town of Enstone was buzzing with gossip about Ann Harrison, whose husband had recently died. It was rumoured that, after having his body interred in the churchyard on 12 January, Ann had entered into an arrangement with bodysnatchers and sold her husband's corpse to them.

The rumours reached such a pitch that the vicar felt compelled to investigate and on 16 February, Mr Harrison's grave was opened in front of a large crowd of people. The gossips were silenced when the body was discovered exactly where it was placed only a month earlier.

Enstone. (Author's collection)

17 FEBRUARY

1899 Robert and Emily Carter appeared at the Bampton West Petty Sessions charged with neglecting their children in a manner likely to cause unnecessary suffering or injury to their health.

When the Inspector for the Oxford and County Society for the Prevention of Cruelty to Children called on the Carters' home in Filkins on 25 January, he found eleven-year-old Robert, six-year-old Beatrice and twenty-two-month-old Nellie in a terrible state. All of the children were filthy and dressed in rags and all were crawling with fleas and other vermin. The cottage was dirty and unkempt and the mattress on the bed on which the three children slept was soaked with urine, while their bedclothes consisted mainly of old sacks.

Both Mr and Mrs Carter were in work, he earning 12s a week with his accommodation and an allotment provided free, while she earned 9d a day. However, it was the Carters custom to go straight from work to the pub, where they habitually stayed until closing time, leaving their children to fend for themselves.

'I will do the best I can if you will let me off this time and I won't have any more beer,' wheedled Carter as he pleaded for leniency from the magistrates, while his wife complained, 'I have done my best, I'm sure. I spend my money as well as I can and am not in debt.'

The Bench retired for a few minutes to consider an appropriate sentence, returning to award Robert and Emily three months' imprisonment with hard labour each. It was their second sentence for a similar offence, the first having been in June 1896.

18 FEBRUARY

1888   Twenty-one-year-old railway clerk Henry George Williams visited the Radcliffe Infirmary for treatment for a boil on his face, and on his way home he purchased a box of fifty cartridges for his revolver. He spent the afternoon out with his dog and was seen by the Oxford canal, apparently firing his gun at a tree. At about three o'clock he went to his parents' home near Woodstock for his tea, after which he announced his intention of going out again.

Neither of Henry's parents knew that he possessed a gun and when his mother heard a loud crack, she believed it was a fog signal. She thought no more about it until she went to the outside lavatory and found herself unable to open the door, which was slightly ajar.

Mr Williams senior was in bed, having worked a nightshift, when his wife woke him. He forced the lavatory door open to find his son sitting on the toilet leaning slightly forward, bleeding from his ears and a wound in his forehead.

They immediately assumed that he had committed suicide but from the nature of the wound and the position in which Henry was found, investigators were able to establish that his death was accidental, caused by the sudden exploding of a cartridge.

19 FEBRUARY

1887   Gypsy family Charlie and Lucy Smith and their two children, Oshey and Prince Albert, were camping on common land near Headington. They were visited by friends on the afternoon of 18 February, who noticed that Lucy appeared to have been beaten and, when questioned, Charlie explained that the beating related to something she had done almost thirty years ago. 'Let it go. Forgive her,' Charlie was told, but he was too stubborn.

At four o'clock in the morning of 19 February, Oshey woke to hear her father shouting at her mother and, as the seventeen-year-old girl watched,

Charlie picked up a hammer and began to beat Lucy. He continued to thrash his wife until he was exhausted, then fell asleep. Lucy crawled out of the tent towards the nearby stream but didn't return and, when Oshey went to check, she found her mother lying dead.

Oshey seized her younger brother and ran for help. The police were called and Charlie calmly greeted them with the words, 'Good morning. I have got a dead 'un this morning.'

While Charlie swore that Lucy had fallen over, a post-mortem examination showed that she had been beaten to death and when a bloodstained hammer was found concealed under the straw bed in the makeshift tent, Charlie was arrested and charged with wilful murder.

At his trial at the Reading Assizes in April 1887, the defence argued that Lucy Smith's death was manslaughter. The jury disagreed and, having been found guilty of wilful murder, Smith was executed by James Berry on 9 May.

20 FEBRUARY

1869 A petty argument at The Black Boy public house in Headington ended in a fight between Thomas Shorter and Richard Lambourn. Although Shorter initiated the fight, he got the worst of it and fell over several times until eventually Lambourn walked away, leaving Shorter to make his way home.

He fell over again and had to be helped by his friends and, once home, complained of pain in his belly. A surgeon was called but Shorter died two days later and a post-mortem examination showed that he had a perforation in his intestines.

Coroner Mr W. Brunner held an inquest and several witnesses to the fight testified. One claimed to have seen Lambourn kneeling on Shorter, while another swore that Lambourn kicked Shorter while he was on the ground.

The inquest jury didn't believe that Shorter's injury could have been inflicted in a fair fight and returned a verdict of manslaughter against Lambourn, who was committed to appear at the Oxford Assizes on the coroner's warrant.

Twenty-two-year-old Lambourn did not have long to wait, since the assizes opened on 27 February. He pleaded guilty to manslaughter, thus forfeiting his trial and placing his fate in the hands of the judge, who was satisfied that the fight was fair and that Shorter had provoked Lambourn into fighting. He discharged Lambourn with a caution, binding him over in the sum of £20 to keep the peace towards all of Her Majesty's subjects in future.

21 FEBRUARY

1762 Oxfordshire and all of its surrounding counties endured gales and heavy falls of snow, which resulted in severe damage to property and loss of life. Between Cassington and Yarnton, shoemaker James Slatter lost his bearings in the blizzard and wandered into the River Isis, where he drowned. Another person was lost in Blenheim Park, while David Knapp died between Dorchester-on-Thames and Wittenham. Although Knapp had sought shelter among some bushes, the snow was so deep that he was standing almost upright when he was found dead.

22 FEBRUARY

1899   Twenty-eight-year-old tailor James Bowerman appeared at Oxford City Court charged with neglecting his six children in a manner likely to cause suffering and injury.

Gorden Walsh of the Oxford and County Society for the Prevention of Cruelty to Children told the Bench that Bowerman was addicted to drink and, although he earned £2 9s a week, he spent most of it on alcohol and failed to provide for his children.

When Walsh visited the house on 15 February, the children were suffering from bronchitis and Mrs Bowerman explained that she was unable to afford a doctor. She had only 3½d to her name and the previous week, her husband had given her only 5s.

Bowerman's employers told the Bench that they had given him chance after chance but had now terminated his employment. Bowerman himself said that it was 'all through drink' and pleaded with the magistrates to be given one more chance, promising never to touch a drop again. However, magistrates recalled that he had made similar promises in May 1898, when he served a one-month prison sentence for a similar offence.

At that time, he had been provided with everything he needed to make a comfortable home for his family but, in the words of the magistrates, had 'gone from bad to worse.' They sentenced him to two months' imprisonment with hard labour and the OCSPCC proposed to try and keep his home and family together until he was released.

23 FEBRUARY

1890   Coroner Mr E.M. Challenor held an inquest at The Swan, Cholsey, on the death of eighteen-month-old Percy Edward Smith.

Two days earlier, Percy was left in the charge of his twenty-year-old sister, Sophia, who was indoors doing housework while keeping half an eye on Percy, who was playing just outside. Suddenly, she saw him toddling determinedly up the garden path towards the open well.

Sophia rushed outside and called for Percy to come back but instead of obeying her, he ran full tilt into the well. Sophia could see him floating on the surface of the water and immediately went for help but could not find anyone to assist her. It was at least a quarter of an hour before she located William Rumble, who fetched a ladder and climbed down into the well to extricate Percy, by which time, the toddler had drowned.

The inquest jury returned a verdict of 'accidentally drowned', suggesting that the open well should be provided with a cover to prevent any similar tragedies in future.

24 FEBRUARY

1900   It was said that there was no happier family in Charlbury than that of Alfred William Jones. He and his wife had been married for ten years and their three children were clean, well-behaved and obviously much-loved.

On 24 February, Mary Jane Jones sang as she did her housework. She bought some bread, putting aside a shiny new penny from her change, which she told the baker's boy would please her children. At 3.15 p.m. she chatted briefly with a neighbour and appeared her normal, cheerful self but less than an hour later, Mr Jones arrived home from work and,

Church Street, Charlbury. (Author's collection)

finding his tea not ready, went in search of his wife. He found her lying on their bed with the bodies of her daughters beside her, their throats cut. Fortunately, eight-year-old Alfred Thomas Jones was out playing that afternoon, otherwise he may well have shared his sisters' fate.

Although two-year-old Lilian Mary and nine-month-old Marjory Alice were dead, Mary was still alive. Her husband called his sister, who lived opposite, who sat with Mary while Jones went for a doctor. Mary was able to answer questions using whispers and gestures, and indicated that she alone was responsible for harming the children, having cut their throats with a razor but, even though she lived until the following morning, she did not explain why.

An inquest was held by coroner Mr Westell, who reminded the jury that, as Mary's husband, Alfred Jones was not bound to reveal any facts that incriminated himself or his wife. In the event, Jones did little more than formally identify the bodies.

Nobody could think of any possible reason why Mary Jane Jones might murder her children then commit suicide. There was no family history of insanity and Mary was happily married and a devoted mother. It was said that she was concerned that one of the girls was suffering from influenza and that her sleep had recently been disturbed as a result. Marjory's birth had also been quite difficult, although that was nine months earlier.

The inquest jury questioned where Alfred Jones was at the time of the murders but the police assured them that Alfred had an unshakeable alibi for the relevant period. Satisfied, the jury returned verdicts of wilful murder against Mary Jane in respect of her children and suicide while temporarily insane on her own death.

25 FEBRUARY

1852 Sixteen-year-old Mary Westall worked for saddler and harness maker Christopher Maisey at Faringdon. However, when she fell pregnant by her master, Mary's outraged parents took her home and forbade her to

Market Square, Faringdon, 1950s. (Author's collection)

have any contact with Maisey.

On 25 February, Mary sneaked out of her parents' home and was later seen entering Maisey's house. Yet when Mary's parents confronted Maisey, he denied having seen her. A watch was kept on the house and the following day Mary emerged looking weak and ill. She was taken back to her parents' house, where a doctor confirmed that she had recently given birth.

Mary insisted that she had never seen her baby and had no idea what became of it. After she gave birth, Maisey carried her to the hay loft, where she was given a meal of tea and bread and butter and told to hold her tongue about the child. When Maisey left the house, Mary managed to crawl to a neighbour.

On 13 June, a baby's body was dredged from a nearby pond. It was wrapped in a piece of carpet which matched that in Maisey's house, and was therefore assumed to be Mary's child. Although the child had been in the water for some months and was badly decomposed, several of its bones were fractured and its joints were dislocated, as if it had been violently treated. Surgeons were certain that the child was born alive and an inquest returned a verdict of wilful murder against Mary Westall and Christopher Maisey.

Mary was tried at the Oxford Assizes on 12 July and acquitted, the jury having accepted that she knew little about the fate of her baby. Maisey had fled and a warrant was issued for his arrest for wilful murder.

He was eventually apprehended at Liverpool, from where he was apparently planning to flee the country disguised as a woman. At her own trial, Mary gave an account of the birth, saying that the child 'fell out of her' onto the brick floor in a passage at Maisey's house. The jury at Maisey's trial at the Oxford Assizes on 28 February 1853 weren't convinced by the medical evidence that the baby was born alive and thought that the baby's injuries may have resulted from it dropping onto the brick floor. They gave thirty-three-year-old Maisey the benefit of the doubt and he was acquitted.

26 FEBRUARY

1899 Elizabeth Hutt from Osney was cooking Sunday lunch and removed a baking tin containing potatoes and water from her oven, placing it on the floor. Moments later, her son, George Vincent Hutt, who was nearly four years old, tripped and sat down on the edge of the tin, scalding his buttocks.

Elizabeth dabbed the scald with linseed oil and later obtained a mixture of linseed oil and lime water from a neighbour, with which she anointed George's bottom. The scald didn't seem too serious and George seemed unperturbed by it until two days later, when he happened to scratch it overnight. From then on, he seemed really poorly and, as a precaution, his parents moved him into their bed.

At three o'clock in the morning on 3 March, Harry Hutt noticed that his son's jaws appeared stiff. Hutt went for a doctor but although he asked two or three, none was prepared to come out to the child in the middle of the night. Eventually, George died at ten minutes to five that morning.

The coroner requested a post-mortem examination and Dr Arthur Percy Parker found a severe ulcerated wound on George's right buttock. Parker believed that the cause of George's death was acute blood poisoning and gave his opinion that even if a doctor had attended when Hutt requested, the child would have died anyway. The inquest jury returned a verdict in accordance with the medical evidence.

27 FEBRUARY

1844 Between two and three o'clock in the morning, the watchman doing his rounds of Oxford discovered a fire at St Ebbe's Street. He immediately roused the occupants of the premises, who were Rabbi Aaron Jacob (or Jacobs) and his family and their lodgers, John Tubb and his wife.

Tubb managed to drag his wife out of the building but the staircase was soon impassable and the other occupants went to a rear window. Twelve-year-old Rachel Jacob was lowered onto a neighbour's roof, followed by her mother. Rachel's brother jumped from the window, landing on his head and badly injuring himself, but Aaron Jacob and his eldest daughter, Rebecca, failed to escape. It was thought that Aaron went back into the flames to try and save his valuables, which were found close to his body when the flames were eventually doused, while the floor collapsed under Rebecca before she could escape, plunging her into the cellar where her body was discovered.

An inquest on the two deaths was held by coroner Mr Brunner at The Horse and Chair public house in St Ebbe's and returned two verdicts of 'accidental death'. It was determined that the blaze spread from the shop below the living quarters, where several women's gowns hung close to the fireplace and probably caught fire.

Note: Some reports suggest that Tubb had a son, who was rescued by his father.

28 FEBRUARY

1871 At Witney Station, a group of porters and clerks were playing a game of 'Duck', which involved each of the men throwing stones at a target stone.

Sixteen-year-old clerk Charles Harris threw his stone then bent to pick it up. As he did so, Porter Henry Mortimer loosed his stone, which struck Harris on the temple, knocking him unconscious. He was carried home, where he was attended by a surgeon, but did not survive.

At an inquest on his death, the jury were told that the 14lb stone had already left Mortimer's hand when Harris bent down. All of the participants in the game insisted that the accident was Harris's fault, since he got in the way of Mortimer's shot. The jury attributed no blame, returning a verdict that Harris 'died from injuries received by being accidentally hit with a stone.'

29 FEBRUARY

1888 Gamekeeper George Lewis was out with his gun at North Aston when he spotted a young woman lying in a hide. He shouted to her several times and fired his gun into the air but, receiving no response, concluded that she was either ill or dead and went for the police and a doctor. When Dr Turner examined her, he noted that she had a frostbitten nose and hands and that there were also traces of frostbite on her head. The woman was young and well-nourished and Turner determined that her death resulted from exposure to the cold.

Three letters were found in the woman's pockets and they led the police to identify her as twenty-one-year-old Annie Florence Lambeth, originally from Birmingham. Annie's mother, Elizabeth, told the inquest into her daughter's death that she hadn't seen Annie for fifteen months and that she was last heard of living in Hampshire. Although she came from a respectable family, Annie was something of a wayward young woman who had often run away from home and had even been placed in a 'home' in Liverpool because her parents couldn't control her.

There were no signs of violence on Annie's body, nor were there any indications that she had struggled before dying. It seemed as if she simply lay down in the hay on the hide and succumbed to the bitterly cold weather and the inquest jury returned a verdict of 'death from exposure to the cold.'

MARCH

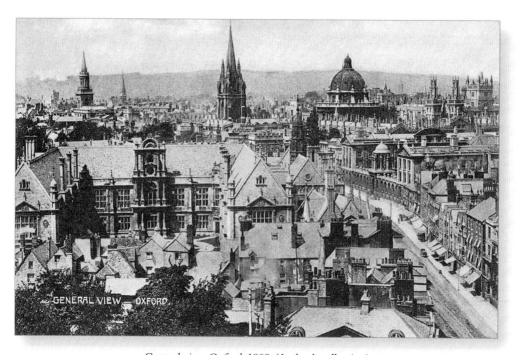

General view, Oxford, 1909. (Author's collection)

1 MARCH

1884 Ellen Kelly of High Street, Oxford, was boiling greens in a large pot that held about two gallons of water. When the vegetables were cooked, she lifted the pot from the stove and placed it in a corner. There were children running in and out of the house and two-and-a-half-year-old Daniel Nicholls overbalanced and sat down in the pot of boiling water.

High Street, Oxford, 1920s. (Author's collection)

Mrs Kelly swiftly pulled him out, stripped off his clothes and floured his burned bottom and, as soon as he had fresh clothes on, Daniel continued to run about and play. When he was in pain the next day, more flour was put on the burns, followed by oil.

It took four days for Daniel's parents to take him to the Radcliffe Infirmary, by which time the boy was seriously ill. Always a weakly child, he gradually deteriorated and died two days later and surgeon Mr A.F. Street gave the cause of his death as scalds to the buttocks, which did not seem inclined to heal.

At an inquest on his death, the jury returned a verdict of 'death by accidental scalding'.

2 MARCH

1830 Thomas Beesley appeared at the Oxford Assizes charged with the wilful murder of John Barrett at Wolvercote on 3 July 1829.

Beesley and several other young men were making a nuisance of themselves in the village, chasing the cows and horses, until Beesley put a duck from the village pond in his pocket.

William Robinson and William Eeley remonstrated with him, saying that he should know better than to destroy other people's property, at which Beesley denied having picked up a duck. He was proved a liar by the loud quacking coming from his coat pocket.

One of Beesley's companions struck Eeley before the group drifted off. However, shortly before six o'clock, they returned to Wolvercote looking for trouble. They started a fight with some of the local youths, during which Beesley flourished a bludgeon, hitting several people. At one stage, he walked up to sixteen-year-old John Barrett and poleaxed him with a single blow to the right-hand side of his head.

When Barrett died from his injuries, Beesley was charged with wilful murder, although the jury at his trial eventually found him guilty of the lesser offence of manslaughter, on the grounds that there was neither premeditation nor malice. Nevertheless, the judge commented on the aggravated nature of the offence, sentencing Beesley to fourteen years' transportation.

Interestingly, Beesley was followed into the dock by a man named William Newell, who was charged with killing a sheep. Newell was sentenced to death for his offence, as were John Sage for breaking into a house and stealing clothes and bacon and Abraham Wheeler for stealing a pair of shoes and a waistcoat worth 4s. All three were later reprieved.

3 MARCH

1947   Coroner Harold Franklin held an inquest into the death of forty-seven-year-old Blanche Ruth Beamsley, who died at the Oxford County and City Mental Hospital at Littlemore, where she had been a voluntary patient since 1943.

Having heard medical evidence that Miss Beamsley died from asphyxia due to manual strangulation, the inquest jury returned a verdict of 'murder by some person or persons unknown.'

When the coroner pointed out that this meant that Miss Beamsley was most likely murdered by another patient, the foreman of the jury insisted that they were not prepared to go as far as that and were neither exonerating nor blaming anyone for the murder.

4 MARCH

1873   Police Sergeant Henry Hawtin was on plain clothes duty in Cowley, when he saw Isaac Cripps coming towards him. Cripps was a near neighbour of Hawtin's and, until fairly recently, had been a teetotaller. However, he had taken to drink and, when drunk, became violent and abusive.

As Cripps drew closer, he shouted, 'Where's that ******* Sergeant Hawtin? I will blow his bloody brains out tonight.' Hawtin saw that Cripps was pointing a gun at him and, seizing the barrel, pushed it away, asking Cripps, 'Do you mean it, Ikey?'

'Yes, you *******, I do. I'll swing for you,' Cripps replied. He kicked Hawtin hard on the shin and pointed the gun at him again, pulling the trigger.

Somehow, Hawtin managed to lodge his thumb beneath the pistol's hammer, so that it failed to fire. Cripps tried again and Hawtin succeeded in throwing him to the ground. As he did, Cripps's son, Giles, ran up and snatched the gun from his father's hand, handing it to the landlady of the nearby Maudlen Arms for safekeeping. Cripps told Hawtin that he would go quietly but as soon as the policeman tried to handcuff him, Cripps fought like a man possessed.

Hawtin was battered and bruised but not seriously hurt and Cripps was charged with attempted murder and with wounding Hawtin with intent to do him grievous bodily harm. He was tried for both indictments at the Oxford Assizes. The court heard that Cripps harboured a grudge against

Hawtin for something that occurred between the policeman and Cripps's brother and that, after suffering a head injury, Cripps was adversely affected by even small quantities of alcohol.

The jury found Cripps guilty of the lesser offence of wounding with intent to do grievous bodily harm, but Mr Justice Denman felt that Cripps was lucky that he hadn't killed Hawtin. Pointing out that Cripps had committed a wicked offence – going out armed with a gun and deliberately seeking revenge for a perceived grudge – Denman sentenced him to twelve years' penal servitude.

5 MARCH

1824 John Packer and Richard Harding appeared at the Oxford Assizes charged with three counts of feloniously cutting William Cox, with intent to murder him, with intent to maim and disfigure, and with intent to do grievous bodily harm.

Cox, the Burford police constable, had a warrant for Packer's arrest. He apprehended him on 19 December 1823 but Packer managed to escape by flinging himself into a river.

That evening, Cox heard that Packer was drinking in The Six Bells Inn at Burford and went there to arrest him. As Cox walked through the front door, Packer ran for the back door but Cox seized him by the coat. The two men scuffled and Harding piled in to assist Packer, while another constable tried to help Cox. However, Harding and Packer seized the constables' staves from them and belaboured Cox about the head and neck, before escaping through a window.

Summoned to the pub, surgeon William Pitt found Cox insensible. His hair was matted with blood and he had four wounds on the back of his head, which, according to Pitt, were 'calculated to produce dangerous results'. Yet, while Cox was adamant that the wounds were made by Packer and Harding hitting him over the head with police staves, Pitt was equally certain that a staff couldn't have caused the type of wounds he observed on Cox's head, believing them to have been made by a poker or similar instrument, which had a sharp edge.

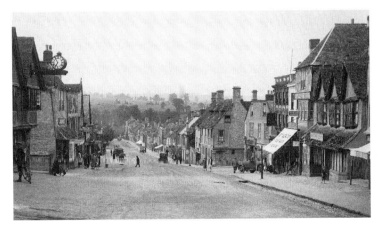

Burford, 1920s. (Author's collection)

Pitt described the injuries as 'incised wounds', explaining that a blunt instrument would have caused more swelling and bruising than was evident on Cox's head. The prosecution immediately called witnesses who testified that a poker had been used to hit Cox, but their evidence was far from convincing.

Mr Justice Park explained to the jury that the charges against the prisoners were for 'feloniously cutting' and, technically, a blunt instrument could not be used to stab or cut. If there was nothing to prove that anything but a staff had been used, the prisoners were entitled to be acquitted of the capital charges against them.

The jury found both defendants not guilty and both were immediately charged with violently assaulting the constables in the execution of their duty. On the advice of their counsel, both pleaded guilty. Observing that, but for a point of law, both men would probably have forfeited their lives, Park sentenced Packer to eighteen months' imprisonment with hard labour and Harding to twelve.

6 MARCH

1846 After attending a steeplechase and enjoying dinner at Bicester, livery stable keeper John Clarke set off with several other gentlemen to ride home to Oxford. The riders were proceeding at a brisk trot but George Alexander Helvert (or Hulvert) was riding faster than the others and soon pulled ahead.

Twenty-two-year-old Henry More William Singleton took exception to this and set off after his friend Helvert. As he caught up with him, the two men galloped on, playfully flourishing their whips at each other when, without any warning, they suddenly came upon the unlit turnpike gate at Gosford.

Singleton's horse attempted to jump the gate, ploughing through it and unseating its rider, who landed some 9 yards away. He fractured his skull on landing and died soon afterwards from an extraversion of blood on the brain.

At the inquest, the jury closely questioned the gatekeeper, William Clarke, who stated that he heard the sound of horses approaching at a rapid rate and rushed to open the gate but by the time he reached it, the accident had already happened. Even though he knew that there would be a lot of people returning from the steeplechase and the oil was provided for him, Clarke argued that he only lit the lamps on dark nights and considered that it would not have helped on this occasion.

The inquest jury disagreed and, although they fell short of any official censure, in returning a verdict of accidental death, they were unanimous in their opinion that much blame was attached to Clarke for failing to light the lamp.

7 MARCH

1848 Coroner Mr J. Churchill held an inquest in Adderbury on the death of seventy-eight-year-old Elizabeth Townsend.

Mrs Townsend was staying with her son and went out for a stroll. Meanwhile, boatman Joseph Fisher was taking a barge load of coal along the canal from Banbury to Heyford.

Adderbury, 1919. (Author's collection)

The laws of the Canal Company deemed that, on reaching the bridge, bargemen should unfasten the rope connecting the horse to the barge while the horse was taken up to the road and down on the other side to re-join the towpath. However, on this occasion, Fisher allowed the rope to be stretched across the road.

John Auger approached the rope on horseback and Fisher shouted to him to wait for a few moments until he could unfasten the rope. Auger pulled up and waited and, moments later, another horse approached at a gallop. Although Auger and Fisher both shouted at its rider to stop, Thomas Huxford's horse was bolting and he had no control over the animal. It barrelled into the rope, which immediately snapped, one end striking Mrs Townsend, whose face and neck were so badly injured that she had died before the arrival of the Adderbury surgeon.

Although they returned a verdict of 'accidental death', the inquest jury asked the coroner to censure Fisher for flouting the canal laws. The contemporary local newspaper reported that during the course of the inquest, no less than three other boatmen were observed with their ropes stretched across the road.

8 MARCH

1845 Twenty-three-year-old John Clanfield was working in a stone quarry at Cuddesdon when a young boy appeared at the quarry's edge. The child, who was about ten years old, was employed as a bird scarer and carried a gun under his arm.

Clanfield asked the child to 'let him have a shoot' and went to take the gun. As he did so, the gun went off, discharging its load of lead shot into Clanfield's right side. He was taken to the Radcliffe Infirmary but was beyond medical assistance and died the next morning.

The inquest jury returned a verdict of 'accidental death', asking the coroner to reprimand the boy's employer for allowing so young a child to carry a loaded gun. The farmer immediately protested that the child had been issued with powder only, so that the gun made a noise and scared away the birds – he had taken it upon himself to load the gun with pieces of lead and had done so against the farmer's orders, having been scolded only the day before for shooting rather than scaring the birds. The coroner severely reprimanded the boy for disobeying his master, cautioning him against doing so again.

9 MARCH

1899   George Thomas Cox and his wife Annie, of St Ebbe's, appeared at Oxford Police Court charged with neglecting their children in a manner likely to cause them unnecessary suffering on various days during the past six months.

Inspector Cole from the National Society for the Prevention of Cruelty to Children visited the house on 3 March and found it to be in a filthy condition, with decomposed food and human waste on the floor. The children slept in one bed and, according to Cole, their sheets were stiff with dirt. There were three children there – John (7), Lilian Clara (6) and Louisa (5) – all of whom were seriously underweight. They were inadequately clothed and covered in infected flea bites. Louisa had a bad case of rickets and could barely walk and, when they were later examined by a doctor, he remarked that every hair on their heads had a nit on it. While the Inspector was at the house, the eldest child, nine-year-old Irene Caroline, came in, having been sent to buy beer for her mother, who was drunk. Irene was in the same dirty, emaciated state as her siblings.

Cox earned good wages as a cabinet maker but his wife spent every penny on drink and had even pawned his tools on occasions, which prevented him from working. Several people had tried to help the children in the past but Annie Cox refused charity and had thrown their well-meant gifts of food into the garden.

Her husband seemed almost resigned to appearing before magistrates, saying that he had tried to persuade his wife to do better but without success, adding that he had expected to be prosecuted, given the way Annie behaved. In reaching their verdict, the Bench considered Cox's apparent good character, although they stressed that he couldn't shirk the responsibility of attending to his children. He was therefore fined 40s, with 22s 6d in costs, while his wife was sent to prison for four months with hard labour.

10 MARCH

1847   The trial of William Cave for wilful murder took place at the Oxford Assizes. Although he was married, Cave and widow Hannah Treadwell (or Tredwell) were engaged in an affair that had lasted several years. Hannah was a very jealous woman and, having fallen on hard times financially, seemed to believe that Cave should support her. She began following him through the village of Thorley demanding money and abusing him.

On 4 August 1846, Cave was walking to the outskirts of the village, where he owned land, when Hannah began to berate him for making eyes at the wife of one of his neighbours. Cave denied doing any such thing and continued walking, with Hannah at his heels scolding and nagging.

Suddenly, a shot rang out and, seconds later, Cave hurried nervously back through the village. Hannah lay dead on top of a bank near his land, a single gunshot wound beneath her chin, which severed her carotid artery, killing her instantly.

Cave freely admitted shooting Hannah, saying, 'I have done it. I must suffer the law and it will be a warning to others.' When he was apprehended, his pistol was loaded and he claimed to have reloaded it after shooting Hannah with the intention of killing himself, but decided that he should have some time to repent first.

Cave gave several different explanations for Hannah's death, saying that he had intended to hit her with the pistol, which had gone off by accident, and also suggesting that she provoked him by telling lies about him and throwing stones.

Cave was lucky to have a sympathetic jury, who took ten minutes to agree that he was sufficiently provoked to merit a verdict of guilty of manslaughter. Commenting on the 'merciful construction on the facts' displayed by the jury, Mr Justice Maule gave Cave the severest possible sentence for manslaughter, that of transportation for life. He died in prison in December 1847, while waiting to leave.

11 MARCH

1884 Baby Eric Arthur Sealey of Queen Street had recently had a bad cough, although he had almost completely recovered after treatment from a surgeon. As he sat in his high chair at the breakfast table, he suddenly began to cough and seemed unable to draw breath.

His mother snatched him out of his chair and pulled a piece of chewed bread from his mouth. However, Eric continued to gasp for breath and gradually went black in the face.

Eric's father ran for a surgeon, who arrived within minutes. However by that time Eric was dead from what the jury at his inquest would later determine was 'accidental choking'. He died on his first birthday.

12 MARCH

1859 Edward Faulkner was seen by witnesses leading two horses from a field at Great Haseley. Moments later, one of the horses galloped past towing Faulkner behind it, both of his feet apparently somehow attached to the animal's tail. People rushed to try and help him but, by the time they reached him, he had fallen and the horse had bolted.

Faulkner was dead. His tattered and torn clothes had been dragged over his head and his face was cut to ribbons. His left ankle was shattered, the foot attached only by a sliver of skin, and the ribs on his left-hand side were smashed.

Doctors theorised that the broken ribs and possibly the ankle injury were caused by a kick from the horse but could not suggest how fifty-six-year-old Faulkner came to be entangled with its tail. At an inquest held by coroner Mr J.H. Cooke, the jury was equally baffled, returning a verdict of 'accidental death'.

13 MARCH

1858 Mrs James of Brize Norton complained to a neighbour that she had sickness and diarrhoea, coupled with an unpleasant sensation in her throat.

The neighbour suggested a drop of gin but it did not help Mrs James, whose condition worsened until she died on 24 March.

On the day of her death, both her husband and son were taken ill. A neighbour volunteered to walk to Bampton to summon a doctor for them and was rewarded with a glass of gin, but he too was taken ill, vomiting violently on his way to fetch the surgeon. The two carpenters who had made Mrs James's coffin were similarly afflicted, having accepted a glass of gin when they delivered it.

Mr James died on 26 March, leaving the coroner with a mystery. Everyone who had drunk gin at the James' house had been ill and Mr and Mrs James, who had each drunk more than one glass, had died.

Post-mortem examinations on both bodies showed no signs of poisoning but suggested that Mrs James had died from bronchitis and her husband from epilepsy. The coroner adjourned the inquests and contacted the Secretary of State for permission to send samples to analyst Mr Herapath for testing.

Surprisingly, the Home Secretary refused the coroner's request and, when the inquests concluded on 16 April, the jury suggested sending the samples for testing at their own expense. There is nothing to suggest that this was ever done – the jury returned verdicts according to the medical evidence on both deaths and the gin was safely disposed of, just in case.

14 MARCH

1877 Shoemaker William Patrick spent all day drinking in The Ship and Anchor in Chipping Norton, running up a slate for his drinks. Eventually he called for some rum and the landlord's wife, Susan Cotton, refused to serve him any more until she received payment for what Patrick had already drunk. Patrick used a foul profanity and when Mrs Cotton left the room he followed her, seizing her arms and saying that if he had a pistol he would blow her brains out.

Later that evening, Mrs Cotton went to visit an aunt and bumped into Patrick, who intimidated and threatened her. As she was running home,

Chipping Norton. (Author's collection)

he leaped out of the shadows and asked her to forgive him for insulting her that afternoon. Mrs Cotton told him that he was barred, at which he again threatened to kill her.

Terrified, she broke away from him but tripped over as she was running for home. Patrick, who was chasing her, fell on top of her and told her that if she would allow him to have intercourse with her, he wouldn't hurt her. Mrs Cotton refused and Patrick stabbed her three times, wounding her left thigh. Luckily, her injuries were not too serious and she managed to escape.

Charged with 'unlawfully stabbing and wounding Susan Cotton with intent to do her grievous bodily harm', Patrick appeared at the Oxford Assizes in July. His defence was that he was very drunk at the time of the offence and had been wildly waving the knife about when it accidentally struck Mrs Cotton's thigh.

The jury found Patrick guilty of the lesser offence of unlawfully wounding, much to the chagrin of the presiding judge, who questioned how a wound could be made 'unintentionally' after the defendant had persistently threatened his victim with violence and tried to stab her three times. Nevertheless, the judge was powerless to change the jury's verdict and, remarking that he thought that they had been very lenient, he sentenced Patrick to six months' imprisonment with hard labour.

15 MARCH

1859   Coroner Mr J.H. Cooke held an inquest at Pyrton into the death of seventeen-year-old James Jordan.

Jordan went with Bracey's carters to collect some timber for his employer. On returning to Pyrton, Jordan busied himself with unharnessing the horses. As he did so, a piece of timber fell off the waggon, striking him hard on the back of the neck.

Jordan just had time to gasp 'Oh!' before falling down, dying within minutes. A later post-mortem examination showed that he had a dislocated vertebra in his neck, which had proved fatal. The inquest jury returned a verdict of 'accidental death'.

16 MARCH

1942   Thirty-one-year-old Private William Henry Lovelock of the Oxford and Bucks Light Infantry appeared before Mr Justice Charles at the Oxfordshire Assizes, charged with the wilful murder of his wife, Edith Elizabeth Lovelock, and Norman Whalley.

Lovelock pleaded not guilty to the two counts of murder but guilty to two counts of manslaughter. The court heard that, on finding his wife in bed with Whalley, Lovelock snatched up a loaded revolver that was lying on the bedside table and, according to Mr Justice Charles, was 'provoked beyond anything that a reasonable man could be supposed to bear' when he shot his wife and her lover.

The guilty pleas were accepted by the prosecution, who freely acknowledged that Lovelock had taken no weapon of any kind with him when he went to look for his wife but had simply grabbed the revolver on impulse. He was sentenced to twelve months' imprisonment on each charge, the sentences to run concurrently.

17 MARCH

1892 A double execution took place at Oxford Prison. The two condemned men were thirty-one-year-old Charles Raynor and thirty-five-year-old Frederick Eggleton, who were found guilty at the Buckinghamshire Assizes of the wilful murder of two gamekeepers at Pitstone, near Aylesbury on 12 December 1891. Under normal circumstances, the executions would have taken place at Aylesbury Prison but since that had recently been converted to a women's prison, the men were transferred to Oxford for their appointments with executioner James Billington.

Oxford Prison (now a hotel). (© R. Sly)

Contemporary newspapers stated that the previous double execution at Oxford took place almost sixty years to the day before this one, on 19 March 1832. On that date, John Gibbs was executed for arson and George Lay for highway robbery. Since then there had been ten executions, all for murder. The newspapers commented that, of the forty-one executions that had taken place in Oxford since 1778, twenty-seven were in the month of March.

18 MARCH

1899 'Last week, we reported that Mrs M. Moores had three fingers bitten off by a horse' wrote the reporter from *Jackson's Oxford Journal*. The newspaper then went on to give a corrected account of Mrs Moores' injuries.

They related that Mary Moores and her daughter were returning to Little Milton from Oxford in the carrier's cart. The carrier, Mr Dashpur (or Dashper), had purchased a horse in Oxford that day and Mrs Moores volunteered to hold the end of the halter rope, so, instead of tying the cob to the back of the cart, Dashpur passed the rope through the trap window. As the cart went through Cowley, the horse began to buck and plunged backwards, the rope ripping off four of Mrs Moores' fingers.

High Street, Little Milton. (Author's collection)

Mrs Moores and her daughter pleaded with Dashpur to take them to the hospital in Oxford but he refused. He did stop at Little Milton to seek medical advice and the doctor there immediately ordered him to take Mrs Moores back to the Radcliffe Infirmary where, according to the newspaper, it was hoped that her thumb could be saved.

19 MARCH

1879 Fifteen-year-old farm labourer Edward Shirley was scaring birds at Cuddesdon when Charles Jennings, who was at work in an adjacent field, heard him shouting for help. Jennings looked up and saw the youth staggering towards him clutching his chest.

Shirley collapsed before he could reach Jennings, who ran to him and found that he was bleeding heavily from a gunshot wound in his left breast. Shirley managed to tell Jennings that he was lifting the gun to his shoulder when it caught in his clothing and went off accidentally.

Church Road, Cuddesdon. (Author's collection)

The gun was found in a nearby ditch and Shirley admitted that he had loaded it with shot, against the specific instructions of his employer Mr Chillingworth, who permitted him only to charge the gun with powder so that it made a noise and scared away birds.

In spite of medical attention, Shirley died later that evening and at an inquest held by coroner Mr W.W. Robinson, the jury found a verdict of 'death from a gunshot wound caused by accident', donating their fees to the boy's mother.

20 MARCH

1873 As Elizabeth Gunn walked through Banbury, forty-six-year-old Richard Eden suddenly ran up to her and asked, 'Will you give me my bed?'

Elizabeth, who had bought a bed from Eden five years earlier, protested that she had paid him for it but Eden shouted, 'I will murder you dead' and began to chop at her with a large hook or knife. Elizabeth finally managed to get away and Eden calmly walked into The Windmill public house. Edward Parker Burden, who had witnessed the attack, followed him and Eden told him that he might fetch a policeman if he liked and have him hung.

Burden did just that and Sergeant Morgan arrived to arrest Eden, who handed over the knife and waited quietly for another policeman to assist Morgan in taking him to the station. 'I can stand to be hung,' he told Morgan helpfully, adding, 'I can be roasted, if they like.' Meanwhile, surgeon Francis Hudson had been summoned to attend to Elizabeth Gunn. He found her suffering from loss of blood – one of her hands had been almost amputated and she had a wound on her temple that had penetrated her temporal artery, as well as injuries to her head, back, shoulders and arm.

Eden was charged with maliciously wounding Elizabeth Gunn with intent to murder her and also with wounding with intent to do grievous bodily harm.

At his trial at the Oxford Assizes, his counsel relied on an insanity defence and Eden seemed keen to speak on his own behalf, claiming that he was a bulldog and that he had been persecuted by the people of Banbury for serving the Lord. He related that a drunken old midwife had killed his wife and that he had only lent Elizabeth Gunn his bed and she refused to return it.

However, while Eden's rambling speech seemed to indicate that he was not in his right mind, prison surgeon John Briscoe disagreed, saying that he had found the prisoner completely rational. In his summary for the jury, Mr Justice Denman reminded them that a prisoner was deemed sane unless it was proven otherwise and the jury found Eden guilty of wounding with intent to do grievous bodily harm, making no mention of insanity. Presumed sane, he was sentenced to twelve years' penal servitude.

21 MARCH

1755 Having been found guilty of highway robbery at the Oxford Assizes, twenty-year-old Richard Mansfield and nineteen-year-old Richard Dancer were sentenced to death.

They had robbed a man named Morgan of his purse and a brass counter and both made a full confession in the run up to their execution. However, both swore that the purse contained just two shillings, rather than the one guinea that Morgan claimed had been stolen.

On the day of their execution, a cart waited at the door of Oxford Castle to receive them. Suddenly, a bulldog rushed out of the crowd and seized the horse by the throat, refusing to let go. The horse took fright and bolted and, with the bulldog still hanging on to its throat, dragged the cart through the crowds of people who had assembled to watch the execution.

By a miracle, only two people were injured – an elderly man was knocked over and badly bruised, as was a pregnant woman.

Note: Some sources give the date of the double execution as 22 March.

Oxford Castle. (Author's collection)

22 MARCH

1762 Gypsy Shadrach Smith was executed at Oxford for highway robbery, having been found guilty at the assizes of robbing and stripping a girl in a lane near Chalgrove Field. It was reported that Smith 'used the young woman very cruelly' and, if it hadn't been for the intervention of his ten-year-old son, would most probably have killed her. The boy was the chief witness for the prosecution at his father's trial and was imprisoned for his own safety in the run up to the opening of the assizes.

After receiving the death sentence, Smith seemed quite philosophical about his fate, remarking lightly that he did not mind being hanged, as 'it would save his keeping.'

23 MARCH

1870 Ten-year-old Joseph Hawse was employed by a farmer near Wantage to drive rooks from the newly-sown corn. Because of his age, Joseph wasn't allowed to have a gun but he managed to get hold of some gunpowder, which he kept in his pocket.

Somehow, the gunpowder exploded and set Joseph's clothes on fire. Another boy scaring birds in the next field was quick to rush to his aid and did all he could to put out the blaze but, finding himself unable to do so, resorted to running as fast as he could for help.

Abraham Carter hastened to the field and found Joseph sitting quietly, totally enveloped in flames and smoke. Carter put out the fire and cut off what little remained of Joseph's clothes, then carried the boy home and fetched a doctor. Sadly, Joseph's legs were so badly burned that his bones were actually charred and he died the following evening.

An inquest jury later returned a verdict of 'accidentally burnt'.

24 MARCH

1878 At about half-past four in the morning, a young man getting up to go to work in Lockinge realised that the house next door to his own was on fire. The occupants were his grandparents, James and Frances Prior, who were both in their seventies. Mrs Prior had a bad leg and was in the habit of dressing it by candlelight when she retired to bed. Only two days earlier, she had accidentally set fire to her bedclothes and now the cottage's thatched roof was ablaze.

The Priors daughter and son-in-law managed to gain entrance to their cottage by breaking a window but when they reached their parents' bedroom, they found the door locked. Before long, the roof caved in.

Although the Wantage Fire Brigade were quick to arrive, they could do little apart from damping down the flames with the object of searching the debris and, at eight o'clock, two dreadfully charred bodies were removed from the burned-out cottage. They were unrecognisable but were assumed to be all that remained of Mr and Mrs Prior.

At the inquest, the jury returned verdicts of 'accidentally burnt' on both bodies, bemoaning the fact that there was no portable fire escape in the village.

25 MARCH

1899 Brook Alder was returning to his house in East Challow at around ten o'clock at night when he heard a moaning noise coming from behind a hedge. Peering over, he saw something in the canal and realised that it was a woman and a bicycle. The canal was frozen and the woman's head and shoulders and the front wheel and handlebars of the bicycle had gone through the ice into the water.

With difficulty, Alder managed to get the woman's head out of the canal but he was unable to pull her up the bank without assistance. Supporting her upper body, he shouted until help came. The woman was carried to The Coach and Horses Inn, where she was wrapped in blankets and given brandy. Dr Woodhouse was summoned and found her suffering from shock and hypothermia and, although she was still alive when he arrived, she stopped breathing soon afterwards. Woodhouse tried artificial respiration for almost an hour but to no avail.

After her death, the woman was identified as forty-four-year-old Annie Ellen Plummer who was cycling home after visiting friends in Stanford-in-the-Vale. It was a clear night and there was a full moon and nobody could suggest how Mrs Plummer could have cycled into the canal. At the inquest on her death, the jury returned a verdict that she died from the effects of shock having accidentally ridden a bicycle into the Wilts and Berks Canal at night time.

26 MARCH

1828 The Stroudwater coach changed horses as usual at The Crown and Thistle, Abingdon and continued its journey, carrying a man and a woman inside and three ladies and four gentlemen outside. The coach had not gone more than a few yards, when one of the horses began to kick and plunge, throwing the passengers into a state of panic.

One of the male outside passengers jumped off and, as the coach progressed, one of its wheels lodged against a wall. It scraped along the wall for some 50 yards, during which time, another male passenger jumped off, scaring the horses, which promptly bolted at full speed. With the assistance of a male passenger, coachman Mr Thomas managed to steer the horses into a wall, stopping them in their tracks. As he did, a woman fell from the coach, landing in front of the wheels, although fortunately she was not injured.

Passer-by Mr Dutton helpfully held the bridles of the leading horses while they were uncoupled from the coach but as soon as they were freed, they whipped round and began to kick out at Dutton, who found himself trapped by the horses on one side and a crowd of spectators on the other. Unable to escape, Dutton flung himself onto the wall of a bridge, where he lay face down.

Unfortunately, he was still within range of the horses, one of whom kicked him hard on the hip, knocking him over the edge of the wall. He managed to grasp the coping but the horse kicked him again, this time severing one of his fingers and almost severing a second. Dutton dropped off the bridge into the river below, although, luckily, he was a good swimmer and managed to reach the bank, where he was pulled from the water bravely insisting that he wasn't hurt.

Later that day, the bridge was the scene of a second accident, when a boy leading a blind horse across it strayed too near to the wall and the horse fell over, landing on a pile of wood below and breaking its back.

The contemporary local newspapers indignantly pointed out the bridge's inadequacies, stating that it was the main thoroughfare into the town and was more than 250 yards long and so narrow that carriages could not pass each other on it. Furthermore, the walls were so low in places that several people had fallen over them in recent years.

27 MARCH

1871　Coroner Mr Brunner held an inquest at Oxford City Gaol into the death of seven-week-old Alfred Timms, whose mother had been imprisoned the previous day for failing to obey an order to enter the Workhouse.

The woman was a widow, who already had three young children to support when she gave birth to illegitimate twins. Dependent entirely on parish relief, her payments were stopped as soon as she was considered to have recovered sufficiently from childbirth to move into the Workhouse. When she was gaoled, she had received no money for two weeks.

Alfred and his twin were both sickly babies, who had problems suckling from birth. Unable to afford milk, their mother fed them on pap made from bread and water, on which the children failed to thrive. At his death, Alfred weighed less than half the normal weight for a baby of his age and his twin was in a similar condition and was not expected to survive.

At the inquest into the baby's death, it was pointed out that Alfred and his siblings were all clean, well dressed, and had been cared for as well as their mother was able, considering her circumstances. The coroner took the view that, in sending Mrs Timms to gaol, the magistrates were acting in the best interests of her children, since she refused to go to the Workhouse where they would be taken care of properly. Even so, Mr Brunner apparently believed that Mrs Timms was to be pitied rather than punished and the inquest jury agreed.

28 MARCH

1930 Farmer Frank Brown of Tackley went out shooting and, as he scrambled through a hedge, the trigger of his shotgun caught on a twig and the gun discharged, shooting him in the stomach.

He was found lying seriously wounded in a hedge by railway ganger Frederick Bull, who immediately rushed off to get help for the injured man. However, as he tried to tell his son what he had found, Bull collapsed at his feet and died.

Brown was taken to Radcliffe Infirmary, in a critical condition, where he later died from his injuries.

29 MARCH

1870 A bull was driven from the cattle market at Reading to Henley-on-Thames and on reaching Duke Street, it suddenly went berserk. It knocked down a child – fortunately without causing it any serious injury – then fell down exhausted. Minutes later, it found its second wind and charged at a group of people nearby.

Sixty-four-year-old Robert Jeshureiah Dence couldn't move fast enough to get away and the bull butted him in the stomach, knocking the breath out of him. He slumped across the bull's back and was carried for a few yards before the beast tossed him into the air. Dence fell on his back with a resounding thud and lay motionless.

The bull stood pawing the ground and snorting and nobody dared to approach Dence for fear it would charge them. Time seemed to stand still for several minutes, until a waggon drove past and distracted the bull's attention, allowing Dence to be carried to safety.

Sadly, he was so badly injured that he died the following day, an inquest returning a verdict of 'accidental death'. The bull was captured and slaughtered.

30 MARCH

1821 Mr Bradbury of Dorchester-on-Thames had suffered from fits from birth and, on 30 March, he became delirious. Escaping from his house, he ran stark naked along the road towards Burcot, showing such an amazing turn of speed that nobody could catch up with him.

The following morning, Bradbury was found dead in a ditch adjoining the turnpike road, his body frozen stiff. There were no marks of violence on his body and doctors supposed that he had died as a result of exposure.

Accordingly, at an inquest held by coroner Mr Cooke, the jury returned a verdict that Bradbury died from the inclemency of the weather.

31 MARCH

1894 James and Eliza Hemmings had been separated for seven months. James took their three oldest children to live with his parents, while his wife worked as a prostitute to support herself and their baby.

On 31 March, Eliza was drinking at The Hope and Anchor in George Street, Oxford, with another man, coincidentally named James Hemmings. Eliza saw her husband and, when she challenged him about supporting her and the baby, he punched her in the face, causing her nose to bleed.

James's namesake fled, leaving husband and wife together, and they went to Eliza's lodgings, where Eliza asked her landlord Mr Clark's permission to bring her husband in. Clark stayed talking to the couple for some time and was later to say that he believed that they were on the point of reconciliation. However, a couple of hours after Clark left the room, the house was roused by the sounds of a violent scuffle and cries of 'Murder!' Mr and Mrs Clark ran downstairs and were just in time to see Hemmings leaving through the front door.

Although Eliza had been viciously beaten, she was well enough to visit the police station the next morning to lodge a complaint against her husband and to appear in court on 3 April, although she fainted after giving evidence. By 5 April, she was so unwell that a doctor arranged for her admittance to hospital, where she died that evening. A post-mortem examination revealed cuts and bruises all over her body but surgeons attributed her death to bruising and inflammation of her heart and brain.

James Hemmings was charged with his wife's wilful murder, appearing before Mr Justice Hawkins at the Oxford Assizes on 30 June. There, two surgeons gave evidence about the extent of Eliza's injuries and both were of the opinion that the bruising to her heart might have been a much earlier injury than all the others, possibly occurring days before. It was suggested in court that Eliza's landlady, Mrs Clark, had fought with her on a couple of occasions over outstanding rent and had actually pushed her over in the course of one such argument.

Eventually, Hemmings's defence counsel offered a guilty plea to the lesser offence of manslaughter, which was accepted by the prosecution. The jury strongly recommended mercy and, after taking the weekend to consider his sentence, Mr Justice Hawkins sentenced Hemmings to five years' penal servitude.

APRIL

High Street, Chipping Norton, 1956. (Author's collection)

1 APRIL

1858 Eleven-year-old Reuben Wilkins was a ploughboy employed by farmer Mr Keene at West Hendred. On 1 April, Reuben was taking a team of three horses from the field back to the farm. The lead horse was blind and, as he often did, Reuben jumped onto its back to save his legs.

Unfortunately, one of the other horses barged into the horse that Reuben was riding, startling it and sending it off at a canter. It reached the banks of a brook and kicked up its heels, sending the boy flying over its head into the water, before toppling off the bank and landing heavily on Reuben. He was carried home in a state of collapse, in which he remained for forty hours before rallying slightly. However, his internal injuries were so severe that they eventually proved fatal.

The inquest was told that the blind horse was known as a vicious kicker but that it was otherwise quiet and Reuben frequently rode it home. In returning a verdict of 'accidentally killed' the jury expressed a strong view that the carter, who was some distance behind Reuben at the time of his accident, should not have left so young a child in charge of the horses. The jury also stated that Mr Keene should not have permitted the boy to ride.

2 APRIL

1830 John Broadest took his master's horse to a pond near Burford for a drink. While it was drinking, he scrambled onto its back, frightening the animal and causing it to bolt.

Almost three miles later, the horse neared the Upton toll gate and, as it approached at a gallop, Broadest yelled to seventy-four-year-old Thomas Little to close the gate. Little did as he was asked, standing before the gate with his arms held aloft to try and stop the horse. Unfortunately, the horse had other ideas and, with Broadest still clinging on desperately, it leaped the gate. Little was knocked over and died soon afterwards from his injuries.

Coroner Mr Cecil held an inquest at Burford, at which the jury strongly censured Broadest for getting on the horse, which was seriously injured by its jump over the gate. They returned a verdict of 'accidental death' on Little.

3 APRIL

1925 Juray Parker, described in the contemporary newspapers as 'a negro', had lodged with Sarah Ann Tanner in Summertown for almost a year. He was said to be 'very strange in temper' and on 3 April, he suddenly announced over breakfast that Mrs Tanner would have to die that day, adding that he was going to be hung and that his time had come.

Parker then left the house and witnesses described him travelling around Oxford by bus, shouting in pidgin English, 'Me do murder,' 'Me no care,' and 'Me only die once'. He returned to his lodgings for supper, which he ate calmly and quietly but, as soon as he had finished eating, he attacked his landlady with his table knife, cutting her throat.

Fortunately for Mrs Tanner, the knife was not that sharp and, although Parker inflicted a wound almost six inches long, it was superficial. Meanwhile, Parker fled and nothing more was seen of him until the early hours of the following morning, when he appeared in a railway signal box at Yarnton and announced that he had 'done a woman in.'

Parker was tried for attempted murder at the Oxford Assizes and although his defence insisted that the offence was due to a sudden explosion of temper and that Parker had neither motive nor intent to commit murder, the jury found him guilty. He was sentenced to four years' penal servitude.

4 APRIL   **1885** Coroner Mr W.W. Robinson held an inquest at The Fox Inn, Sandford-on-Thames on the death of thirty-eight-year-old labourer Edward Bampton.

On 2 April, Bampton and William Pollard were employed to empty a cesspool at Sandford, which took them almost until midnight. During the course of their work, the ladder on which Bampton was standing broke, plunging him into the cesspool. Naturally, his clothes were in a disgusting state and the servants of the house washed them for him. Since he had no spare garments, he was forced to dress in his wet clothes to walk home.

As Bampton and Pollard set out to walk to Littlemore, Bampton excused himself, saying that he needed to retire into a field and would catch up with Pollard momentarily. Pollard saw him open a field gate and go inside but reached home before Bampton caught up with him and went to bed. It wasn't until Pollard was on his way to work the following morning that he learned that Bampton had not arrived home.

A search was made for the missing man, who was found lying on his back under a tree in the field where Pollard last saw him. He was insensible and his body was completely rigid, although he could still move his fingers when commanded to do so.

Bampton was carried to The Fox Inn and laid before the fire but died before he could be examined by a doctor. When Dr Duff arrived at the inn just minutes after Bampton's death, he could find no signs of any injuries, nor were there any indications that Bampton had been drinking. He was known to be epileptic and the doctor theorised that he might have suffered a fit, although he believed that the principal cause of death was exposure to the cold night in wet clothes. The inquest jury found 'that deceased died from natural causes and that his death was hastened by exposure to cold.'

5 APRIL   **1939** Pilot Officer Peter Shennan of No. 15 Bomber Squadron was killed in an accident at Abingdon.

Shennan, who was stationed at RAF Abingdon, was a member of the crew of a plane piloted by Flying Officer P. Chapman, which was engaged in bombing practice. Chapman made three attacks on a target before turning the aircraft and climbing. At a height of 900ft, he turned back towards the target and began to dive to gain speed.

As he did, he noticed something falling out of the rear cockpit of the aircraft. He manoeuvred the plane so that he had a good view of the falling object, realising to his horror that it was Shennan.

An inquest held that evening recorded a verdict of 'death by misadventure'.

Abingdon, where an RAF officer fell to his death in 1939. (Author's collection)

6 APRIL

1856 Coroner Mr F. Westell held an inquest at Ducklington into the death of twelve-year-old Joseph Jordan.

Jordan was employed with a carter to help roll grass on parkland at Ducklington. As a team of four horses pulled a heavy granite roller over the grass, the roller accidentally mounted a pile of stones. The horses set off at a brisk trot and Jordan was knocked down, the roller passing over his body and squashing him flat.

Jordan died instantly and the inquest jury returned a verdict of 'accidental death'.

7 APRIL

1894 Husband and wife Sarah Ann and Bond Gibbs were residents at Banbury Workhouse and, on 7 April, Bond was out all day selling nuts. He and Sarah then drank a large quantity of rum, after which they began quarrelling. Sarah pulled Bond's whiskers and, after he threatened to dash her brains out with a hammer, she kicked him hard in the testicles.

Over the next few days Bond became more and more unwell and on 18 April, he was seen by Dr Griffin of Banbury, who ordered him to be admitted to the Workhouse Infirmary. At that time, Bond was suffering from 'extravasations of urine', with urine leaking from his bladder and collecting in his scrotum. Griffin couldn't determine whether this was due to violence or to a 'stricture' but he believed that Gibbs had a ruptured urethra and that his lower abdomen was gangrenous.

Because Gibbs was so ill, a deposition was taken at his bedside, in which he accused his wife of kicking him. Sarah was charged with causing grievous bodily harm and, when Bond died on 19 April, the charge was upgraded to one of manslaughter.

Thirty-eight-year-old Sarah appeared before Mr Justice Hawkins at the Oxford Assizes. From the outset, Sarah maintained that she had not kicked her husband, merely pushed him with her foot, and that she had only done that because he was pinning her to the ground by her throat.

Her defence counsel insisted that, if Sarah had injured her husband, it had been in self-defence and produced witnesses who had seen red marks on her throat on the morning of 8 April. Several people testified to Bond's previous violent behaviour towards her, including two of Sarah's three young children.

The jury gave Sarah the benefit of the doubt and, after deliberating briefly, pronounced her 'not guilty'.

8 APRIL

1871   An inquest was held into the death of Hannah Messenger, the wife of the inn keeper at Stokenchurch.

Thirty-six-year-old Hannah, who already had five children, was heavily pregnant when she died from 'uterine haemorrhage'. However, a post-mortem examination conducted by Mr Hayman revealed that she also had a head injury. The inquest was told that Hannah and her husband argued shortly before her death and Hannah threw a book at her husband, who promptly threw it back, hitting her on the head.

Coroner Mr Dixon adjourned the inquest for a second opinion on the injury and whether it had played any part in Hannah's death. Surgeon Mr Taylor conducted another post-mortem examination and corroborated Hayman's findings, both surgeons agreeing that the injury was very slight. Neither thought that it had contributed to Hannah's demise, although both surgeons pointed out that the 'great mental excitement' of a quarrel might have induced the miscarriage that ultimately killed her.

Once the inquest re-opened, the jury returned a verdict that 'the deceased died from uterine haemorrhage but how induced there was not sufficient evidence to show.'

9 APRIL

1880   Former soldier George Illing had been courting Miss Smith, much to the chagrin of her mother, who didn't approve of the relationship. Eliza Smith sent her daughter to London to get her away from Illing and, on 9 April, he called at her house in Woodstock to remonstrate with her. Neighbours heard screams, shouts of murder and shots and ran to see what was happening, finding Mrs Smith bleeding from her face and Illing standing over her with a pistol.

Thomas Margetts bravely attempted to disarm Illing and the pistol went off as the two men struggled. 'Take it, take it,' Illing said, thrusting the pistol at Margetts, who took it to the police station. Meanwhile, Illing walked into The Bear Hotel and asked the landlord to fetch a policeman as he wished to give himself up. When Sergeant Dyer arrived, Illing told him, 'Yes, I did it, but under great provocation; she has served me very bad and driven me to madness. I did not know what I was doing.'

The bullet fired at Eliza Smith passed through her right-hand jaw bone and lodged in the left, from where it was later removed. Although the wound wasn't fatal, erysipelas set in and Eliza's life was despaired of. Fortunately, she recovered to see Illing sentenced to ten years' penal servitude for her attempted murder at the Oxford Assizes of 8 July.

The Bear Hotel and Town Hall, Woodstock, 1950s. (Author's collection)

10 APRIL

1899 At an inquest held by coroner Mr Westell in Chipping Norton, the jury seemed intent on putting to rights a serious problem with the delivery of mail in the area.

The deceased was thirty-four-year-old Walter Williams, who had driven the mail coach between Chipping Norton and Oxford for nine years. On 8 April, the coach horses bolted and Williams was thrown, sustaining a fractured skull. Two passengers were also injured in the incident and the jury believed that the horses were unmanageable. They questioned the witnesses in great detail, establishing that one horse, a little chestnut, had bolted twice before and that Williams had specifically asked passenger John Thomas Barnett to accompany him, as he was having problems coping with the horses.

The coroner repeatedly tried to subdue the jury, telling them that they were only required to look into the cause of death. However, the jury insisted that the horses that Williams was expected to drive were some of the worst that could be found and wanted to indict the owner for manslaughter.

Town Hall, Chipping Norton. (Author's collection)

A horse–drawn coach. (Author's collection)

'It is well known that the way in which the mail cart is horsed has been a disgrace to the neighbourhood,' protested a juryman, but the coroner flatly refused to have anything to do with what he deemed 'sly allegations of manslaughter', saying that in order to bring in a verdict of manslaughter, the jury needed proper evidence.

The jury eventually agreed that Walter Williams received fatal injuries when the horses he was driving became unmanageable for reasons unknown. 'That rather feebly expresses our intentions on the subject,' the foreman added, making the point that the horses were notoriously vicious. Although the jury weren't quite prepared to go as far as returning a verdict of manslaughter against the horses' owner, they wanted the coroner to order him to provide better horses in future.

'I won't do it,' protested the coroner and the matter was eventually settled when the jury insisted on calling Williams's widow. Harriet Williams testified that, although her husband had made written complaints about the horses in the past, he had not specifically complained about this particular team, which he had driven for three weeks.

11 APRIL

1883 Blacksmith John Butler of Banbury and his wife Ann appeared at the Oxon and Berks Assizes charged with administering a noxious substance to Mary Vincent at Neithrop, with intent to procure her miscarriage.

Mary, an orphan, told the court that having known the Butlers since she was a child, she formed a relationship with their son, Charles, which she believed would lead to marriage. However, at the beginning of July 1882, Mrs Butler questioned her about whether or not she was 'in the family way' and if Charles had attempted to do anything with her. Mary chose not to reply but Mrs Butler inferred from her silence that she was pregnant and told her that Mr Butler would get some stuff to make her miscarry.

A few days later, Mary was summoned to the Butlers' house, where she was given some inky liquid to drink and told to take the rest of the bottle home with her. The liquid made her violently sick within minutes and she couldn't bear to take any more.

Although the banns for her marriage to Charles were read, John Butler forbade the union and, when Mary gave birth to a baby on 8 January 1883, she had to summon Charles for paternity. She had saved the remaining liquid and handed it over to the police, who had it analysed and found it to contain perchloride of iron. According to analytical chemist Mr T. Beesley, it would be noxious to a pregnant woman and, being eight times stronger than the formula in the British Pharmacopoeia, would almost certainly cause a miscarriage. Butler's brother was a porter at a chemist's shop in Banbury and told the court that he had obtained the 'medicine' for his brother-in-law, who had been taking it in weak doses for many years.

At that point, the presiding judge asked the prosecuting counsel if he believed that he could prove the charge against the prisoners. The judge pointed out that the whole case rested on Mary's evidence and that she had quarrelled with the Butlers after they put a stop to her marriage plans. She made no complaint against them until after the bastardy summons was disputed and, by taking the liquid home with her to take more of the solution she was an accomplice to the act. The jury determined that they had heard enough evidence and, after a short consultation, acquitted the prisoners, who were discharged.

12 APRIL   **1883**   At the Oxon and Berks Assizes, twenty-year-old musician William Macbeth was tried for two offences – indecently assaulting eight-year-old Florence Wicks on 16 March and unlawfully committing an unnatural offence with a boy on 17 March.

When the jury found him guilty of both offences, judge the Honourable Sir James Fitzjames Stephen dealt with the second indictment first, sentencing Macbeth to twenty years' penal servitude. For the indecent assault on Florence, Macbeth received a nominal sentence of one day's imprisonment although Stephen did say that he would have passed a very severe sentence, had that offence stood alone.

13 APRIL   **1909**   An inquest into the deaths of an entire family concluded in Oxford. On 5 April, the grocer's shop in Oxford owned by James Thomas Barber remained closed long after it should have opened for business. There was no sign of Barber and his wife and family, who were eventually found dead in the living quarters attached to the shop. Eleven-year-old Edgar James Barber lay in the kitchen, a puncture wound in his throat and severe injuries to his forehead, apparently inflicted by a hatchet. Mr Barber was found in bed,

still dressed in his nightclothes, with a deep stab wound in his throat. His thirteen-year-old daughter, Winifred, was badly bruised and had two neck wounds, while Mrs Emily Constance Barber had fatal injuries to her throat.

Since the premises were securely locked, all the evidence suggested that Mrs Barber had killed her husband and children before committing suicide and a note was found in her handwriting which read, 'Refer to Miss Morgan, Tubney, Abingdon', directing whoever found the bodies to contact Mrs Barber's sister.

The motive for the murders was unclear. Mrs Barber was known to have been upset after the death of her brother and had written to Miss Morgan saying, 'My head is so bad I do not know what to do.'

At the inquest, private detective Edwin Bullivant testified that Mrs Barber had consulted him in May 1906 with suspicions that her husband was having an affair. Bullivant followed Barber several times but had never found any evidence to substantiate his wife's suspicions – now he told the inquest that Mrs Barber had threatened to kill her husband if she ever caught him being unfaithful, adding that she would also kill her children as she couldn't bear to leave them behind.

The inquest jury found that Mrs Barber wilfully murdered her husband and children before committing suicide during a temporary fit of insanity.

14 APRIL

1758 People visiting The Chequer Inn at Oxford could pay one shilling – roughly equivalent to £7 in today's money – to view something that 'a gentleman skilled in anatomy' believed to be 'the greatest curiosity that ever yet appeared in Europe.'

The attraction in question was the preserved body of a baby recently stillborn in Witney, which had 'but one head, yet two faces, four eyes, two noses, four cheeks, two ears, two chins, two backs, four arms, four hands, twenty fingers, four thighs, four legs, four feet and twenty toes, all compleat and perfect' [sic].

15 APRIL

1899 Ellen 'Nellie' Herman appeared at Oxford Police Court charged with neglecting her son, William.

The case was brought to court by the Oxford and County Society for the Prevention of Cruelty to Children and Inspector Alcock, who made several visits Nellie's home in Bath Court and invariably found her drunk in bed. The house was furnished only with a chair and table and seven-year-old William was usually naked except for a shirt. He was seriously underweight and frequently bruised.

Mrs Herman was warned several times about her conduct and was once even persuaded to sign the pledge, promising never to drink alcohol again. In court, she denied that William was dirty or that he had been neglected, saying that she would be wicked to ill-treat her only child and that she would rather injure herself than hurt the boy. However, the magistrates believed that the evidence proved that Nellie was an unnatural mother and sentenced her to two months' imprisonment with hard labour. William was sent to the Workhouse.

16 APRIL

1893   Maria Stanley, the landlady of The Three Tuns public house at Chipping Norton, served a Sunday lunch of cheap beef, which she purchased the day before from butcher George Kempson. The family used the leftovers to make two or three more meals until on 20 April, Maria died in agony after two days of sickness and diarrhoea. Doctors were convinced that her death was caused by ptomaine poisoning, arising from eating diseased or decomposed meat.

Only Maria's mother-in-law remained free from illness and she was the only person in the family who had not eaten the beef. Several other families who had purchased beef from Kempson were also taken ill and at Maria Stanley's inquest, the jury returned a verdict of manslaughter against the butcher.

The Inspector of Nuisances at Chipping Norton retrieved several joints from the consignment of meat, which the purchasers had salted. The meat was putrid and when a small amount was fed to a dog it suffered the same symptoms as those humans who had consumed it.

Kempson was tried at the Oxford Assizes charged with 'feloniously killing and slaying' Maria Stanley. Although he insisted that he and his family had eaten meat from the same cow with no ill effects, as had his cowman, the fact that Kempson had sold the beef so cheaply aroused suspicions that it was of inferior quality. In addition, farmer Ernest Woolliams testified that on 23 March, he sold two sick cows to Kempson, both of which were incapable of walking and had to be conveyed to his premises on a sledge.

The case was complicated by the fact that the weather between the cow being slaughtered on 3 April and the meat being sold on 15 April was unseasonably warm. In addition, the Stanley family had stretched the beef over several meals and there were questions about how the meat was stored. However, the deciding factor for the jury was that Kempson had bought and sold the meat very cheaply, from which they inferred that he knew that it was substandard and, in selling it knowing its condition, had committed a criminal offence. He was found guilty and sentenced to eight months' imprisonment with hard labour.

17 APRIL

1826   Fifty-six-year-old baker Edward Arnatt of Eynsham was a heavy drinker and was extremely violent when drunk, when his wife and daughters frequently called on their neighbours to protect them.

Such was the case on the night of 17 April, when Ann Arnatt shouted, 'Murder! Pray some of you come in, or I shall be murdered tonight.' Thomas Maley, John Cox, Mary Rickson and Richard Davis went into the house and took a large stick from Arnatt, with which he had been beating his wife.

Arnatt sat down calmly in the kitchen but his wife begged the neighbours not to leave, for fear of another row. After sitting quietly for a few minutes, Arnatt suddenly seized his shotgun from a beam and shouted, 'Damn your eyes, I'll shoot you!' With that, he fired the gun through the closed door at the group of neighbours standing talking to his wife in the passage beyond it.

The charge hit Thomas Maley in the chest, lacerating his heart, and he died from his injuries almost instantly. An inquest returned a verdict of wilful murder against Arnatt, who was committed for trial at the next Oxford Assizes.

Numerous people testified that Arnatt was normally a respectable, kind-hearted, peaceable man, who wouldn't hurt a fly when sober. The jury found him guilty of the lesser offence of manslaughter and, warning Arnatt of the dreadful consequences of giving way to passion, the judge sentenced him to twelve calendar months' imprisonment.

18 APRIL

1860 Twenty-two-year-old servant Ann Barkus and her thirteen-month-old illegitimate son, Charles, stayed at a cottage near Ipsden for three weeks before leaving on 18 April. She was seen by several people on the road to Henley – where she planned to visit her aunt – sometimes with her son, sometimes alone. She told one person who enquired that Charles was dead and another that he was with a woman named Moore at Witheridge Bottom.

His true location was revealed on 19 April, when James Grace and another man walked past a disused well in the vicinity. They paused to drop a couple of stones down the well and, as they did so, a child began to cry from the depths. The two men raised the alarm and ploughboy James Tuck volunteered to be lowered into the well, bringing up Charles in his arms. The child was very badly bruised, particularly on his back, and had a large contusion on the back of his head. He was also cold, thirsty and very hungry.

The well was around 150ft deep and a little over 3ft in diameter. When questioned on 20 April, Ann explained that she tripped while carrying her son and that he flew out of her arms into the well. She told PC Joseph Rogers that she waited by the well for two hours and that she had heard Charles crying – however, she gave no explanation why she hadn't raised the alarm and had left her child for almost thirty-six hours without mentioning his whereabouts to anybody.

It took just ten minutes' deliberation for the jury to find Ann Barkus guilty of attempted murder and she was sentenced to death, although Mr Justice Byles was quick to reassure Ann that her life would be spared.

19 APRIL

1847 Coroner Mr Brunner held an inquest at The Dashwood Arms, Kirtlington, into the death of William Paine, a stonemason from Woodstock.

Paine was employed building bridges on the Oxford and Rugby Railway and took a walk with his family to show off his work. At Tackley, labourers had laid a plank across the River Cherwell but as Paine tried to

The Dashwood Arms, Kirtlington. (Author's collection)

walk across it, he missed his footing and plunged into the river below. A non-swimmer, he drowned in 18ft of water, in full view of his wife, child and sister, as well as several other spectators. The inquest jury returned a verdict of 'accidental death'.

20 APRIL

1893 James Jennings of Benson was well known as a kindly old man, who often gave the village children pennies and halfpennies. However, according to twelve-year-old Alice Annie Costar, his reasons for doing so were not born of kindness.

Alice was later to state at the Oxford Assizes that, on 20 April, she met Jennings sitting on a bank at the side of the road and he asked her to sit with him for a while. He then grabbed her arm, pulled her to the ground and sexually assaulted her, only releasing her when they were disturbed by a passing cart. Alice walked away making no complaint to anyone about the assault for fear that her mother would give her a thrashing. When, after two weeks, Alice finally told her mother what had happened, Mrs Costar went straight to the village constable and Jennings was arrested that evening, protesting his innocence.

At Jennings' trial at the Oxford Assizes in June, the defendant swore under oath that he was resting on the bank when Alice asked if she could sit down next to him. When he agreed, Alice rifled through his pockets and extracted a penny and a halfpenny before leaving. The cart driver was called as a witness but was only able to state that he saw Jennings and Alice walking off in different directions as he approached them.

It was revealed in court that Alice had twice before accused other men of assaulting her and that the second of her alleged attackers had been brought before magistrates and subsequently discharged. In his summary of the case for the jury, Mr Justice Pollock told them that Alice was obviously in the habit of accusing men of molesting her and that, in the absence of any corroborative evidence against Jennings, they should find him not guilty.

The jury complied and Jennings was discharged. 'I thank thee Lord that thou hast delivered me from lying lips and deceitful tongues,' he said before leaving the court.

21 APRIL

1894 Forty-year-old Edwin John Warland was cleaning windows at Brasenose College when a portion of the stonework crumbled and gave way beneath his feet. Warland fell 15ft to the ground, landing heavily on his head.

Brasenose College. (Author's collection)

He was admitted to the Radcliffe Infirmary suffering from a compound fracture of the left leg, a fractured right kneecap, a severe wound extending all the way across the top of his skull and a possible fractured spine. He was lucid enough to explain to doctors how his fall occurred, saying that it was a pure accident and that he didn't blame anyone.

Warland survived until 11 May, when he succumbed to inflammation of the spinal cord extending upwards into his brain. The jury at his inquest returned a verdict of 'accidental death'.

22 APRIL

1757 When John Franklin was tried at the Oxford Quarter Sessions for the murder of his wife, he refused to take his trial seriously and was so confident of an acquittal that he offered to take wagers at odds of two or three to one. Yet Alice Franklin had obviously been cruelly mistreated before her death – her skull was fractured and her head bore the scars of many old wounds. She was due to give birth and, when surgeons opened her body, even her unborn baby was bruised.

Her husband, a notorious criminal, was well known for his brutality towards his wife and, on his arrest and committal to Oxford Gaol, he was chained to the floor to prevent his escape. Found guilty of wilful murder, he was executed at Green Ditch on 23 April.

During his trial, a main supporting beam in a gallery in the court broke and the floor began to tilt alarmingly. Someone shouted, 'Fire!' which caused people to begin to clear the building immediately – had they not done so, the gallery would most probably have plunged to the ground under the weight of the crowds.

23 APRIL

1908 Coroner Mr H. Franklin held an inquest on the death of forty-two-year-old Edward Harris, a fitter for the Oxford Gas Company, who died while making a connection between the gas main and a house at Cowley. Harris's assistant, Mr Joyce, told the inquest that as Harris was working in a hole that was between twelve and fifteen inches deep, he suddenly slumped forwards.

Joyce immediately dragged him out and, with the assistance of two passing doctors, began artificial respiration, but their efforts were unsuccessful.

The cause of death was given as coal gas poisoning and Joyce related that his colleague had been fine one minute and unconscious the next. A representative of the gas company stated that the workmen were not provided with respirators because the job was not considered dangerous. The inquest jury returned a verdict of 'accidental death'.

24 APRIL

1857 During the day, shoemaker John Talbot walked several miles to deliver his shoes and by eleven o'clock at night was returning home to Wantage.

John was seen lying on the road by numerous people, who walked by assuming that he was drunk. Only Charles Bosher stopped to ask if he was all right, to which John replied that he had lost his way, trying to stand up but falling down again.

Concerned, Charles went to fetch his parents but by the time they got back to John, he had died. A post mortem examination revealed that he had drunk no alcohol.

At the inquest held by coroner Mr W.D. Wasbrough, several people testified to seeing Talbot lying in the road between eleven o'clock at night and four o'clock the next morning and, in returning a verdict that he died from exposure, the inquest jury remarked that any one of them could probably have saved John's life.

25 APRIL

1836 Samuel Petty (aka Duncan Petty) appeared before magistrates in Oxford. It was alleged that, on two separate occasions, he had lured a little girl into fields and tried to take off her clothes. One of the children, Maria Freeman, screamed and Petty dragged her to a nearby river and threw her in, leaving her to drown. Fortunately, a passer-by heard her cries and rescued her from a certain death.

Petty was committed for trial at the Oxford Assizes, where the charge against him is recorded as 'robbery' – he stole a handkerchief from the pocket of his second victim, Rebecca Slater. Found guilty, Petty was sentenced to death but then reprieved and sent to Oxford Gaol.

Having been released, he offended again and appeared at the Oxford Assizes on 26 February 1842, this time charged with 'assault on an infant with intent to ravish.' He was acquitted due to insanity.

26 APRIL

1858   In a case brought by the Royal Society for the Prevention of Cruelty to Animals, twenty-year-old John Humphries and his eighteen-year-old brother Charles appeared at the Wantage Petty Sessions charged with cruelty to a cat.

The cat belonged to their neighbour, Police Superintendent Millard, and the brothers decided that it might be sport to pour spirits of turpentine on the animal's 'fundament' (anus), causing it to suffer the most excruciating agony.

The brothers pleaded guilty to the offence and were each fined 10s. In default of payment, both were sent to Abingdon Gaol for twenty-one days.

27 APRIL

1877   Mild-mannered Oxford shop assistant James Grainger was admitted to hospital for surgery to remove a tumour on his hip. The tumour arose from an incident on 10 January when, on his return from work, Grainger was asked by his wife to fetch some gin. When he refused, Marion Louise Grainger stabbed him in the left buttock with a stiletto.

The police and a surgeon were called and, having examined the injury, the doctor put a piece of sticking plaster on it and advised Grainger to rest. Although it bled copiously, the stab wound did not appear to be life-threatening and, indeed, Grainger was well enough to return to work the next day, although he was limping badly and was obviously in severe pain. In due course, Marion was brought before magistrates for wounding with intent to do bodily harm, but her husband insisted that the incident was an accident and was so reluctant to testify against her that the case was dropped.

Although Grainger's injury healed externally, an internal aneurism formed the large 'tumour' around the scar. On 27 April, Grainger was admitted to the Radcliffe Infirmary for surgery to remove the tumour, which was found to consist of blood and blood clots. Yet although the surgery appeared to have been successful, Grainger went rapidly downhill and died on 16 May. The cause of his death was given as 'unhealthy inflammation of the blood vessels', which had not healed properly after the operation.

Grainger's surgeon, Mr E.L. Hussey, was not only the senior surgeon at the hospital but was also the city coroner and it fell to him to preside at the inquest on Grainger's death. Incredibly, Hussey did not declare an interest and the jury found a verdict of wilful murder against Marion Grainger.

She was tried at the Oxford Assizes on 1 July, where, having expressed indignation at Hussey's conduct, her defence counsel pointed out that there was no way of knowing whether the victim died as a result of the wound, or as a result of the operation. Reminding the jury that nobody had initially thought Grainger's injury serious and that Grainger himself had dismissed it as an accident, he asked them to consider whether or not death resulted from the wound in his buttock and, if so, was it inflicted by the defendant and was it done deliberately or accidentally? The jury took just ten minutes to find Marion Grainger not guilty.

28 APRIL

1755 Robert Randall (or Randell) was executed on the Castle Green, Oxford, having been found guilty of sheep stealing at the last assizes. As he reached the place of execution and ascended the ladder preparatory to being hanged, he called for silence. The assembled crowd fell quiet as Randall addressed them.

He declared that, in the course of his dissolute and ill-spent life, he had been guilty of many crimes but swore that he was innocent of that crime for which he was about to die. Unfortunately for Randall, his protestations of innocence had no influence on his executioner.

29 APRIL

1857 At the Wantage Petty Sessions, Martha Smuggs was charged with assaulting Sarah Swimmings on 15 April. Sarah's mother accompanied her to court and Martha accused her of bewitching her, alleging that Mrs Swimmings was deliberately making her ill using a book of spells.

Although nobody was able to prove any supernatural wrongdoing by Mrs Swimmings, the original charge of assault against her daughter was upheld following the testimony of an eyewitness. Sarah was fined 14s plus costs but was allowed a fortnight's grace to pay.

30 APRIL

1875 Surgeon Edward Horne of Wallingford went rowing with two friends. Twenty-year-old Robert Unowlsby Sibley, who lived with Horne's family, accompanied them in his canoe.

At Benson Lock, the party were overtaken by a Thames Conservancy Board tug and the captain offered to give Horne's boat a tow. Keen not to be left behind, Sibley grabbed the side of the boat, while Horne grasped the front of Sibley's canoe.

After travelling for some time at speeds of up to 10mph, Horne's wrist began to ache and he shouted that he needed to let go of the canoe. Sibley seemed to be having difficulty either hearing or understanding what Horne was saying but Horne's companions urged Sibley to let go of the boat and, when it seemed that the young man had got the message, Horne relinquished his hold on the canoe. Unfortunately, Sibley did not let go.

The canoe swung round and Sibley fell out. He clung to the side of the boat but his weight pulled it down and seeing the boat shipping water, Horne's friends rushed to the bow to redistribute the weight. In the ensuing commotion, Sibley lost his grip and disappeared from view while the tug steamed on, oblivious to what was happening in its wake.

It had travelled for more than 50 yards before the rowing boat could be disconnected and the occupants were able to return to where they last saw Sibley. While his companions went for help, Horne tried to find Sibley but the water was deep and muddy and his body wasn't found for almost an hour.

At an inquest held by coroner Mr H. Dixon the jury returned a verdict of 'accidentally drowned'.

MAY

Iffley lock and River Isis. (Author's collection)

1 MAY

1857 An inquest was held at Woodstock on the death of drayman Eli Ashfield, who worked for Messrs Wootten's Brewery in Oxford.

The previous day, Eli and his fellow drayman were returning from Woodstock to Oxford with their dray. Both men had been drinking heavily during the day and Eli's companion fell asleep.

He woke to find Eli missing and, when the drayman retraced his route, he discovered that Eli had fallen from the dray between Campsfield and Begbroke, the wheels passing over his head. His sleeping colleague didn't even notice as the horses continued on their familiar journey home without needing the guidance of their driver. Meanwhile, Eli was conveyed to The Star Inn at Woodstock, where he was found to be dead.

The inquest jury returned a verdict of 'accidental death'.

2 MAY

1852 Plasterer Elijah Noon of Jericho went to The North Star public house to collect his wages but instead of taking them home to his wife, he stayed out drinking. Eventually, Eliza Noon was forced to go and drag her husband out of the pub.

She nagged her tipsy husband all the way home, calling him a good-for-nothing villain. Although thirty-three-year-old Elijah held his tongue, he grew angrier and angrier and as soon as he arrived home, he fetched an old sword from a cupboard, drew it from its sheath and struck Eliza on the back with the flat of the blade.

The couple's twelve-year-old daughter grabbed her mother's arm and tried to pull her outside but Elijah ran the sword into his wife's left side. Eliza collapsed across the threshold then managed to get to her feet and walk to a neighbour's house, where she collapsed again. Then, helped by her daughter, Eliza staggered back home, where Elijah was calmly sheathing the sword and replacing it on the shelf. Eliza fell to her knees before him, begging him to hold her hands, as she was dying.

Elijah sent their daughter out for brandy and when she returned, her father had undressed her mother and put her to bed. A doctor was called and dressed Eliza's wound, leaving her in the care of her neighbours. Elijah refused to leave her bedside – neither he nor Eliza made any attempt to hide the cause of her injury and Eliza stated several times before witnesses that she forgave her husband.

When Eliza died the next day, she left five children motherless, one of whom had not yet been weaned. A post-mortem examination revealed that the sword had penetrated her body nearly ten inches, passing between her seventh and eighth ribs. It had nicked her lung, diaphragm and coronary artery and gone through one side of her stomach and out of the other.

Elijah was charged with wilful murder, appearing at the Oxford Assizes in July 1852. His defence counsel tried to convince the jury that Eliza had fallen backwards onto the sword as her daughter tried to pull her away. There were numerous witnesses to Elijah's previous good character and the jury eventually found him guilty of the lesser offence of manslaughter. He was sentenced to two years' imprisonment.

3 MAY

1900 Richard Dunn and John Stockford were asked to collect some timber from Marsh Gibbon by their employer. Accordingly, the men set out in two carts, each pulled by two horses.

Stockford's horses were slightly faster than Dunn's, so he was ahead for much of the time. The two carters met at The Fox Inn at Bicester, where they rested the horses and had something to eat and drink. They next met up at the crossroads at Middleton Stoney, shortly before attempting to go down the steep hill near the village.

Both carts were fitted with skids, which prevented them from going too fast downhill when carrying heavy loads, although it was debatable whether the gradient of the hill at Middleton Stoney or the weight of Stockford's load were sufficient to necessitate their use. It began to rain and Miss Lizzie Togwell noticed Stockford doing something to his cart at the top of the hill – the next thing she saw was the horses galloping past her, with Stockford trying desperately to stop them. Miss Togwell bravely attempted to stop the horses but was unsuccessful.

Meanwhile, Dunn had caught up with Stockford and found him lying on the road. He called to Miss Togwell, 'My mate's knocked over,' and she went to see if she could help. She stayed with Stockford while Dunn went for assistance, returning with a policeman, who helped convey the badly injured carter to The Jersey Inn, where he died soon afterwards from shock and loss of blood arising from a severe compound fracture of his leg.

Stockford's horses were quiet, reliable animals and although marks on the road showed that he had employed the skids, it was suggested that they had somehow come off, allowing the wagon to descend the hill unchecked. Although conscious, Stockford was not able to say how the accident happened and neither Miss Togwell nor Richard Dunn had seen anything more than the aftermath. Hence, with very little evidence to explain Stockford's demise, the inquest recorded a verdict of 'accidental death'.

4 MAY

1886 Nineteen-year-old Charles Dixey appeared at the Oxon and Berks Assizes charged with unlawfully and indecently assaulting his nine-year-old stepsister, Ellen Beechey, at Bampton on 12 October.

After evidence from a surgeon corroborated the child's account, the court was told that Ellen, her father and mother, Dixey and four of his

Market Square, Bampton. (Author's collection)

brothers slept in two beds, in the same room of a small cottage. It was said that Ellen was 'frequently outraged' and that although Charles Dixey was on trial, any one of his brothers could have taken his place in the dock.

He was found guilty and sentenced to eight years' penal servitude.

5 MAY

1900   Four-year-old Frank Arnold was taken for a walk by his nursemaid, fourteen-year-old Emily Barrett. Emily was pushing Frank's baby sister in her pram, while Frank ran on a little ahead. As he crossed the bridge at Binsey Lane, Frank appeared to trip and, before Emily could react, he slipped between the rails of the bridge and fell into the stream below.

Emily raced down to the side of the stream, which was only 2ft deep. She could see Frank floating face down in the water but was unable to reach him from the bank and, as the fast current carried him swiftly downstream, she abandoned the attempt and ran for help.

She approached a passer-by, who declined to help with the rescue but promised to pass on a message that there was a child drowning. He kept his promise, calling at The Osney Arms public house and notifying the landlord John Taylor, who immediately jumped on his bicycle and pedalled to the scene. He pulled Frank from the water and gave him artificial respiration for more than fifty minutes, although, sadly, his efforts were in vain.

An inquest was held by coroner Mr Galpin, at which the city engineer Richard Charles Long testified that the bridge was properly constructed and in perfect order. It was suggested that Frank had tripped over the projecting nuts that bolted the railings to the road, which protruded almost an inch from the ground and Long conceded that the bridge was probably dangerous for young children, although in fairness, he would expect children to be supervised by an adult as they crossed it. Hearing that there had been two similar accidents in recent weeks, Long agreed that it would be simplicity itself to put some wire netting behind the rails.

The inquest jury returned a verdict of accidental death, requesting that the authorities should act to make the bridge safer and asking the coroner to commend John Taylor for his efforts.

6 MAY

1878   Coroner Mr E.L. Hussey held an inquest at The Waterman's Arms, St Aldate's, into the death of six-year-old Harry Cox.

Bricklayer Edward Green stated that he was walking over Folly Bridge the previous afternoon when someone had told him that there was a child in the water. Green spotted a little boy floating just under the surface of the river and pulled him out but, sadly, he was dead.

The only witness to Harry's death was his six-year-old playmate Henry Benting. Henry, who was considered too young to be sworn, told the inquest that he and Harry were playing together when Harry lay on his stomach on a wall overlooking the water, moving his arms and legs.

'Look at me – I can swim,' he shouted excitedly. Tragically, when he overbalanced and fell headfirst into the water, Harry discovered that he could not.

Folly Bridge, Oxford. (Author's collection)

7 MAY

1849   As James Layton and his wife were walking near Great Bourton a shot rang out and Martha Layton fell to the ground. James then threw down the pistol with which he had just shot his wife and calmly cut her throat.

Martha was attended by Dr Robert Stanton Wise, who stitched up the wound in her throat and removed a piece of lead shot that was embedded in her forehead. Martha gave a deposition before magistrates the next day, confirming what had happened but saying that she forgave her husband. According to Martha, the couple had not been quarrelling but James was swearing at her and had threatened to kill her, as he had done numerous times in the past. (Unbeknown to her husband, Martha was contemplating separating from him.)

Martha survived for twenty-two days and a post-mortem examination revealed that her death was caused by a fragment of skull bone that was driven into her brain when she was shot, causing an abscess.

James was charged with wilful murder and appeared at the Oxford Assizes on 11 July, where he refused to plead on the grounds that he believed that his wife was still alive. Eventually, it was decided that, if Martha was still alive, then James could not have murdered her and his insistence that she was not dead was accepted as a plea of not guilty.

The court heard that James had been unlucky in business and imagined that Martha, her son and her brother were conspiring to defraud him. In the past, he had shown signs of mental illness and the defence produced several witnesses who believed that he was not in his right mind. However, the medical witnesses, including the gaol surgeon, saw no evidence of insanity and the prosecution produced witnesses of their own, who believed Layton to be perfectly rational.

The judge instructed the jury to give the defendant the benefit of any doubts they might have and they found him not guilty on the grounds of insanity. He was sent to the Bethlehem Royal Hospital – the infamous Bedlam – and eventually to Broadmoor Criminal Lunatic Asylum, where he is believed to have died aged seventy-one in 1877.

8 MAY

1839 Eighty-four-year-old Fanny Phillips of Woodcote was a little frail but was able to continue living in her own cottage with a lot of help from her neighbours. Mary Lambden called every morning to help Fanny get up, then put her to bed again at night, but on 8 May, as she approached Mrs Phillips' cottage, she could see that the door had been forced. Mary fetched her husband, James, and they found Mrs Phillips lying dead in bed with terrible head wounds. Henley police constable Henry Stephens searched the cottage, which had been ransacked – even Mrs Phillips's wedding ring had been prised from her finger. There was a small canvas bag on her doorstep containing a few tools and Stephens traced them to a man named John Hore, from whom they were stolen on 25 March.

Police enquiries established that a man named Charles Morley had recently been taking a keen interest in the victim's living arrangements and that, in the aftermath of the murder, he seemed to have come into some money. When his cottage was searched, another file belonging to Hore was found.

Although Morley was the chief suspect in the murder of Fanny Phillips, the police only had sufficient evidence to charge him with the theft of Hore's tools. Morley had previous convictions and, when he was found guilty, he was sentenced to be transported for seven years.

Under the impression that, having been convicted of theft, he could not be prosecuted for murder, Morley began to boast about his haul from Mrs Phillips' cottage. Morley's cell mate contacted the police, who conducted a further search of Morley's cottage, finding two bags of money concealed in the thatched roof. Morley was officially charged with wilful murder and, having been found guilty at the Oxford Assizes on 2 March 1840, was executed on 23 March.

9 MAY

1893 Servant Elizabeth Lambourn worked at The Druid's Head public house in Oxford and was described by the landlady Sarah Ann Goodwin as 'a most aggravating girl'. On 9 May, Mrs Goodwin heard screams and, when she went to investigate, saw Elizabeth being pursued upstairs by the pub's general handyman, Daniel Jones, who was brandishing a poker. Although Mrs Goodwin didn't actually see Jones hit the servant, Elizabeth ended up with two wounds on the top of her head, a bruised forehead and a broken finger on her right hand.

Jones was tried at the Oxford Assizes charged with maliciously wounding Elizabeth, who swore that she had done nothing to merit such violence and suggested that Jones was jealous because she had a boyfriend.

However, Mrs Goodwin and several of the pub's customers testified that Elizabeth and her attacker had been 'wrangling' on the day before the attack after Jones accused her of telling lies about him and blackening his character, since when Elizabeth continuously put her tongue out at Jones or thumbed her nose at him. The jury took the view that Elizabeth provoked Jones by taunting him and found him not guilty.

10 MAY

1886 Coroner Mr Bromley Challenor held an inquest at The Isis Tavern, Iffley, into the death of twenty-year-old housemaid Sarah Cooper.

Sarah was employed by Revd Sparks of the Military College, Cowley, and on 7 May, she took four of his children, aged thirteen, nine, five and three-years-old, for a walk at Iffley. They passed a punt tied to a post and the children clamoured to be allowed to sit in it. The boat drifted about a yard into the river and Sarah tried to paddle it back to the bank but minutes later, the cord tethering the punt broke and it began floating downstream.

Contemporary reports do not make clear how many of the children were still in the punt at this time but the oldest, Winifred, and the youngest were definitely there, and possibly one of the other children. Two men tried to reach the punt with a boat hook but couldn't and so told Winifred and Sarah to grab the chain that stretched across the water near Iffley Mill to stop boats going over the weir. They managed to do this but the punt bumped against a post in the river marked 'Danger' and they fell out.

Sarah clung to the side of the punt with one hand and the youngest child's dress with the other but she was unable to hold on and was swept away. James Martin saw the child drifting under the bridge and threw a lifebelt, which Sarah grasped and managed to hold on for a couple of minutes before she grew too exhausted.

All of the children were rescued alive but Sarah was sadly drowned and, at the inquest on her death, the coroner was appalled by the behaviour of bystanders who, with the exception of Martin, acted with what the coroner referred to as 'barbarous apathy'. There was plenty of time to shut the lock gates but neither the lock keeper nor his assistant lifted a finger to do so, which the coroner described as 'monstrous' and 'one of the most inhuman things he had ever heard in his life.' Although the stand-in lock keeper, Thomas Martin, couldn't be held legally responsible for Sarah's death, the coroner called him morally responsible, saying that he stood by and watched the accident unfolding without bothering to walk a few yards to see if he could help. The inquest jury concurred, recording a verdict of 'accidental death' while rueing the fact that it should have been preventable.

11 MAY

1899 Eliza Earle died at the Littlemore Asylum and a post-mortem examination showed that the cause of death was shock, arising from four broken ribs, five dislocated ribs and severe bruising all over her body. It seemed as though Eliza had been severely beaten.

Until her admission to the asylum on 6 May, Eliza lived with her husband, James, near Henley-on-Thames. On 20 April, she began to show signs of madness and was visited at home by a surgeon, who didn't think that her condition was sufficiently serious to warrant hospitalisation, although he continued to visit every two days to monitor the situation. A local woman, Mrs Bull, was employed to look after her in her own home but by 4 May, Eliza was so deranged that it became necessary to tie up her hands and legs to restrain her.

When Eliza died and it was discovered that her husband had knelt on her to subdue her, he was charged with her wilful murder, although the charge was later reduced to manslaughter. Earle appeared before Mr

Justice Day at the Oxford Assizes in June, where the crux of the case for the jury was to determine whether or not Eliza's death resulted from her husband's actions. The court heard that Eliza twice tried to harm herself at the beginning of May, by throwing herself against a tree and by throwing herself downstairs, but, according to one witness, her injuries were caused by her husband's violence.

Eliza Earle was both strong and violent in her madness and, having deliberated for twenty minutes, the jury returned to court to say that there was insufficient evidence for them to convict Earle of her manslaughter. He was pronounced not guilty and discharged.

12 MAY

1894 The all-male Bullingdon Club is an exclusive Oxford students' club, allegedly founded in 1780. Originally centred on hunting and cricket, the club is now better known as a dining club, with a reputation for hell-raising.

On 12 May, the club held a dinner at Christchurch College, which ended in what the contemporary newspapers described as 'an orgy of destruction.' All of the lights and the 468 windows of the quad were smashed, along with numerous doors and blinds. As a result, the club was banned from holding any meetings within a fifteen-mile radius of Oxford.

13 MAY

1844 Workers on the Blenheim Estate celebrated the birth of a new Earl of Sunderland, George Charles Spencer-Churchill, by firing a salute in the grounds with cannons. Twenty-five-year-old Henry Sumner was assisting the porter and labourers employed by the Duke of Marlborough, and incautiously opened the end of a cartridge of gunpowder and rammed it into a cannon that had just been fired.

He made no attempt to check if the cannon had been cleared after firing and it was thought that some burning paper or wadding remained in the breach of the cannon, which exploded as soon as it made contact with the opened cartridge. Sumner was blown off his feet, his eyes and hands dreadfully injured. Although a surgeon was immediately summoned and Sumner was taken to Radcliffe Infirmary, he died from his injuries soon afterwards.

At the inquest held by coroner William Brunner, the jury returned a verdict of 'accidental death', commenting that it might have been better to choose someone who had even a vague grasp of how to load and discharge cannons to assist in the salute.

Blenheim Palace. (Author's collection)

14 MAY

1763 Edmund Tomkins was considered the greatest tennis player in England when, on 14 May, he went down to Iffley with a group of friends. They intended to return by boat but the current was so strong that it soon became apparent that they were about to be swept into the mill sluice.

One man jumped from the boat and was lucky enough to land on the river bank, while a second landed a yard away and scrambled to safety. A third was swept away by the current but managed to grab a post at the bridge near the mill. He shouted until the people at the mill heard his calls for help.

The fourth member of the party was still sitting safely in the boat. Once his friends jumped out, the boat turned sideways and jammed across the entrance to the sluice. However, there was no sign of Edmund Tomkins, whose body was not found until the following morning. Although an excellent swimmer, there was a large contusion on the side of the dead man's head, which was thought serious enough to have stunned him and prevented him from swimming to safety. He left a wife and several children.

The Pool, Iffley, 1908. (Author's collection)

15 MAY

1936 A clover rick and a straw rick burned at Stadhampton and, once the fires had burned out, a body was discovered. Only charred scraps of clothing remained but the man was identified from a name on his leather belt as Canadian Thomas Patteson Moss, a twenty-one-year-old undergraduate at Balliol College. A popular student, who was well liked by all who knew him, Moss was said to be a cheerful man, with no apparent worries.

Moss had fragments of partly burned straw in his air passages, suggesting that he was alive when the fire started and that the ricks had initially smouldered, rather than burst into flames. It also suggested that Moss was unconscious, since, had he been sleeping, the inhalation of the straw fragments would have roused him.

Home Office Analyst Dr Roche Lynch analysed the contents of Moss's stomach and duodenum and also examined a small, empty bottle that was found near the body. Lynch theorised that the bottle may have contained some hypnotic drug but found no traces of poison, alcohol or other discernible drugs in Moss's stomach.

Home Office Pathologist Sir Bernard Spilsbury agreed that Moss was unconscious, although he was unable to discover what might have rendered him so. Moss was a healthy man, with no indications of natural disease and no history of epilepsy or fainting. There were no marks of violence on the body, no bruising or swelling and no abnormalities of the internal organs, neither was there any smell of petrol or other accelerants. Moss did have two broken arms and a fractured skull but Spilsbury concluded that these were caused by the fire. Spilsbury ruled out suicide, saying that only a raving lunatic would set himself on fire. He had also considered that Moss might have been knocked down by a car but was unable to find any indication of injury.

At the inquest, which concluded on 18 June, Spilsbury opined that Moss lay down on damp straw between the two ricks and fell asleep. By some mischance, the straw became ignited and Moss was then rendered unconscious and fatally asphyxiated by the gaseous products of combustion and the lack of fresh air.

The police made exhaustive enquiries and traced a witness who believed he had seen Moss walking towards Stadhampton. Another witness saw a speeding car, with a man apparently slumped in the passenger seat. However, even with the assistance of Scotland Yard, it proved impossible to find how Moss got to the ricks or why he went there.

Eventually, the inquest jury returned an open verdict that Moss asphyxiated from the burning of the ricks but there was no evidence to show how he came to meet his death.

16 MAY

1863 'Another fatal accident from crinoline' announced *Jackson's Oxford Journal*, reporting on the tragic story of seventeen-year-old Sarah Lapper.

Sarah worked at Great Barford for a farm labourer, whose wife had been bedridden for twelve months. While preparing an evening meal, she was chopping onions with her back towards the fire when her voluminous dress went up in flames.

In a blind panic, Sarah ran upstairs to her mistress's bedroom, where she blundered about setting fire to the bed curtains. Almost everything in the room was consumed by the fire and, if it hadn't been for the bravery of a young man from the village who spotted the fire and carried the invalid Mrs Edgington to safety, she would doubtless have perished.

Sarah lingered in agony for two days before succumbing to her terrible burns. 'We trust that the above melancholy occurrence will prove a warning to all who wear crinoline, especially those engaged in domestic duties,' ended the newspaper report.

17 MAY

1899 Twenty-two-year-old gamekeeper Thomas Hoster left an agricultural show intending to go to Hanborough. He left there for home at about eleven o'clock at night, sober and in a cheerful mood but never arrived and the following afternoon his body was found at the bottom of a railway embankment near Clift Wood. Initially, it seemed as though Hoster had been hit by a train but, although he often used the railway as a shortcut, there was no reason whatsoever for him to have been on that particular stretch of line. He was walking a familiar route home and his body was found more than 100 yards from where he would normally have left the track and continued his journey by road.

His hat and watch and chain were found some distance from his body, the watch having stopped at 1.20 a.m. The back was open. A post-mortem examination showed that Hoster had a serious wound on his left temple. His skull was fractured and the bone had been driven into his brain, turning it to a pulp, and Dr H. Caudwell from Woodstock favoured a blow to the head from a sharp, angular instrument as being the cause of Hoster's death. Every train driver who had passed along the relevant section of track that evening was questioned and none had noticed their trains hitting anybody. Furthermore, there were no marks of any kind anywhere on the trains suggesting that they may have been involved in an accident.

Coroner Mr F. Westell told the jury that the evidence as to the actual cause of Hoster's death was very weak, advising them to consider their verdict very carefully since, being a gamekeeper, the deceased was likely to have made enemies. The jury returned an open verdict of 'found dead'.

18 MAY

1855 Ann Phipps of Chipping Norton was heavily pregnant, a fact that didn't stop her husband from beating her. On 18 May, Henry Phipps added a new torture to his catalogue of cruelty, kicking Ann heavily in the genitals. Three days later, she was delivered of a stillborn baby girl and so bad was her confinement that her life was despaired of.

Although weak, on 6 June Ann managed to make a statement detailing her husband's violence and saying that she believed that her baby died as a result of his brutality. 'I have been dangerously ill but my medical attendant tells me I am getting better,' Ann stated.

Sadly, she died days later and when coroner Mr Westell held an inquest into her death, several neighbours testified that they had seen cuts and bruises on Ann's body and that she had complained that her husband had inflicted them. One neighbour even witnessed Henry beating and kicking his wife on 18 May, but even so the inquest jury found that there was insufficient evidence to prove that Ann had died from Henry's ill-treatment. Instead they returned a verdict of 'natural death from inflammation etc. after delivery.'

Phipps was charged with an aggravated assault upon his wife and was committed for trial at the Oxford Assizes. On 2 July, he was found guilty of assault and inflicting actual bodily harm and sentenced to twelve calendars months' imprisonment.

19 MAY

1952 A distressed young man ran up to the railway signal box at Moor Hill near Horley and asked the signal man to call the police as he had just murdered a girl. 'She dared me to do it,' he insisted, leading the police to where Rose Margaret Meadows lay strangled beneath a hedge.

Rose and her strangler, Oliver George Butler, were both employed at 'the Ally' – the Northern Aluminium Co. Ltd, Banbury – and although Butler was already married, he and Rose had fallen in love. However,

Butler insisted that Rose was obsessed by death and frequently talked about murder and suicide, saying that a fortune teller had predicted that she would be murdered and asking Butler to be the one to kill her.

When he was tried at the Stafford Assizes, Butler stuck to his story that Rose had deliberately provoked him into killing her, adding a new detail that she had a weak heart and that her death had been a terrible accident, which happened only because she had egged him on. The jury found him guilty but gave a strong recommendation for mercy.

In spite of an appeal on the grounds that Mr Justice Hallett had misdirected the jury by telling them that this was a case of murder when the defence maintained it was an accident, Butler became the last person ever executed at Oxford Prison on 12 August 1952.

20 MAY

1878   At one o'clock in the morning, PC Day was patrolling his beat in Oxford when he came across his colleague PC Green rolling around in the street with shoemaker Henry Grimsley. Day went to Green's aid but Grimsley bit him hard on the leg and it eventually took both policemen to subdue him. Even then, he was so wild that he had to be strapped to a stretcher to be taken to the police station.

Green explained that he had heard Mrs Grimsley shouting for help, her husband having beaten her. Green spoke to Grimsley, who promised that he would go indoors and behave himself for the rest of the night, but then punched the policeman hard in the face. Grimsley would later insist that Green deliberately knocked him over, whereas Green maintained that Grimsley was too drunk to stand. Whatever happened, the men grappled for some time while Green tried to handcuff Grimsley, who, during the course of the struggle, bit the policeman's thumb.

Brought before magistrates at Oxford City Police Court, Grimsley turned on the tears, begging the magistrates to be lenient with him. Since it was his first offence, he was fined 5s with 6s 6d costs or fourteen days imprisonment, and bound over in the sum of £20 to keep the peace for the next six months.

21 MAY

1921   In his book *Three Men in a Boat*, author Jerome K. Jerome described Sandford Lasher:

> The pool under Sandford Lasher, just behind the lock, is a very good place to drown yourself in. The undercurrent is terribly strong, and if you once get down into it you are all right. An obelisk marks the spot where two men have already been drowned, while bathing there; and the steps of the obelisk are generally used as a diving-board by young men now who wish to see if the place really IS dangerous.

One of those who lost his life there was Michael Llewellyn-Davies, the adopted son of author J.M. Barrie. Michael went to bathe with a friend, Rupert E.V. Buxton, on 21 May and their bodies were not recovered until the following day. An inquest later returned verdicts of accidental death on both men.

Sandford Reach and Mill. (Author's collection)

Other victims of the Lasher include John Richardson Currer (1840), Richard
Philmore and William Gaisford (1843), Edward John Templar (1864), George
William Manuel Dasent (1872) and Clarence Sinclair Collier (1879).

22 MAY

1900 Daniel Sabin was walking home to Hook Norton, his dog running
ahead of him. The animal suddenly turned into a field and almost
immediately, Sabin heard it yelping. He ran to see what the matter was
and found the dog with its paw almost completely cut off.

The dog was taken to veterinary surgeon Alban Bull, who immediately
contacted the police. PC Gooding went to interview the owner of the
field, William Tustain, who stated that he had thrown an axe at the dog
because it tried to steal his lunch. Tustain was convinced that the axe
hadn't actually hit Sabin's dog.

There was no love lost between Sabin and Tustain, who was summoned
to appear at the Chadlington Petty Sessions, charged with unlawfully
wounding a dog without cause. In his defence, Tustain said that he hadn't
meant to hit the dog and was still positive that he hadn't. He explained that
Sabin owned several dogs, all of which were a complete nuisance, chasing
his cattle and worrying his sheep. Had the dog belonged to anyone else but
Sabin, said Tustain, he wouldn't have cared if it had run off with a sheep.

Sabin presented a veterinary surgeon's bill to the magistrates and also
claimed that he had sustained a loss of 30s on account of the dog's injuries.
Although magistrates found Tustain guilty of cruelty to a dog, fining him
5s with 15s costs, they dismissed Sabin's claims for financial restitution.

23 MAY

1921 An inquest was held in Oxford on the death of a young woman,
whose body was found in the River Thames that morning.

On the previous day, two rowing boats collided and capsized on the
Thames and their occupants were thrown into the river. Four men
and two ladies who were out for an evening pleasure trip on the river
were rescued by PC Tindall and Mr Harry Round, who saw the disaster
unfolding from the bank. However, they were unable to locate twenty-

year-old Dorothy Riley, who was drowned. Dorothy, from Manchester, was visiting Oxford with her mother.

The inquest jury returned a verdict of accidental death, commending Tindall and Round for their heroic efforts.

24 MAY   **1819**   Coroner Mr Cecil held an inquest at the Radcliffe Infirmary on the death of sixteen-year-old Edward Adkins.

Stallions were often paraded about the public streets for the purpose of showing them off and, on 15 May, Edward was standing at the roadside in Queen Street with his father's cart. A stallion walked past and suddenly kicked out, fatally injuring him.

The inquest heard that the horse's owner kept many stallions and had never before allowed any of them to be on the public street for the purpose of exhibiting them. The stallion in question was considered very quiet and had never kicked out before. Furthermore, the boy in charge of it had it on a very short rein and was walking down the middle of the road, away from pedestrians and parked carts.

Taking all this into consideration, the jury returned a verdict of 'accidental death'. However they asked that the city magistrates should prevent what they called the 'shameful practice' of exhibiting stallions on market days, which had become very prevalent in recent months. (On the day of the inquest alone, there were three stallions on the street where Edward was kicked.) The jury were unanimous in their condemnation of the practice as 'dangerous in the extreme'.

25 MAY   **1891**   Some years earlier, the area around Ock Street in Abingdon was supposedly haunted by a ghost. Now the local newspapers reported on renewed poltergeist activity in the town, this time centred on West St Helen Street.

The so-called supernatural antics attracted huge crowds every night, as people hoped to see the ghost with their own eyes. Meanwhile, the occupants of the small tenements insisted that they could get no peace

because of a constant barrage of missiles through their windows. The poltergeist delighted in throwing things through glass, including potatoes or lumps of coal or coke.

The missiles seemed to come from all directions, in full view of the spectators and usually appeared to be thrown over the roofs of the houses. Ladders were fetched and the roofs searched on the assumption that someone was hiding there, but to no avail.

The police took a keen interest in the goings-on and, on 8 June, arrested a local man, Alfred Carter, on suspicion of being the ghost. However there was absolutely no evidence against him and when the stone-throwing continued unabated while Carter was confined in the lock-up, the police were forced to release him without charge.

26 MAY

1874 Eighteen-year-old Fanny Wiggins of Witney went to a club feast and, while walking home, sat down for a rest. She soon fell asleep but was rudely awakened by something biting her neck.

Initially, Fanny seemed to suffer no ill-effects from the bite and was well enough to go to work the next day and also to attend another club feast the following evening. However, while she was at work two days later, her neck suddenly began to swell. It continued to swell alarmingly until 2 June, when Fanny died in agony.

Doctors could only theorise that she had been bitten by a viper or something similar but could not explain why it took more than two days for the effects of the bite to be felt.

27 MAY

1900 Labourer William Franklin of Bladon quarrelled with his wife about her son from a former marriage and the argument rumbled on until Franklin eventually stormed off.

Mrs Franklin went to bed but her husband came back and began to abuse her. Hoping that he would go to sleep, she went into the garden but the argument continued after her return. Finally, Mrs Franklin threatened to leave, at which her husband picked up the heavy wooden implement used to pound potatoes for the pigs and smashed her over the head.

She slumped over the sofa and was aware of her husband rummaging through the cupboard where the razors were kept. When he left the house, Mrs Franklin went to a neighbour and was taken to Woodstock

Union Infirmary, while the police began a search for her husband. He was found in a barn in Cassington, having cut his own throat, but missed all the major blood vessels.

Franklin was charged with the attempted murder of his wife and with attempted suicide, appearing at the Oxford Assizes to answer both charges. Having pleaded guilty to the second charge, the trial dealt with the attempted murder, to which Franklin pleaded not guilty.

It emerged that Franklin had a long history of beating his wife and was well known to the Woodstock police. Offered the opportunity to testify, Franklin declined and it was pointed out by the defence that they only had Mrs Franklin's word for what had happened but, since she appeared in court swathed in bandages, there was little doubt that she had been assaulted.

The jury returned a verdict of guilty wounding with intent. The judge remarked that he believed that guilty of attempted murder would have been more appropriate, since Franklin obviously had a violent temper and was unable to control himself. Announcing his intention of protecting Mrs Franklin from her husband, the judge sentenced him to five years' penal servitude.

28 MAY

1920 An inquest was held at Oxford into the death of George H.T. Richards, aged twenty, an undergraduate of Magdalen College.

Richards was among a party of five friends who went out on two punts. As they were returning to Oxford, the punt pole appeared to stick in the mud and Richards fell overboard into deep water.

It was dark at the time and although John F. Fleming dived at the spot where the punt pole remained, he was unable to find the body. He made several attempts before exhaustion set in and he was forced to admit defeat. It was some time before Richards' body was recovered and, although artificial respiration was attempted, it proved impossible to resuscitate him.

The inquest jury returned a verdict of 'accidental death'.

29 MAY

1924 During the traditional beating of the bounds ceremony at Charlbury several boatloads of people had been safely ferried over the River Evenlode, when a punt suddenly capsized, throwing all on board into the river. Sixteen-year-old Evelyn Pickett was rescued by a fourteen-year-old boy, clinging round his neck as he swam with her on his back. However, just before they reached the safety of the bank, exhaustion forced Evelyn to relinquish her hold and she was drowned. Her body was later dragged from the river, as were the bodies of thirteen-year-old James Bishop and ten-year-old Cyril Smith.

An inquest into the deaths of the three children was held the following day and heard from the chairman of the parish council, Mr Taylor, who was in the punt and attributed the cause of the disaster to the children standing up. The inquest returned verdicts of 'accidentally drowned' on all three victims.

30 MAY

1880 Coroner Mr C. Duffell Faulkner held an inquest at The Three Pigeons Inn near Banbury into the death of a baby, found two days earlier in the nearby canal.

The inquest was scheduled for eleven o'clock in the morning and, by order of the coroner, Dr Hudson visited the inn at seven o'clock to conduct a post-mortem examination. Knowing that the jury would have to inspect the body, Hudson borrowed a tea tray from the publican, which he covered with a sack and placed on a table in the shed. He laid the infant's remains on the sack before upending a heavy iron pig trough, which he placed over the body.

Sometime later, a man saw the local butcher's dog emerging from the shed, carrying something in its mouth. Since the witness was unaware of what was being stored in the shed, he paid no attention to the animal but a little later, a second dog was seen in the pub yard, again carrying something in its mouth. Only now did someone remember the tiny corpse in the shed, which had vanished.

The second dog was followed home, where it was relieved of the infant's head, but there was no trace of the body and it was assumed that the butcher's dog had either eaten it or buried it. The loss of the body was not the only disaster as, just when the first witness at the inquest was about to testify, a tremendous crash shook the building. It was caused by a runaway horse and cart, which attempted to negotiate a turn into Castle Street at full gallop and collided with the pub. One of the cart's shafts went through a window, narrowly missing three men sitting nearby.

The inquest jury eventually accepted Dr Hudson's evidence that the baby had been stillborn and returned an open verdict.

31 MAY

1893 Mr and Mrs Giles Pilcher and their son were visiting Giles's mother at her home in Norham Gardens, Oxford. On 31 May, four-year-old Lewis Theodore was left in the charge of his nurse, Elizabeth Sibley, while the adults went to Godalming.

Lewis begged to go fishing for minnows, so his nurse took him for a walk towards Medley Weir at Port Meadow on the River Thames. When they didn't return for lunch, two servants went out to look for them and found the nurse's cap floating on the surface of the water a few yards from the weir. Nearby, the bodies of Elizabeth and Lewis were clearly visible on the riverbed.

Several witnesses had seen them together near the water and it was surmised that Lewis toppled in and that his nurse died trying to save him. Coroner Mr E.L. Hussey held an inquest that evening at which the jury returned a verdict that both of the deceased were found drowned but that there was no evidence to show by what means they came into the water. At the conclusion of the inquest, the coroner revealed that so far nobody had been able to contact the boy's parents, who were thus still unaware of the terrible tragedy that had befallen their family.

JUNE

Chipping Norton police officers. (Author's collection)

1 JUNE

1847 Five young men went on an excursion down the river from Oxford and, having reached their destination, four decided to bathe. Two were good swimmers, one could swim a little and the fourth, Charles Sewell, could not swim at all.

Suddenly, Sewell shouted that he was out of his depth. John George Stilwell swam to his assistance and managed to get Sewell onto his back. However, Sewell clung so hard to Stilwell's neck that he couldn't swim.

Alfred Joy, Henry Ramsey Taylor and Charles Hawkins were on the river bank and Joy, who considered himself a weak swimmer and had therefore decided against bathing, took off his coat and plunged into the river to try and rescue his friends. By the time he reached them, Stilwell had sunk but Joy managed to grab Sewell's head. Panic stricken, Sewell immediately dragged Joy underwater and Joy was forced to relinquish his hold to save himself.

Sewell's body was dragged from the river two hours later and Stilwell's soon afterwards. An inquest held by coroner Mr Brunner into Sewell's death returned a verdict of 'accidentally drowned', while University coroner George V. Cox recorded that Stilwell's demise was 'accidental death while trying to save Mr Sewell.' The jury commended Alfred Joy's rescue attempt, which was particularly remarkable since he was at best an indifferent swimmer, who had not swum for five years.

2 JUNE

1828 Coroner Mr Cecil held an inquest at Headington into the death of five-day-old John Burrows.

The inquest was told that the baby was suffering from colic and that a relative, Elizabeth Lambourn, gave him a large spoonful of syrup of poppies, which killed him.

Elizabeth produced the bottle of medicine at the inquest. It bore no label and she explained that she had purchased it to treat the 'griping bowels' suffered by her own eight-month-old child.

The coroner called William Rose of Headington, who described himself as a blacksmith and horse doctor. Having examined the bottle, Rose admitted that he had made up the mixture with twenty-five drops of laudanum to one ounce of syrup, following directions from *Buchan's Medicine Book*. Rose insisted that he would not have recommended giving the mixture to so young a baby as John and that the maximum dose for a baby would be three or four drops, not a spoonful.

The inquest jury returned a verdict that 'the child died in consequence of having too large a dose of syrup of poppies administered by an ignorant person, without intention of doing harm.'

3 JUNE

1893 Coroner Mr W.W. Robinson held an inquest at The Plough Inn, Wolvercote on a double drowning.

Thirty-three-year-old Rosa Gibbings was visiting her father at Summertown, accompanied by her little boy, four-year-old Sidney John. Rosa had recently been ill with general unspecified weakness and pains in her head and her doctor had recommended a change of air.

On 2 June, mother and son went for a walk. They were seen walking alongside the canal towards Wolvercote by Cyril Quiller-Couch, who then stopped to talk to a friend for around twenty-five minutes. When he continued walking towards Wolvercote, Quiller-Couch spotted something in the canal and realised that it was a woman.

Rosa Gibbings was standing upright in about 5ft of water, which reached to her forehead. Sidney was also upright but was about nine inches underwater. There were no signs on the canal banks that anyone had slipped and no injuries on either body.

The coroner delayed the inquest until 3 June so that Rosa's husband might attend. The jury learned that she had no history of insanity, fits, fainting or light-headedness and that, although she had been ill for two years, she had never expressed any desire to end her life. She left a half-finished letter to her husband at her father's house, having told her brother that she would finish it when she returned from her walk.

Coroner Mr Robinson could only suggest that the two deaths were accidental, yet Quiller-Couch and his companion were in earshot and heard no splashes or cries for help. In the absence of any more specific evidence, Robinson suggested to the jury that they returned open verdicts and the jury immediately agreed on 'found drowned'.

4 JUNE

1882   Coroner Mr C. Duffell Faulkner held an inquest into the death of James William Hutchings, the son of the occupier of the Broughton Drying Mills near Banbury, who died on 2 June.

On the previous Saturday, twenty-five-year-old James and a friend went on an extended pub crawl. They rode back to the mill and had tea before setting off for Bloxham, where they visited yet more pubs and drank numerous glasses of beer. They ended up in The Red Lion and James found his way into a room where a dance was being held. However, he was so drunk that he fell over and the landlady asked him to leave.

High Street, Bloxham, 1950s. (Author's collection)

Outside, James drunkenly offered to fight anyone and everyone and eventually Thomas Baughan took off his coat and squared up to James, hitting him on the nose. James swung his fist at Baughan but missed completely, falling over and dragging Baughan with him.

Baughan got up and walked away but James complained of pain in his 'lower regions'. Unable to mount his horse, he was put in a cab and taken home, where a surgeon was called to attend to him. In spite of the doctor's treatment, Hutchings died and a post-mortem examination revealed that his bladder had burst.

Surgeon Mr Franey found no marks of external violence on Hutchings and theorised that he was injured when Baughan fell on top of him during their brief fight, at which time Hutchings almost certainly had a very full bladder due to the volume of liquid he had consumed that day. Legally, it was possible for Baughan to have been charged with his manslaughter but the verdict of the inquest jury was one of 'excusable homicide' and Baughan faced no charges.

5 JUNE

1900 William Trinder appeared before magistrates at Oxford City Court charged with cruelly ill-treating two ducks. Alongside him in the dock were Harry Hearn (11), Sidney Cox (12), Bertram Cox (10), Reginald Scragg (10), Horace Scragg (9), Percy Talboys (9) and Thomas Derrick (11).

The magistrates were told that on 29 April, Trinder put his dog into the duck pond at Grandpont, Oxford, scattering the ducks in all directions. He then encouraged the children to throw stones at them, resulting in one duck losing an eye and another sustaining a broken wing and having to be put down.

Although Harry Hearn swore that he had thrown nothing, in finding them guilty, magistrates insisted that all the boys must be dealt with alike. Trinder, who was older, was fined 2s 6d with 5s costs, while all of the others were fined 1s each with 1s costs.

6 JUNE

1885 George Lawrence Hanson and his wife Sarah Ann of Thame made their first appearance before magistrates at County Hall, Oxford, charged with the wilful murder of their five-month-old daughter, Georgina, on 4 June.

Upper High Street, Thame. (Author's collection)

The first witness was Dr Herbert G. Lee, who was called to Georgina and found her throat cut. Lee recalled remarking that it was a sad affair, at which both Mr and Mrs Hanson accused each other of being responsible for their daughter's death. An inquest had already recorded an open verdict, the jury unable to determine who cut Georgina's throat.

It seemed certain that the murder was committed by Sarah, who was suffering from severe puerperal melancholia, or post-natal depression, and at the Hansons second appearance before magistrates, it was put to her that she was responsible.

'I wish to say I done it but I was very ill at the time,' she admitted.

Twenty-seven-year-old Sarah was committed for trial at the next Oxford Assizes, where she was acquitted on the grounds of insanity and ordered to be detained during Her Majesty's pleasure. She was sent to Broadmoor Criminal Lunatic Asylum and is believed to have died there in 1929.

7 JUNE

1852 The new Public Baths and Wash-Houses at Oxford were opened with great ceremony. However, not fifteen minutes after the speeches given by various local dignitaries had finished and the baths were declared open to the public, there was a tremendous rumbling noise, followed by a heavy crash. There had been an explosion of steam in the hot water system, which resulted in the hot and cold water cisterns falling down, demolishing nearby walls as they fell.

Stoker John Wordsworth was badly hurt and died from head, back and chest injuries later that day. Nine-year-old Tom Cambray Burchell was killed outright and several more people were injured. For some time, it was feared that there were many more victims buried in the rubble but fortunately those fears proved unfounded.

An inquest later ruled that both deaths were accidental.

8 JUNE

1891 William Painton appeared at the Abingdon Division Petty Sessions charged with wounding twelve-year-old Henry Griffin, with intent to kill and murder him.

There was bad blood between Painton and Griffin, who were neighbours at South Hincksey and who worked for the same farmer. Eighteen months earlier, Painton was charged with breaking into the house of Griffin's widowed mother. Griffin gave evidence against him and Painton was sentenced to three months' imprisonment, since when Painton had held a grudge against Griffin and had often been heard to threaten to kill him.

On 29 May, a publican saw Henry walking towards his home, covered in blood. Seeing that the child could scarcely walk, William Brain escorted him home and Henry's mother took him straight to the Radcliffe Infirmary, where he was found to have three lacerations on his skull, the longest of which was four inches in length. The wounds had split the boy's scalp to the bone but, according to the house surgeon, were not life threatening. Police Sergeant Weekes was informed of the assault on Griffin and tracked Painton to Bilston in Staffordshire, where he was arrested on 2 June. He admitted hitting Griffin 'five or six times' with a hoe, adding that he didn't care whether the boy was dead or alive.

At the Petty Sessions, Henry's head was still swathed in bandages and he fainted while waiting to give evidence. Painton had nothing to say in his own defence and was committed for trial at the Reading Assizes, where he was found guilty of wounding with intent to do grievous bodily harm and sentenced to twenty months' imprisonment.

9 JUNE

1900 Caleb Hughes woke at five o'clock in the morning to go to work. Thirty-four-year-old William Hughes came into his house and they had two cups of tea and some bread and butter, before walking to Letcomb Bassett, where they were to spend the day hoeing mangolds.

At about half-past nine, the two men stopped for 'lunch' of bread and cheese, washed down by cold tea. When they started work again, William began complaining about the heat, saying he felt thirsty. He made three trips to the well of a nearby cottage to fetch water but it didn't seem to help to cool him down and before long he began to stagger. Caleb took his hand and William collapsed, shivering and groaning almost constantly.

Eventually a cart was procured to take him to the surgeon at Wantage but he died moments before he arrived. Dr Emerson had no doubt that William's death was due to sunstroke and, at the inquest into William's death, the jury returned a verdict in accordance with the medical evidence.

Note: It has not proved possible to establish any relationship between William and Caleb Hughes.

10 JUNE

1871 Eighteen-year-old Mary Ann Sutton had worked for the Turner family in St Giles's, Oxford, since October 1870 and was entirely satisfactory until 10 June, when she complained of feeling unwell.

Mrs Elizabeth Turner gave her some brandy and within half an hour, Mary Ann felt better. However, Mrs Turner thought she looked a little stout and asked her if she might be pregnant. Mary Ann denied her condition and got on with her work as normal but later that afternoon, Mrs Turner couldn't find her servant and, when she went to look for her, she found Mary Ann in her bedroom. Her clothing was disarranged and there was a chamber pot containing a large blood clot on the floor.

Mrs Turner sent for surgeon Edward Robert Owen, who verified that Mary Ann had recently given birth. Mary Ann continued to deny having done any such thing, until Owen produced several blood-soaked cloths from the trunk in her bedroom. Only then did Mary Ann admit to having had a baby, which she confessed to hiding in the coal yard.

Owen retrieved the body of a baby boy from beneath a pile of small coals. On washing the body, he found that the baby's skull was smashed like an eggshell on one side and the infant had several deep cuts on its neck and some broken ribs. Owen was satisfied that the child was born alive and died from blows with a blunt instrument.

When an inquest found a verdict of 'wilful murder' against Mary Ann Sutton, coroner Mr W. Brunner committed her for trial at the next assizes and magistrates at the City Police Court followed suit. Mary Ann Sutton was tried at the Oxford Assizes on 12 July but, in spite of the overwhelming evidence against her, the jury found her guilty only of concealing the birth of her baby and she was sentenced to fifteen months' imprisonment.

11 JUNE

1892 Joseph Jones worked as a carter at Bloxham Grove Mill and was asked to deliver sacks of flour to the Co-Operative Stores at Claydon and Banbury. As it was Saturday, Jones took his seven-year-old son Frederick and his two nieces along for the ride.

The children were travelling in the bed of the waggon but Frederick persisted in climbing out and riding on the footboard. His father remonstrated with him several times, eventually threatening, 'If you don't get in, my lad, I'll hit you with this whip.' Frederick finally did as he was told but, as he was climbing back into the waggon, he slipped and tumbled off and before his father could stop the horses, the wheel went over his head. He died in his father's arms minutes later.

The inquest on his death was held at The Plough Inn, Little Bourton, by coroner Mr G. Coggins. The jury returned a verdict of 'accidental death', saying that Frederick's demise arose from his own disobedience although they laid part of the blame on Joseph Jones. They believed that he was wrong to have taken the children with him, saying that he had enough to worry about controlling three horses, without having to control three children as well. The jury further stated that they believed that Jones should have stopped the cart immediately his son began to misbehave and, had he done so, the boy's life would undoubtedly have been spared. At the jury's request, the coroner called Jones back into the room and admonished him for his carelessness.

12 JUNE

1880 At about nine o'clock in the evening, Eliza Tame filled a lamp with benzoline in the sitting room of her cottage at Long Wittenham. Five of Eliza's children were in the room at the time, including eleven-year-old Eliza Ann.

Whenever Eliza filled the lamp, she normally wiped any spills from the outside. However, on this occasion, she forgot to do so. She lit the lamp with a Lucifer match then slipped out of the room for a few moments and, when she returned, the lamp was on fire. Eliza picked it up and tried to blow out the flames but within seconds, the burning lamp became too hot to hold. Eliza threw it away from her and, to her horror, her daughter Eliza Ann's dress immediately burst into flames.

In a panic, Eliza Ann ran out of the house and into the yard, where the fresh air fuelled the flames. By the time her clothes were extinguished, she was dreadfully burned and, in spite of the attentions of a surgeon, died soon afterwards.

An inquest was held at The Vine Cottage Inn at Long Wittenham, at which the jury ruled that Eliza Ann Tame met her death by 'burns from benzoline'.

13 JUNE

1900   The Oxford City Coroner held an inquest at the Radcliffe Infirmary into the death of two-year-old Edith Kate Loder.

Just before one o'clock on 11 June, terrible screams were heard in Thames Street, St Aldate's. Neighbours rushed to investigate and found Mrs Loder standing in the hall trying to extinguish her burning clothes by smothering the flames with a greatcoat. Sadly, when Edith heard her mother's screams, she rushed into her arms and her own clothes ignited.

Neighbours put Edith and Mrs Loder in a cab to the hospital, where Edith died later that evening from shock arising from burns to her face, arms and hands.

Mrs Loder was severely burned on her arms, face and chest and, detained in hospital, was too ill to attend the inquest. She told her husband, Frederick, that she had thrown a drop of paraffin oil onto the fire in the wash house and the can exploded in her hand, setting light to her clothes. At the time, Mrs Loder was standing very close to the cradle in which her one-month-old baby was lying and could only think of running away so that the cradle was not ignited by her burning garments. Unfortunately, Edith ran into her arms and was herself set alight.

The coroner offered to adjourn the inquest in the hope that Mrs Loder would recover sufficiently to attend but the jury did not find it necessary and returned a verdict that Edith died from accidental burns. They donated their fees to her father.

14 JUNE

1882   Neighbours of the Wyatt family in Banbury heard a child screaming, followed by prolonged moaning. Less than an hour later, William Wyatt called them into the house, where his wife's son, John Thomas Side, lay dying on his mother's lap. Wyatt explained that the toddler had fallen off a chair, the chair then falling on top of him.

A post-mortem examination showed the cause of death as an extraversion of blood on the brain, which surgeon Mr Franey believed was caused either by a heavy blow from a fist or blunt instrument, or by a kick from a booted foot. Franey thought it remotely possible that the fatal injuries could result from a fall but only one from a considerable height – the surgeon was adamant that a fall from the chair would not suffice.

If John didn't fall then only his stepfather or his mother, Anne, could have caused his fatal injuries and the inquest jury returned verdicts of wilful murder against both of them. At the Oxford Assizes, the Grand Jury ignored the bill against Anne, leaving only William to stand trial for his stepson's murder.

William was a widower with three children when he met and married Anne. Her illegitimate son was a healthy little boy until he moved into his stepfather's home, when he regularly appeared bruised. Neighbours frequently heard him screaming and William constantly complained about the child's 'filthy habits' and about his inability to walk properly.

Two weeks before John died, Anne explained some bruising on his face to neighbours by saying that he had fallen down the stairs. At Wyatt's trial, it was pointed out that Mr Franey had suggested that the toddler's fatal injuries might have been caused by a fall and presiding judge Lord Justice Bowen made much of the burden of proof.

To convict Wyatt of murder, the jury must believe that John died from being beaten and that Wyatt deliberately inflicted the blows with the intention of killing him. Bowen pointed out that there was another person in the house at the time – Anne Wyatt was prevented from giving evidence since she was married to the defendant – but the jury must be sure that, if John died from violence, it was inflicted by William, not Anne, and it was done intentionally. The entire case was Franey's word against the defendant's and Wyatt was entitled to the benefit of any doubts the jury might have.

The jury were divided, some wishing to find Wyatt guilty of manslaughter, others wishing to acquit him. Pushed to decide, they found Wyatt not guilty and he was discharged.

15 JUNE

1860   Coroner Mr T. Pain held an inquest at The Crown Inn, Banbury, into the death of seventeen-year-old Charles (or William) Byles of Charlbury.

Byles was running an errand for his employer and was riding a pony along Banbury High Street when a butcher's cart ploughed into the pony, knocking it over. Byles was so severely injured that he died the following morning.

At the inquest, it was determined that fourteen-year-old Henry Armitt, was driving recklessly and very fast and the jury returned a verdict of manslaughter against him, which was supported by the magistrates.

Henry was sent for trial at the Oxford Assizes on 11 July. In considering the case, the Grand Jury found that there was insufficient evidence against Armitt to support a conviction but, since he was committed on the coroner's warrant, he was forced to appear. He was acquitted and discharged with a warning to drive more carefully in future.

High Street, Banbury, 1916. (Author's collection)

1899 The trial of Joseph Slatter and Robert James for wilful murder concluded at the Berkshire Assizes.

On 3 April, Isaac Day, the landlord of The Chequers Inn at Harwell, asked the police for assistance in removing Slatter and James from his premises. They were not keen to leave and scuffled with PCs Hewitt and Charlton and, when the policemen succeeded in getting them out of the pub, they began to fight in earnest.

High Street, Harwell, 1950s. (Author's collection)

Hewitt was punched several times in the head and face, blackening both of his eyes and breaking his nose. Eventually, the pub landlord and other bystanders came to Hewitt's assistance and he managed to handcuff Slatter, while James fled. Meanwhile, PC Charlton had been kicked unconscious and died the next day.

James was arrested on 4 April and maintained that he, Slatter and both policemen were all drunk. He insisted that the constables had challenged himself and Slatter to a fight and that both policemen had been hitting out with their police staves and had used unnecessary violence, against which he had simply acted in self-defence. However, numerous witnesses testified that the policemen were sober and that they had done nothing more than defend themselves against a vicious, unprovoked attack.

The inquest into the death of Joseph Charlton returned a verdict of wilful murder against Slatter and James and magistrates subsequently committed them for trial at the next Berkshire Assizes. They were found guilty of manslaughter and, describing their crime as 'as close as possible to murder', the presiding judge sentenced them each to twenty years' penal servitude.

PC Charlton left a wife and four young children and, only five years earlier, his seven-year-old son also died in tragic circumstances, being run over by a cart on 6 September 1894.

17 JUNE

1871 Coroner Mr C. Duffell Faulkner held an inquest at Chalford into the death of widow Ann (or Hannah) Thomas. On 15 June, Ann was helping to brew beer in the brew-house of the farm owned by Mark Bayliss and was just about to ladle the hot liquid from the copper when a large flitch of bacon fell onto her shoulder. The bacon was suspended from the ceiling by a cord but rested on a ledge in the wall and somehow fell off.

The blow knocked Ann over and she landed with her back on the edge of a large tub. Although a doctor was immediately summoned from Chipping Norton, Ann's back was so badly injured that she died before he arrived.

The inquest returned a verdict of 'accidental death'.

18 JUNE

1838 Richard Claydon, James Trotman and William Widdows were shooting rabbits on Lord Dillon's estate between Charlbury and Woodstock. During the evening, they split up, agreeing to meet again later but when Widdows and Claydon arrived there was no sign of Trotman.

As the two men waited for him, they heard somebody say, 'Damn your eyes, if you are in the hedge, come out or I will shoot you.' Minutes later, gamekeeper Joseph Chapman approached Widdows and Claydon and asked them what they were doing. When they explained that they were out shooting rabbits, Chapman told them they would have no rabbits that night.

When Trotman appeared, all four men walked along together until Trotman shouldered his gun and told Chapman, 'If a rabbit passed that light, I would shoot it before your face.' Chapman assumed that Trotman was pointing the gun at him and objected. His companions persuaded him that no threat was intended but Chapman was still arguing. 'Would you shoot a rabbit here if you were to see one?' he asked Trotman, who replied that he would.

'If you did, I would shoot you,' Chapman insisted, raising his gun and adding, 'Damned if I don't shoot you.' Claydon protested but Chapman laughingly passed the gun to him, telling him that it was not loaded. The argument niggled on a while longer before the men separated again.

Half an hour later, Claydon heard his name being called and found Widdows with Joseph Chapman and Joseph's brother, William. Joseph asked where Trotman was and soon afterwards, Trotman came walking towards the group. Immediately, Joseph began to goad him about having a rabbit in his pocket. Angrily, he and Trotman aimed their guns at each other and, sensing trouble, William Chapman knocked the muzzle of his brother's gun upwards while Claydon attempted to disarm Trotman, who refused to relinquish his weapon. As William grabbed his brother's gun, it fired and Trotman fell to the floor, dying.

Joseph Chapman was charged with wilful murder and appeared at the Oxford Assizes on 28 February 1839. Although he insisted that the shooting was an accident and he would not have fired if his brother hadn't grabbed his gun, Chapman was found guilty and sentenced to death. His sentence was later commuted to one of transportation for life and he sailed for Van Dieman's Land on 9 July 1839.

19 JUNE

1899 Benjamin Green appeared at the Oxford Assizes charged with having unlawful carnal knowledge of a girl between the ages of thirteen and sixteen years old. He was additionally charged with indecent assault.

The victim was Green's youngest daughter, Eva, and Green gave an emotional speech in his own defence. He told the court that he had been married for twenty-eight years and had nine children. The allegation of sexual misconduct with Eva was a wicked, evil and malicious attempt by his wife to get him locked up as revenge for boxing her ears.

Since a surgeon who examined Eva could find no evidence to support the allegations against her father, Benjamin Green was acquitted.

20 JUNE

1857 Coroner Mr W.D. Wasbrough held an inquest at The Wheatsheaf Inn, Wantage, into the death of fourteen-month-old Charles Deacon.

The toddler's ten-year-old brother, Henry, was left to babysit the boy but neglected to keep his eye on Charles, who toddled into the road and was run over by a fully-laden waggon. The wheel of the waggon passed completely over his body, causing severe internal injuries and Charles died about ninety minutes later.

The inquest jury returned a verdict of 'accidentally killed', adding a rider to state that they completely exonerated the driver of any blame in the tragedy. They were less sympathetic towards Henry, who narrowly avoided criminal charges in respect of the death of his brother.

21 JUNE

1937 Assistant chef John Edward Allen from Burford approached a police officer in London and told him that he was wanted for 'the job in Oxford.' Allen was the last person seen with seventeen-month-old Kathleen Diana Lucy Woodward before her strangled body was found hidden in long grass near her home.

The child's father was a waiter, who worked with Allen at The Lamb Inn, Burford and, on 19 June, Allen went to his home and told Mrs Woodward that her husband wanted him to take the baby out for an airing. Allen

The Lamb Inn, Burford. (Author's collection)

had taken the baby out before but when he didn't return after two hours, the alarm was raised.

Allen was tried for baby Kathleen's wilful murder, his trial at the Oxford Assizes concluding on 21 October 1937. Allen alleged that Mrs Woodward was in love with him and that they were having an affair. He insisted that Mrs Woodward had strangled her daughter and that he had offered to take the blame as he had previously spent time in a mental hospital and thought he would be acquitted.

The jury found Allen guilty, although they recommended that enquiries should be made into his mental state. Having passed the mandatory death sentence, Mr Justice Finlay promised the jury that he would write to the Home Secretary and Allen was ultimately declared insane and sent to Broadmoor Criminal Lunatic Asylum. Apparently a model inmate, in July 1947, he escaped by climbing a sixteen-foot outer wall and remained a fugitive until May 1949, when he was recaptured in north-west London.

22 JUNE

1872   Samuel Clark of Headington lost several cabbages from his garden and kept a look out to try and catch the thief red-handed. When he caught seventy-five-year-old Richard Cooper in the act of cutting a cabbage Clark went to the local constable.

Cooper, the village Parish Clerk, was absolutely mortified at being served with a summons to appear before the magistrates and spent a sleepless night before going to the church and hanging himself in the bell tower.

Coroner William Brunner held an inquest the following day at The White Hart Inn, Headington, at which it emerged that another villager had told Cooper to help himself to as many cabbages as he wanted – the old man had simply got the wrong garden and couldn't bear to be branded a thief.

23 JUNE

1887   At Wroxton, John Ward and two brothers, Henry and George Cad, indecently assaulted a five-year-old child named Rose Alice Taylor. The boys, who were aged between ten and thirteen years old, appeared at the Quarter Sessions on 27 June, from where they were sent for trial at the Oxfordshire Assizes.

When their trial opened on 4 July, John and Henry were prepared to plead guilty to indecent assault. However, George insisted on pleading not guilty, exposing the boys to a formal trial by jury. The assault on Rose was proved to the jury's satisfaction and they found all three defendants guilty.

The judge remarked on the precocity of the offence, bemoaning the fact that he could not sentence the boys to a 'thoroughly good whipping'. He adjourned overnight to allow himself time to ponder the most appropriate sentence, returning to court the next morning having apparently had a change of heart.

He called Ward's mother and the Cads' grandmother into the witness box and asked if they would consent to have the boys whipped. When both women agreed, the judge made arrangements for the Inspector at Banbury police station to carry out the whipping with a birch. Once the judge was satisfied that the boys would be punished, he told them that they were very naughty boys but added that he didn't like to send such young children to prison. With that, he discharged them to the Inspector, on their own recognisances to keep the peace for one year and to come up for judgement if called upon to do so.

24 JUNE

1880 An inquest was held by coroner Mr Coggins into the death of thirty-seven-year-old Edwin Betteridge.

On the night of 23 June, there were several rumbles of thunder around Over Norton and one particularly loud bang brought villagers rushing to their doors. They saw Betteridge lying flat on his back in the street, completely insensible. Nobody was able to revive him and he died within minutes.

Betteridge was carried back to his own cottage and laid on the floor. Surgeon Mr Mowbray Jackson was summoned and, finding no immediately obvious cause of death, requested that the dead man was taken upstairs to his bed and undressed.

Early on 24 June, Jackson returned to examine Betteridge's corpse more closely. He discovered 'a great discolouration' behind the dead man's left ear, which extended down his back as far as his calves. Jackson concluded that 'death was occasioned by shock to the system from the electric fluid' – in other words, Betteridge had been struck by lightning.

The inquest jury returned a verdict of death due to shock from lightning, donating their fees to Betteridge's widow.

25 JUNE

1849 George Carr appeared at Oxford City Court charged with annoying his landlord and neighbour, Thomas Clark of Plantation Road.

The Bench were told that after Clark gave his tenant notice to quit, Carr took to decorating the front door of his cottage with drawings of coffins and gallows, from which men who bore a resemblance to Clark were depicted hanging. Clark was a somewhat nervous man and decided to seek assistance from the magistrates rather than confronting Carr directly.

A solicitor acting for Carr maintained that his client was at liberty to indulge his taste for drawing on his own front door. However, Clark's solicitor countered with the fact that, if it could be shown that such conduct was intended to annoy another, it was punishable by a fine of up to 40s. Furthermore, if necessary, Clark's solicitor stated that he could produce four witnesses who had heard Carr indulging in abusive language towards his client outside his house, which constituted a breach of the public peace.

Magistrates asked if Carr was prepared to apologise for his conduct and agree to vacate the house within two weeks. When Carr agreed, he was discharged, on payment of 6s costs.

26 JUNE

1871 The body found in a pond at Little Barford was quickly identified as that of four-year-old Edward 'Teddy' Patrick Busby.

When Rachel Busby moved in with Thomas Castle at Barford St John, he promised to marry her. Castle was bringing up his one-year-old daughter,

Sarah, and, with her illegitimate son, Teddy, Rachel fully expected them to become a family. However, the promise of marriage was never fulfilled and, after the first month, Castle began to mistreat Teddy, beating and starving the little boy and forcing him onto the streets to beg for food.

'The child always seemed to be in the wrong place; it always seemed to be in the way,' Rachel said later, adding, 'we scarce went to bed but there was a row about the child.'

After Teddy's body was found, Rachel Busby and Thomas Castle were arrested and charged with his murder. Before magistrates, Rachel made a full confession to killing her son, so that 'he should be out of his miserable little life.' Although Rachel insisted that the tragedy would never have happened if Castle had kept his promises, married her and been a father to her son, she took full blame for the tragedy, stressing that Castle was innocent.

When the case came to trial at the Oxford Assizes, the Grand Jury found 'no bill' against Thomas Castle and Rachel pleaded guilty to the charge of wilful murder, adding that she believed that she was pregnant.

Mr Justice Lush assembled a jury of matrons and a surgeon to examine Rachel and they found that, if she was with child, she had not yet quickened (reached the stage of pregnancy at which the foetus could be detected). Lush had no alternative but to pass the mandatory death sentence on Rachel, although she was later reprieved and her sentence commuted to one of life imprisonment, which she served at Knaphill Female Convict Prison in Woking.

27 JUNE

1849 Fourteen-year-old John Gale was shooting rats on his father's farm at Cuddesdon. His brother, Henry, was going about his chores in the farmyard and saw that John had rested the gun against the wall of the pig sty and was walking along the top of the wall.

Henry had his hand on the door of the cow house, when he heard the sound of a shot and turned to see John fall off the wall. 'Oh dear, what will father and mother say?' John asked as Henry carried him into the house. 'I shall die, for the shots are gone into my stomach,' John informed his brother, as Henry laid him on the sofa.

Although Henry ran for a surgeon, John died later that evening. At an inquest held by coroner Mr Brunner, the jury were informed that John was accustomed to handling a gun and that Henry believed that he was walking along a wall to get to the furthest pigsty, where he had shot several rats earlier that day. According to Henry, John accidentally knocked the gun off the wall and it fired when it hit the ground. The inquest jury accepted his explanation, returning a verdict of accidental death.

28 JUNE

1883 Sarah Cooper appeared at Chipping Norton Police Court charged with being drunk and disorderly in Spring Street on 26 June. The magistrates heard that Sarah was married to a navvy working on the construction of the Banbury and Cheltenham Railway. After a day spent drinking, Sarah quarrelled with her husband and began belabouring him with her fists.

Mr Cooper gained a black eye and several other facial injuries before two passing clergyman managed to pull his wife off him, but, as soon as they let her go, she flew at her husband again and continued beating him. The police were summoned and had no choice but to arrest Sarah.

Sarah was actually brought before the magistrates on 27 June but was found to be still 'in such a filthy state of intoxication' that they were forced to remand her for another day to allow her time to sober up. She was eventually found guilty and fined 10s.

29 JUNE

1870 Mr Chaundy's chemist and Hall and Ridley, tailors, stood on the intersection of St Aldate's Street and Pembroke Street in Oxford. Between them was the residence of waiter William Ebenezer Collis. Mr Chaundy and his family lived over their shop, as did Mr Hall.

On the night of 28 June, the Chaundys and Halls were long since in bed when Collis returned from work. Within a few minutes of him retiring for the night, two labourers walking past the outside of the buildings noticed smoke pouring from between the shutters on his windows. One of them ran to the police station while the other attended to a female passer-by, who had fainted in shock. Once he had done that, he made no attempt to rouse the occupants of the buildings but simply stood watching the fire as it blazed out of control.

The Chaundys and the Halls managed to escape the conflagration as did Mr Collis, who was forced to jump into the street from a first-floor window. However, Collis's sister-in-law and servant were trapped upstairs and someone in the crowd of spectators pulled open the shutters, which ventilated the fire. It proved impossible to reach the two women in the inferno, even though Collis tried again and again, until he fainted from the effort. Eventually Collis's and Chaundy's houses completely collapsed and, as soon as the remains were cool enough, a search was initiated for the bodies of the two women, which were burned so badly that they were not recognisable as human beings.

An inquest held later that day determined that Mary Susan Jackson and servant Fanny Clifton died in the fire, although there was no evidence to show how it started. (The most likely theory was that it was started by the pipe Collis was smoking when he returned from work.) The city's portable fire escape had recently been moved from its customary place in the Town Hall yard – nobody knew where it was located and precious time was wasted in tracking it down.

30 JUNE

1903 An inquest was held at Abingdon into the death of eight-year-old Harry Kimbrey.

Harry's fourteen-year-old brother was firing a gun in an orchard to scare birds when Harry ran out from behind a shelter, straight into the range of the gun. The shot blew away half of the boy's head, killing him instantly.

The inquest jury returned a verdict of 'accidental death'.

JULY

Haymaking, 1911.

1 JULY

1908   Mr P.A. Caton-Thompson and William Astley Cave-Browne-Cave hired a punt at Medley Weir. They had travelled only a few hundred yards when the punt pole snapped, plunging Cave-Browne-Cave into the water.

He made no attempt to swim or save himself and after watching him floating downstream for several yards, Caton-Thompson dived in and swam to his rescue. As soon as he reached him, Cave-Browne-Cave grabbed his friend and clutched him so tightly that he lost consciousness. He remembered nothing more until a punt was launched from the bank and pulled both men out of the water.

Although Caton-Thompson quickly recovered consciousness, Cave-Browne-Cave remained insensible and since nobody knew how to do artificial respiration, he was still unconscious when Dr Harold Thompson arrived some time later. Although the doctor tried to resuscitate Cave-Browne-Cave for an hour, his efforts were fruitless.

At an inquest held by University coroner Mr F.E. Marshall, the jury heard that the pole was a new one and that both pieces appeared perfectly sound. A waterman gave his opinion that the pole somehow got beneath the punt and snapped under the strain.

Cave-Browne-Cave's sister testified that her brother had a weak heart and had suffered an almost identical accident the previous year. On that occasion, he had been completely unable to help himself, collapsing the moment he fell into the water.

The inquest jury returned a verdict of 'accidentally drowned', adding a recommendation that simple instructions for the resuscitation of the drowned should be posted everywhere that boats were hired out.

2 JULY

1898   An inquest was held at Towersey into the death of thirty-four-year-old labourer Edward Bambrook, which the coroner described as the most extraordinary he had ever heard of.

Bambrook died the previous day as the result of an accident. Wanting to bore some holes in a trolley, Bambrook placed a poker in the fire and heated it until it was red hot. As he was hurrying towards the trolley, he tripped and fell and the poker penetrated his left eye. He fell so heavily that he bent the poker and, although his sister managed with difficulty to pull the poker out, Bambrook died before medical help could be summoned.

The inquest jury returned a verdict of 'accidental death'.

3 JULY

1882   Having been tried and acquitted for the murder of his stepson (*see* 14 June), William Wyatt and his wife Anne returned from Oxford to Banbury by train. They were met at the station by a large crowd, who expressed their displeasure at the verdict.

The couple were driven to the home of Wyatt's sister in Windsor Street but the crowd followed and, by midnight, there were several hundreds of people at the house, hissing and booing. People made numerous attempts to get at the Wyatts and were beaten back by six policemen, who were forced to draw their staves in an effort to quell the unruly mob, who broke every windowpane in the house and smashed the doors by pelting them with stones.

At four o'clock in the morning, Wyatt slipped quietly out of town, his destination unknown.

4 JULY

1884   William Henry Smith and Thomas Gibbs were working in Smith's hay field near Woodstock when the heavens opened. They left the field to seek shelter but just as they walked through the gate, they saw Mrs Smith coming along the lane with her husband's dinner. Smith and his wife turned back towards the field and stood beneath an ash tree, while Gibbs sheltered from the torrential rain in a ditch.

Suddenly there was a deafening crash of thunder coupled with a flash of lightning and Mrs Smith screamed. Gibbs ran to her aid, to find Smith lying face down and when Gibbs turned him over, it was obvious that he was dead.

Smith's body was later examined by Dr E.W. Turner, who confirmed that Smith had been struck by lightning. The initial strike was on his shoulder and the current ran down his back and right leg, scorching his skin, burning his clothes and singeing all the hair from his body.

Mr C. Duffell Faulkner held an inquest later that day at which the jury returned a verdict of 'death by lightning'. Meanwhile, at Aston Upthorpe, then in neighbouring Berkshire, two more farm labourers were killed by lightning.

5 JULY

1875   At half-past six in the morning, the village postman found sixty-two-year-old Catherine Cridland sitting almost naked on the floor of her house at Clanfield. Catherine was badly bruised and, although barely able to speak, when asked if her husband had beaten her, she replied that he had. A closer examination of the house showed that the ground around the garden well had been heavily trampled and Catherine managed to indicate that her husband had tried to put her down it.

When Catherine died, a search was initiated for her husband, John, who was later charged with her wilful murder. He appeared before magistrates in Burford protesting his innocence and eventually the police established that he had an unshakeable alibi, having been in Bath on business at the time of his wife's death.

Further enquiries showed that Catherine was an intemperate woman who was addicted to drink, and a post-mortem examination suggested that she had sustained her fatal injuries falling downstairs while blind drunk. Her husband was quickly released from custody.

6 JULY

1577   Belgian Roman Catholic Rowlande Jenkes was tried at the Oxford Assizes charged with supporting the Pope and for uttering scandalous words against the Queen. Found guilty, he was sentenced to be nailed to a pillory by his ears and, in retaliation, is said to have placed a curse on the court and on the city of Oxford.

'There arose such an infectious damp of breath among the people that many there present . . . were then smothered and others so deeply affected that they lived not many hours after,' wrote Anthony Wood, the then registrar of Merton College. On the day of what became known as 'The Black Assize', 600 Oxford residents fell ill, along with around a hundred visitors to the city from nearby villages.

The 'gaol fever' continued until 12 August, claiming hundreds of victims, who Wood described as 'very calamitous and full of sorrow, occasioned by the rage of their disease and pain.' Most of the magistrates died, as did two judges, the sheriff, clerks, the coroner, almost all of the trial jury and 100 Oxford scholars who witnessed the trial, although the curse claimed no women, children or poor people as victims.

Jenkes eventually moved back to Belgium, where he is said to have survived to a ripe old age.

7 JULY

1824   Charles Andrews was among a group of haymakers crossing the river on a punt from Kennington when he accidentally fell into the water. Until the boundary changes in 1974 saw it become part of Oxfordshire, Kennington was in Berkshire and the river formed the boundary. When Andrews's body was found an hour later, it was closest to the Oxfordshire side of the river but people on the banks would not permit it to be landed since, in their opinion, his death occurred in Berkshire.

Accordingly, the body was placed on a boat and taken back to the public house at Kennington, where, once again, people refused to allow it to be landed, claiming that the death occurred in Oxfordshire. The body was taken to nearby Sandford but several persons objected to it being brought ashore there.

Eventually, the unfortunate Mr Andrews was unceremoniously dumped on a tow path while magistrates in Oxford were consulted about what should be done with his corpse. The magistrates ordered the body to be taken to the nearest public house, which happened to be in Kennington.

There the body was placed in a shed to await the attentions of the coroner. Mr Cecil, the Oxfordshire coroner, was asked to conduct an inquest but refused on account of the body not having been officially landed in that county. Eventually it was left to his Berkshire counterpart, Mr Slade, to hold the inquest, at which the jury returned a verdict of 'accidental death' and Slade expressed his disgust at those in Oxfordshire who refused to take in the body.

8 JULY

1899   Although he had been feeling unwell for several days, sixty-two-year-old Henry Clarke of Murcott could not afford to take time off work. He complained of feeling ill to his friends, hence when one of them saw him working at the top of a hay rick, he suggested that Clarke should come down.

'Set me a ladder,' Clarke agreed reluctantly. He had reached the fifth rung from the ground when the ladder suddenly turned over and Clarke fell. People rushed to help him but he insisted, 'Don't touch me, I have hurt myself.' He was placed in a wheelbarrow and taken home, where his wife called the doctor. Clarke was conscious and lucid and able to explain that his fall was nothing more than an unfortunate accident.

He was taken to the Radcliffe Infirmary on 11 July, where he died three days later. A post-mortem examination showed that Clarke had chronic heart disease and that the cause of his death was heart failure brought on by the shock of falling.

9 JULY

1882 Eleven-year-old George Wells died at his father's home in Cropredy from the effects of an accident two days earlier.

At an inquest held by coroner Mr C. Duffell Faulkner, the jury were told that George was employed on a farm to lead the horses while Thomas Dunn ploughed. Everything went well until just after two o'clock, when Dunn turned the plough at the end of a furrow. The reins pulled across the flank of one of the three horses, which kicked out in protest and its hoof caught George in the side, knocking him over.

He was carried home and a doctor was summoned but he died two days later from internal injuries. The inquest jury returned a verdict of 'accidental death'.

10 JULY

1877 Five-year-old Eber Dyer lived with his grandmother in Curbridge, while his mother worked as a servant in Oxford. On 10 July, the little boy fell off his chair at the village school. He immediately complained of severe pain in his leg and the schoolmaster sent him home.

Later that afternoon, Eber asked if he might go to bed. His grandmother put him to bed and, soon afterwards, went to check to see if he was all right. She found Eber sweating heavily and fading in and out of consciousness.

When lucid, Eber was still complaining of pain in his leg and his grandmother sent for surgeon Mr Batt of Witney, who recommended poultices. Yet, in spite of the doctor's treatment and his grandmother's diligent care, Eber died on 11 July. A post-mortem examination revealed that he had sustained severe head injuries in the fall at school, which caused his death.

At an inquest held by coroner Mr F. Westell, the jury returned a verdict of 'accidental death'.

11 JULY

1873 Jane Haines was tried at the Oxford Assizes on charges connected with the death of her son.

When Revd Howard Rice of Sutton Courtney realised that his unmarried maid was pregnant, she was asked to leave. On 4 March, Jane went to Culham Station, intending to return to her parents' house near Wantage, but, while waiting for the train, she went into labour. She gave birth to a baby boy in the station toilet, cut his throat with a pair of scissors and placed the corpse in her carpet bag.

Realising that Jane had spent a long time in the lavatory, stationmaster William Bradshaw went to check on her. As a result of what he saw, Bradshaw sent for a local matron, Mrs Rogers, who established that Jane had recently given birth. All Jane would say about her baby was that it had been born dead, but surgeon Arthur Anthony Harris disagreed. He discovered that the baby's lungs floated in water, which he took as evidence of the infant having breathed independently. Harris also found a three-and-a-half inch cut, severing the baby's windpipe, which in his opinion was sufficient to cause death.

At an inquest into the baby's death, the jury returned a verdict of wilful murder against Jane, although magistrates committed her for trial on a charge of concealment of birth. Jane insisted that her child was two months premature and, at the assizes, the prosecution offered no evidence on the charge of wilful murder. On the charge of concealment of birth, it was pointed out that the law required the concealment to be permanent and, in placing her dead baby in an open carpet bag, Jane had just temporarily placed it in the most convenient place available to her. She was therefore acquitted of that charge too.

12 JULY

1899 Twenty-year-old Ernest Henry Thomas Lamburn (or Lambourn) was a baker, who worked for his father. At eleven o'clock in the morning, Lamburn left with his horse and cart to deliver some bread to Littlemore. That evening, a man called to tell his parents that Ernest had been in an accident on the Iffley Road, Oxford, and was at the home of Dr Wylie. William Lamburn went to collect his son and brought him home, promising to follow Wylie's advice and take Ernest to hospital the following morning.

Ernest was conscious but claimed to remember nothing apart from suddenly feeling very giddy and falling from the cart. Witnesses who saw the accident stated that Ernest was driving at a sensible pace when he suddenly toppled over the side of the cart without warning. Everyone was positive that Ernest was not run over.

In the Radcliffe Infirmary, Ernest was treated for a suspected skull fracture. However, his condition gradually worsened and, after his death on 17 July, a post-mortem examination confirmed that his skull was fractured but the actual cause of his death was determined to be meningitis, or inflammation of the brain. There was some question whether the skull fracture caused the inflammation or whether the inflammation of the brain was the reason for the attack of giddiness that caused Lamburn to fall from his cart. At the inquest held by coroner Mr Galpin, the jury favoured the former explanation, returning a verdict of accidental death.

The Radcliffe Infirmary. (Author's collection)

13 JULY

1882 Coroner Mr W.W. Robinson held an inquest into the death of forty-one-year-old William Busby, who died at the Littlemore Asylum.

Busby, an in-patient since 1876, was described as 'an idiotic patient, who was also deaf, dumb and blind'. At mealtimes, his food was cut up into small pieces for him and he managed to feed himself, using a spoon and his fingers.

On 13 July, dinner was cold meat, suet pudding, potatoes and cabbage, which Busby washed down with half a pint of beer. Soon after the meal, he was observed trying to vomit but seemed unable to do so and, when the asylum attendants checked, they found his mouth and oesophagus completely stuffed with his dinner, which he had not swallowed.

A ward attendant managed to prise Busby's mouth open with difficulty and removed more than two ounces of compacted food with a spoon. The medical superintendent arrived within minutes and attempted to remove the blockage with a probang – a long, flexible rod with a ball or sponge at one end. However, the food was so impacted that he was unsuccessful and Busby died within minutes.

Busby was known to bolt his food and the inquest jury returned a verdict that he 'died from choking, caused by having voraciously eaten his dinner.'

14 JULY

1882 An inquest was held at the Radcliffe Infirmary into the death of six-year-old Joseph Orchard, who met his death two days earlier by running in front of a passenger train at the Port Meadow Crossing, Oxford. The child was so severely injured that his face was the only part of his head to remain intact.

The crossing was known to get extremely busy at times and, on the evening of 12 July, there were between thirty and forty people waiting to cross when Joseph suddenly ran out of the crowd, even though signalman William Stott had announced only seconds earlier that there was a train approaching.

The inquest jury returned a verdict of 'accidental death', asking the coroner to forward their recommendations to the directors of the Great Western Railway and the London and North Western Railway, bringing to their attention the urgency of erecting a footbridge at the site.

15 JULY

1882 The headmaster of Thame Grammar School, William George Plummer, appeared before magistrates at County Hall, Oxford, charged with assaulting one of his pupils.

While playing cricket, George Holloway used profane language to the music master. The profanity was overheard by the headmaster, who ordered Holloway to leave the field and later offered him a choice – he could be expelled or thrashed. Holloway chose the latter and was summoned to the headmaster's study to receive his punishment.

According to Holloway, Plummer shut the windows, closed the blinds and removed his gown before ordering the boy to take off his coat and giving him twelve lashes with the cane across his shoulders. Holloway left the headmaster's study in terrible pain and, later that evening, was found to have six or seven wheals on his back, where the skin was broken, along with severe bruising on his arms.

Although Dr Jones testified before the magistrates that the blows were rather severe for disciplining a boy of thirteen, the case against Plummer was dismissed.

16 JULY

1849 Coroner Mr E. Cowcher held an inquest into the death of eight-year-old William Kent from Ock Street, Abingdon.

William was taken ill and died within a few hours from 'Asiatic Cholera'. However, in the opinion of the medical men who attended him, the child's demise was 'accelerated by the effluvia arising from putrid matter lying in and about the yard and premises.'

The child came from a clean and highly respectable family, yet the jury were appalled by the filthy and disgusting state of the neighbourhood. The local newspaper wrote, 'It therefore behoves all of us who have a public duty to perform to endeavour to arouse those who are exposed to like danger from nuisances in their neighbourhood to resort to prompt and effectual means of removing such, lest they should, when too late, find themselves involved in a direful plague, which the adoption of human means might have averted.'

17 JULY

1858 Seventy-nine-year-old labourer William Lovegrove appeared at the Oxford Assizes charged with 'unlawfully taking Elizabeth Tomlin out of the possession of Messrs W. and G. Pearman, her masters, she being under the age of sixteen years.'

Thirteen-year-old maid Elizabeth seemed to have caught Lovegrove's eye and, on 27 February, he met her in the street at Henley-on-Thames and warned her that he would be taking her away some time during the next week. On 2 March, he made good his promise, abducting her from the streets of Henley as she ran an errand.

Lovegrove took Elizabeth to The Swan Inn at Reading, where he demanded a room for himself and his 'wife'. Realising Elizabeth's age, the landlord instructed his servant to take her to her own room, saying that a separate bed would be found for Lovegrove. However, Lovegrove was determined to sleep with Elizabeth and when landlord Charles Webb wouldn't permit him to do so he left the pub and moved to The Sun Inn.

Webb followed him and spoke to landlord Frederick Thompson about his suspicions. Thompson challenged Lovegrove, saying that Elizabeth was more like his granddaughter than his wife but Lovegrove argued that she would be his wife tomorrow.

Hart Street and Market Place, Henley-on-Thames, 1920s. (Author's collection)

Thompson spoke with Elizabeth, who told him that Lovegrove had taken her from the street at Henley and had promised to take her to London.

That was enough for Thompson, who threw Lovegrove out of the pub, having suggested that some women staying there gave him a 'jolly good flouring'. Lovegrove was dredged with flour and put out into the street, while Thompson contacted Elizabeth's parents, who rushed to Reading to rescue her.

At his trial, Lovegrove denied having abducted or enticed Elizabeth but maintained that she had simply followed him and he couldn't rid himself of her. The jury didn't believe a word and found him guilty. He was sentenced to six months' imprisonment, with hard labour.

18 JULY

1845   Twelve-year-old William Sheppard was employed as a bird-scarer on a farm in the parish of Haseley and was supplied with a gun to shoot into the air. Farm labourers walking by the field where he was working saw him leaning with his head over the mouth of the gun and warned him that he shouldn't treat firearms so carelessly. William laughed at them but, five minutes later, the gun went off and literally blew his skull to pieces.

At the inquest on his death, the jury returned a verdict of 'accidental death' and coroner Mr J.H. Cooke implored any farmers present to spread the word that such young boys should not be trusted with guns loaded with shot, since powder alone made sufficient noise for scaring birds.

19 JULY

1927   The body of seventy-two-year-old Colonel Arthur Mearn Lysaght was pulled from the Thames, along with his overturned canoe.

Lysaght was in the habit of dining at the exclusive Phyllis Court Club in Henley-on-Thames on summer evenings then going out on the river in his canoe. According to the Sports Secretary of the club, he did this on the night of 19 July and was not missed until early the following morning.

The elderly gentleman was habitually bright and cheerful and in good health but was known to fall asleep very easily and it was theorised that he dozed off while in his canoe and capsized. The jury at the inquest into his death returned a verdict of 'accidentally drowned'.

Phyllis Court Club, Henley. (Author's collection)

20 JULY

1872 Elderly labourer William Coombes was assisting with the deer cull at Blenheim Park and had concealed himself in long grass waiting for deer to appear.

Unbeknown to Coombes, a doe was hiding in a clump of bracken nearby. When she was startled by the appearance of the estate gamekeepers, she leaped to her feet and fled. Unfortunately, she bounded straight into Coombes, inflicting injuries so serious that he died in hospital two days later.

At the inquest, the jury returned a verdict of 'accidental death', stating that nobody was to blame for the tragedy.

21 JULY

1878 Ten-year-old Frederick Barrett and his father were fishing in the River Cherwell, with several other people. The party ate lunch as guests of farmer Mr Cooper before resuming their fishing.

The anglers were spread out along the bank, each about 30 yards apart, and William Barrett could see his son, as could Thomas Green, who was fishing on the other side of Frederick's position. Yet within ten minutes, Barrett shouted to Green, asking if he could see Frederick and, when Green realised that he couldn't, both men rushed to the place where the boy was last standing.

There was no sign of Frederick and it was some minutes before his father and Green noticed the child's fishing rod floating downstream near Enslow Mill. When the rod was retrieved, they found Frederick drowned, completely entangled in fishing line.

The river where Frederick was fishing was around 5ft deep and there was a mark on the steep bank that looked as though it was made by someone falling into the river. Even though there were several people nearby, nobody had head any cries or splashing, nor had anyone seen any signs of disturbance of the water, such as might have been made by a person struggling against drowning. An inquest was held on the following day at The Rock of Gibraltar public house, Kirtlington.

The River Cherwell, which claimed Frederick's life in 1878. (Author's collection)

The jury returned a verdict of 'accidentally drowned', professing themselves baffled as to how the boy could have drowned unnoticed in such close proximity to so many people.

22 JULY **1830** John Buckingham, a feeble man who was dying from consumption, appeared at the Oxford Assizes charged with stabbing Emmanuel Jervis with intent to murder him.

Jervis was a farmer from Eynsham and Buckingham was his tenant, although Jervis retained one of the upstairs rooms in Buckingham's rented cottage to store beans.

On 14 June, Jervis sent his servant to collect some beans and when the boy returned without any, Jervis went to Buckingham's cottage to see why. Buckingham refused to open the locked door to the room, which was upstairs in his cottage, so Jervis prised it open with an iron bar. He took what beans he needed then turned to leave but Buckingham had armed himself with a pitchfork and stood on the landing barring his way. Jervis was jabbed several times and received a small wound beneath his ear.

In his defence, Buckingham told the court that Jervis had been on too intimate terms with his wife. However, there was no evidence to support this allegation, which Jervis denied vehemently.

Mr Cannington, who was acting as defence counsel for Buckingham, challenged the legality of the charge against his client. He pointed out that, had Jervis died, Buckingham's crime would have been manslaughter not murder and there was no such crime as 'attempted manslaughter'. After due consideration, Mr Justice Park conceded that Cannington had a point and ordered the jury to acquit Buckingham.

23 JULY **1844** Coroner Mr J. Churchill held an inquest at Banbury into the death of Charles Taylor.

The four-year-old boy was one of several children playing in the top-floor room of a house in Neithrop. One little girl was playing on a swing and, as she swung forwards, her outstretched feet hit Charles and kicked him clean out of the open window. He landed on the street below and died instantly. An inquest jury later returned a verdict of accidental death on the little boy who was one of the children of John Taylor, who had recently been found guilty of burglary and transported.

24 JULY **1762** A double execution took place at Oxford when Susan (or Susannah) Harris was hanged for the murder of her illegitimate daughter and James Costard for matricide.

Having been sentenced to death on 21 July, Susan fainted. She was later to say that she did not 'designedly' take away her daughter's life and could not account for the baby's wounds and bruises. Costard excused himself by saying that he was not in his right mind when he shot his mother and begged others to avoid passion and drunkenness.

In those days, convicted criminals stood on a cart before their execution, hanging when the cart was driven away. Costard prayed quietly to himself as he waited, while Susan repeated the Lord's Prayer, beseeching the crowd, 'Father, pray for me, mother, pray for me, good people all pray for me.'

As the cart drew away, Susan fainted again and the knot in the rope slipped to her chin. Her executioners were obliged to put up a ladder and lift her body until the rope was back around her neck and she could finally be hanged. Both bodies were sent to the Oxford Museum for dissection.

25 JULY

1827 Sabrina Bagley and her son Thomas appeared at the Summer Assizes in Oxford charged with the manslaughter of Joseph Smith at Marston.

The Bagleys and Smiths were travelling families and were camping on the roadside when Sabrina challenged Smith for not paying her son for some work he had done for him. Smith was supposedly very drunk and hurled mouthfuls of abuse at Sabrina, who retaliated in kind.

Smith then hit her on the shoulders with his stick and Sabrina threw a stone at him. Stooping to pick up a second, she urged Thomas, 'Do you pick up a stone and fling as well as me.' Thomas did as he was asked but unfortunately selected a stone weighing more than 2lbs. He threw it at Smith and it hit him on the temple, fracturing his skull and instantly poleaxing him. As Mrs Smith tended to her husband, Sabrina threatened, 'If he gets up again, I'll make him die.'

The jury found Thomas guilty of manslaughter and Sabrina of aiding and abetting him. However, since Smith was thought to have provoked them, each was sentenced very leniently to one month's imprisonment.

Note: Some accounts state that the stone weighed at least 5lbs. The trial date is also variously given as 28 July.

26 JULY

1879 Coroner Mr E.L. Hussey held an inquest at the Radcliffe Infirmary into the death of two-year-old Selina Maria Paintin of Cowley Road, Oxford.

Selina's father was a carpenter and, on occasions, would lift the front gate of his house off its hinges if he wanted to get a trolley through into his garden. On 14 July, Mrs Paintin heard a shriek and noticed an errand boy picking up Selina. She ran to see what had happened and found that the gate had toppled over, landing on top of the little girl.

Edward Kilby told the inquest that he saw the toddler lying under the gate and lifted it off her, saying that Selina seemed incapable of standing unaided. He described a 'bad place' on the side of Selina's head, although remarked that there was no blood. Mrs Paintin placed her daughter in a warm bath but when Selina began vomiting blood, her mother rushed her to hospital, where the little girl initially made good progress and seemed likely to recover. However, on 25 July, she developed convulsions and died.

Doctors were certain that injuries caused by the falling gate were the cause of Selina's death and the inquest jury returned a verdict of 'accidental death'.

27 JULY

1830   Although his wife was eighty years old, Mr Austin was convinced that she was conducting a passionate extra-marital affair with a man named Henry (or Harry) Williams, who was even older. Austin threatened numerous times to kill his wife and frequently called his neighbours in the middle of the night to help search his house, believing that Williams was hiding there. Austin was also under the impression that the couple's son, Tom, was acting as a go-between for his mother and her alleged lover and that Tom had initially sold his mother to Williams.

One evening, Austin came home saying, 'I have done it, I have done it.' When Mrs Austin asked what he had done, her husband crowed, 'You will know soon enough. I have done something for that devil of a Tom for selling his mother.'

When Austin died soon afterwards, Tom was shocked to find that his father's entire fortune had been given away and that the husbands of Tom's two sisters had each been given a promissory note for the sum of £200.

Recognising that Austin had almost certainly been insane, one of Tom's brothers-in-law happily relinquished his promissory note. However, the other, Mr Pritchard, refused to do so. Tom was the executor of his father's will and, when he didn't pay Pritchard the promised amount, he found himself standing as the defendant in the Civil Court at the Oxford Assizes. Neighbours told the court that Tom was a dutiful and affectionate son to both of his parents and, on hearing evidence of Mr Austin's delusions relating to his wife's fidelity, the judgement was awarded in favour of Tom Austin.

28 JULY

1851   Coroner Mr Westell held an inquest at Finstock into the death of forty-three-year-old Maria Low.

Although married, Maria lived with a man named Philip Akers and, after sharing lunch with Akers and a couple of guests, Maria began to sweep the floor of their cottage.

Akers had left his gun leaning against the wall in a corner of the room and Maria asked him to 'take it to pieces' in case there was an accident. Akers did so then, before he could stop her, Maria took the stock and barrel from him and threw them into the oven.

There was an immediate explosion and Maria took a whole charge of shots in her upper body. She staggered backwards, unable to speak, falling into a chair and dying within minutes. Had the shots missed Maria, there was no doubt that they would have hit one of the other people present, who were sitting directly behind her.

Akers told the inquest that they usually kept their linen in the oven and he believed that Maria had thrown the gun there without thinking as she tidied up. The jury accepted his explanation and returned a verdict of 'accidental death'.

29 JULY

1879 Coroner Mr C. Duffell Faulkner held an inquest at Steeple Barton on the death of three-year-old Maud Gammage. Maud was playing with other children in the garden of her cottage when she suddenly disappeared. Unfortunately, nobody remarked on the fact that she was no longer in the garden and it wasn't until some time later that her absence was noticed.

Caroline Hayes told the inquest that she went to the communal well and saw Maud's lifeless body in about 4ft of water. With the assistance of another tenant, landlord William Harper went down into the well and recovered the body, but it proved impossible to resuscitate the little girl.

At the inquest, Harper admitted that the wooden cover on the well was rotten and said that he was intending to have a new one made, adding that he would have done so before had the cottagers informed him that one was needed. The inquest jury returned a verdict of 'accidental death' and apparently apportioned no blame to Harper.

30 JULY

1858 After Alfred Martin stayed at The Star in Abingdon, a large bottle of peppermint cordial was missed. When the police heard of the loss, they questioned stationmaster Mr Fry, who had seen a man carrying such a bottle and was able to identify the culprit as Martin.

He appeared before magistrates on 30 July and was found guilty and sentenced to six week's imprisonment. Amazingly, Martin's only purpose in staying at the inn was to apply for a vacancy for a police constable in the Borough Force. Not only that but the theft of the cordial and his subsequent imprisonment led to the automatic forfeit of two pensions that he was entitled to receive for injuries sustained in the Crimean War.

31 JULY

1882 Coroner Mr A.D. Bartlett held an inquest at The Bell Inn into the death of two-year-old Ernest Brewer at Cholsey.

On 28 July, Ernest was left in the care of his eight-year-old sister, Fanny, while their parents were at work. The little boy had a deformed back and was unable to stand unaided and so spent most of his time being wheeled about in a perambulator. In the afternoon, Fanny went out to play, taking Ernest with her in his pram. As well as having babysitting duties, Fanny was also expected to do the housework and soon afterwards, she left her younger sister in charge of Ernest while she swept the cottage out. The younger sister pushed the pram into a shed before going to play at the other end of the garden, leaving the shed door open in case Ernest cried.

Only minutes later, Fanny came out to fetch her brother, to find that he had fallen out of the pram and landed face down in a bowl containing about eight inches of water. Fanny immediately lifted him out and screamed to a neighbour for assistance but the little boy had drowned and, although his body was still warm, nobody was able to revive him.

The inquest jury returned a verdict of 'accidentally drowned in a washing tray'.

AUGUST

Harvesters. (Author's collection)

1 AUGUST

1937   Lorry driver Wally Noble of Paddington was driving his car at Clifton Hampden when he took a left-hand bend too wide. Two young boys were cycling towards Noble's car and he was unable to avoid hitting them.

Clifton Hampden. (Author's collection)

One was thrown into the air by the impact and his bicycle struck George Pike, a back seat passenger in Noble's car, who was severely injured. Without stopping to check on the welfare of the cyclists, Noble drove to a public house in nearby Dorchester and asked for brandy for Pike.

The landlord told him that he needed a doctor rather than brandy and one was summoned, but Pike later died in hospital from his injuries. Noble was brought before magistrates at Oxford on 21 August, charged with driving a car in a dangerous manner and with failing to stop after an accident.

Found guilty of both offences, Noble was fined £1 for failing to stop and was sentenced to three months' imprisonment for dangerous driving. He was also disqualified from driving for two years.

The young cyclist recovered from the injuries sustained in the accident – by coincidence, he was the son of the Dorchester publican who summoned a doctor for George Pike.

2 AUGUST

1763   Elizabeth Loder was at work picking stones in the fields at Thame. Pausing for a drink, she bent to pick up a bottle and suddenly fell to the ground, shot through the head.

A boy had taken out a gun for the purpose of shooting crows and laid it down on the ground momentarily, close to where Elizabeth was working. A dog trod on the trigger, firing the gun and fatally wounding Elizabeth.

An inquest held by coroner Mr Way returned a verdict of 'accidental death'. The incident was witnessed by the boy working next to Elizabeth and had it not been for his evidence, her death would probably have gone totally unexplained.

3 AUGUST

1852   A fierce thunderstorm hit Bicester and four labourers employed by Sir H. Peyton at Swifts House, Stoke Lyne, took refuge in one of the stables to escape the torrential rain.

Suddenly, the stable was struck by lightning, knocking all four men off their feet and rendering them unconscious. Two escaped with minor injuries and a third was merely shaken but John Blaby of Fritwell was very badly injured. The lightning struck him on the head, setting fire to his hat. The bolt of electricity burned off all of his whiskers and chest hair before exiting his body through his elbow, setting fire to his coat as it did.

When Blaby's workmates came round, they found him unconscious and on fire. Having doused the flames, they ran to the house for help and a messenger was despatched to Bicester for a surgeon. However, in spite of the medical attention, Blaby's chest and brain were so damaged that he is believed to have died from his injuries.

4 AUGUST

1866   A devastating fire broke out in the village of Islip, burning down fifteen cottages.

The fire started when a cottage door was left open and the draught rekindled some live embers in the ashes of a fire. The cottage was thatched and the flames soon reached the roof, spread from property to property by a strong wind.

It was almost three hours before the fire engines arrived from Oxford, by which time the cottages had burned to the ground, leaving fifteen families homeless; their furniture and everything apart from the clothes on their backs completely consumed by the fire.

5 AUGUST

1861   The body of a newborn baby girl was found in a garden in Oxford. Marks in the dirt around the baby showed that it had moved its head and legs and so had definitely been born alive.

On hearing about the baby, Mrs Buckingham of Adelaide Street immediately suspected her servant, twenty-three-year-old Harriet Walton. On the previous day, Harriet and her beau George Lynes went for a walk together and, on their way back, Harriet was suddenly afflicted with violent stomach cramps. Harriet begged George to go for her mistress – she was delirious with pain but, with the assistance of Lynes and Mrs Buckingham, somehow managed to get home. Nobody had suspected that Harriet was pregnant and she denied having given birth, but a medical examination confirmed otherwise.

Harriet was charged with the wilful murder of her baby but surgeon Mr Godfrey was unable to determine whether the baby died from convulsions or exposure. If the child died from convulsions, they were natural causes and, in order to prove that Harriet murdered her baby, the prosecution would have to show intent. Since Mrs Buckingham and George Lynes testified that Harriet was almost crazy with pain, it seemed that she did not know what she was doing at the time of the baby's birth.

With the prosecution at the Oxford Assizes unable to prove a cause of death, Harriet was acquitted. She was immediately tried for concealing the birth but acquitted when the judge pointed out that, in order to be convicted of that she must have buried, secreted or otherwise hidden the dead body of a child. If the child was alive when Harriet was taken home, she could not be found guilty of concealment.

6 AUGUST

1844 An inquest was held at Banbury into the death of carpenter John Duckett.

Employed to do some building on a farm near Banbury, Duckett was crossing the farmyard carrying a piece of timber when the farm's bull charged him. Duckett tripped as he ran away and was gored by the bull, one horn catching him below the ribs and the other hitting him behind the ear.

The bull was shooed away, giving Duckett the chance to scramble to his feet and run into the farmhouse but although a surgeon was immediately summoned, Duckett died from his injuries within the hour. He left a pregnant wife, who was due to give birth to the couple's eleventh child.

The inquest heard that, earlier on the day of his death, Duckett struck the bull to move it out of the way. It was thought that the animal recalled the blow and took revenge on its tormentor at the earliest opportunity.

7 AUGUST

1899 Coroner Mr W.W. Robinson held an inquest at The King's Head, Wootton, into the death of seven-year-old James Seeney, who was run over by a portable steam-driven elevator.

Two days earlier, James walked with his older sister, Hilda, from Wootton to Woodstock. Before they left home, their father cautioned James about riding on vehicles but the lure of a steam engine pulling carriages along the road proved too great for the little boy.

Driver Thomas Walter Hanks stated at the inquest that he was driving an engine and towing a threshing machine and an elevator. He was accompanied by fourteen-year-old flag boy George Gregory and boiler feeder Henry Kearsey. Hanks said that the first that he knew of any accident was when Gregory stopped him and told him that a little boy had been run down.

Gregory stated that he was riding on the elevator when a child climbed onto the pole coupling the elevator to the thresher. Gregory told the boy to get off but the boy just replied, 'Ha,' Gregory told him again and the boy tried to dismount but stumbled and fell under the wheels, which smashed his head, killing him instantly.

The inquest jury attributed no blame whatsoever to the employees of the Steam Ploughing Company, returning a verdict of 'accidental death'.

8 AUGUST

1905 An inquest was held into the death of eighteen-year-old George Sheppard, who died after being struck on the head by a cricket ball during a match at Tetsworth on 7 August.

Sheppard continued playing after being hit and initially appeared to have suffered no ill effects. However, within three hours of the end of the match he began vomiting and suddenly died from a brain haemorrhage, the cause of which was attributed to the blow on his head. The inquest jury returned a verdict of 'accidental death'.

9 AUGUST

1888 Henry Burdock and his wife Mary were no strangers to the magistrates in Oxford. Burdock had a violent temper and had assaulted his wife numerous times. He had recently completed a one-month prison sentence for beating her but had apparently learned nothing from the experience as, on 8 August, he knocked his wife down the stairs when she locked away his boots so that he could not go out drinking.

At lunchtime the next day, people heard screams coming from the Burdocks' house on Speedwell Street and found Mary Burdock being beaten by her husband with an iron bar. As neighbours rushed to help her, Henry disappeared inside the house, emerging with his throat cut.

Mary Burdock was taken to hospital, where her wounds were found to be serious but not life threatening. Henry was loaded onto a cart to be taken to hospital but had bled to death by the time he arrived. At an inquest held at the Radcliffe Infirmary by coroner Mr E.C. Hussey, the jury found that Burdock committed suicide while temporarily insane.

10 AUGUST

1856 Coroner Mr Churchill held an inquest at Hook Norton into the deaths of father and son William and Jabez William Buggins, aged forty-seven and twenty-three respectively.

The two men were employed to sink a well on a farm and before leaving at night they bored holes in the rock walls and filled them with gunpowder. They then dropped a load of burning straw into the well, in the hope that it would ignite the fuses and explode the powder.

The atmosphere inside the well was so damp that the fuses failed to ignite and the straw smouldered all night. When the men arrived for work in the morning, William was let down into the well and, within a short while, his son heard him groaning.

Jabez called to some carpenters working nearby and suggested that they should go down into the well but the men maintained that, since it was Jabez's father, he should be the one to make the descent. Accordingly, he was lowered into the well in the bucket but quickly fell silent and, when the bucket was drawn up again, it was empty.

Assuming that Jabez had fallen out, one of the carpenters agreed to be lowered into the well but was affected by a combination of foul air and choking smoke from the burning straw. Jonathan Gough was next to volunteer and he managed to tie a rope around William Buggins's waist. After Buggins was pulled to the surface, Gough went back down for Jabez but, although a doctor was very quickly on the scene, there was little he could do.

The inquest jury returned a verdict that both William and Jabez died from 'accidental death arising from the smoke of the charred straw and the foul air in the well, whereby the deceased parties were both suffocated and choked.'

11 AUGUST

1828 At about two o'clock in the afternoon, a violent storm broke over Great Tew. Those working outside dashed for cover from the heavy rain and huge hailstones, accompanied by thunder and lightning.

James Holloway and Richard Box were building a wheat rick, along with three other labourers. All five men pressed themselves against the base of the rick to avoid a drenching but Box had left his pitchfork on top of the rick, which acted as a lightning conductor. When lightning struck the pitchfork, the rick burst into flames.

The blaze was quickly extinguished and the fire prevented from spreading to the neighbouring ricks. However, Holloway and Box were killed instantly by the lightning strike and their three colleagues were knocked unconscious and took several minutes to come round.

12 AUGUST

1857 Sixty-three-year-old farm labourer Thomas Goulder was building a wheat rick at Bucknell.

One of his fellow labourers cautioned him to be careful not to slip and Thomas turned to him and cheerfully replied, 'No, I shan't.' Just seconds later, he fell to the ground, landing heavily on his head and also fracturing a rib, which punctured his lung.

Although his employers paid for the best possible medical attention, Thomas never regained consciousness and died from his injuries on 17 August. At his inquest, the jury returned a verdict of 'accidental death'.

13 AUGUST

1868 Twenty-four-year-old John Robert Dunn, the assistant to Dorchester surgeon Mr Byas, was about to commence his annual leave. Byas drove him to Culham Station to catch a train to Reading and, before entering the station, Dunn called at the Railway Station Inn for a drink.

In conversation with the landlord, Dunn mentioned that he had a pistol and the landlord asked if he would mind shooting a cat for him. Dunn was pleased to oblige, despatching the cat before going to the station. Porter Mr Lynes began chatting with Dunn about destroying the cat and asked if he might see Dunn's pistol. Dunn passed it to him, neglecting to mention that it was loaded and as Lynes was examining it, the pistol went off, shooting Dunn in the liver.

Dunn died hours later and an inquest jury returned a verdict of 'accidental death'.

14 AUGUST

1879 Louisa Barnard of Wantage was at the pub when her infant daughter died alone at home. A post-mortem examination showed that baby Ellen was emaciated and had no trace of food in her stomach or bowels and surgeon Mr Barker determined that she had starved to death. (He allowed the baby's mother to be present at the post-mortem, reasoning that he could hardly throw her out of her own living room!) Since Louisa's breasts were still engorged with milk following Ellen's birth, an inquest found a verdict of manslaughter against her mother, who could have suckled her baby but didn't.

She was tried at the Oxon and Berks Assizes in October 1879, where it emerged that Louisa's husband had rowed with her countless times over her neglect of their baby. Nobody had ever seen Louisa ill-treating Ellen but the consensus of the witnesses seemed to be that Louisa was destitute.

She had five other children and spent most of her day hawking fish around the pubs or working in the fields in all weathers to earn enough to feed them and, as a consequence, neglected the latest addition to her family, who was always dirty and rarely fed.

The jury found twenty-eight-year-old Louisa guilty of manslaughter but strongly recommended her to mercy. The judge attributed the offence more to poverty and hardship than malice and sentenced Louisa to one year's imprisonment with hard labour.

15 AUGUST

1856   While visiting a friend at Boddicott, sixty-four-year-old Hannah Flint from Adderbury helped clear up after dinner. She removed the tablecloth and, having given it a shake, folded it and went to put it away. Unfortunately, being in a strange house, she mistook the cellar door for that of the pantry. Having opened the wrong door, she fell down the steps from top to bottom, landing heavily on her head and dying soon afterwards, without regaining consciousness.

At an inquest held at Boddicott by coroner Mr Churchill, the inquest jury returned a verdict of 'accidental death'.

16 AUGUST

1880   Thirty-two-year-old labourer James Wise shared a bed with his six-year-old niece, Elizabeth, whose parents slept in another bed in the same room in their cottage at Mapledurham. After going to bed as normal on 16 August, Elizabeth seemed to be in terrible pain when she awoke the next morning and, when a surgeon was consulted, he found that the child had been raped. Elizabeth's parents immediately sent for the police, at which James tried to drown himself in a water butt.

Wise's defence was that he had absolutely no recollection of doing anything to his niece and, if he did, he must have been very drunk at the time. (Wise had venereal disease, with which he infected his niece.)

Tried at the Oxon and Berks Assizes on 26 October, Wise was found guilty by the jury and sentenced to eight years' penal servitude.

17 AUGUST

1899   Coroner Mr W.W. Robinson held an inquest at Bladon on the death of ten-year-old Florence Soame from Oxford.

Florence and her sister Lily were visiting their aunt at Bladon post office and, on 16 August, they went with their three cousins and another boy to play at Bladon Pits, which were worked-out stone pits now used as a repository for rubbish. When the children arrived, William Woodward had just dumped a load of vegetable refuse from the gardens at Blenheim Palace and four of the children climbed into the back of his horse-drawn cart and clamoured for a ride.

Woodward was a kindly man who had no objection to amusing the children for a few minutes. He was standing at the horse's head drinking water and had every intention of giving them a ride when he finished his drink. However, the horse inexplicably decided to walk backwards and, although Woodward had a firm hold of the bridle, he was unable to stop it as it backed the cart off the edge of the pit and crashed more than 20ft to the bottom.

Park Street, Bladon. (Author's collection)

The cart landed upside down and, by a miracle, three of the children were found beneath the upturned cart with only minor injuries. Sadly, Florence was pinned to the ground by the side of the cart and died instantly from internal injuries.

The inquest heard that the cart horse was eleven years old and was known as a quiet, steady animal. Nothing had happened to frighten it, it was not being annoyed by flies and it had not moved in response to the children in the cart touching the reins, as they were unable to reach them.

The coroner ruled that there was no blame attached to anyone for the child's tragic death, which appeared to be a pure accident caused entirely by the horse. The jury concurred, returning a verdict of 'accidental death'.

18 AUGUST

1886 Twenty-eight-year-old Florence Anne Nutting of Leamington died in the Radcliffe Infirmary, having fallen from a train at Culham two days earlier.

At an inquest held by coroner Mr E.L. Hussey, the chief witness was Miss Mary Jane Mitchell, Florence's friend and travelling companion. Mary stated that Florence suffered from weak ankles due to rheumatic fever as a child. Hence when Florence asked her to reach a book from a rack in the centre of their first-class carriage, Mary stood up to oblige. She turned her back on Florence for a second or two and when she turned around again it was to see Florence falling backwards out of the carriage door.

Florence was picked up from the track insensible and taken by carriage to Oxford, from where she was conveyed to hospital in an ambulance. Meanwhile, the train continued to Oxford, where stationmaster Robert Davis questioned Mary and conducted some tests on the carriage door.

Mary insisted that her friend had not made any sound as she fell. The train had travelled from Paddington Station without stopping and Mary was positive that she would have noticed had the door been open even a fraction. Davis was equally certain that if the door was improperly closed, the wind would have blown it wide open long before the train reached Culham. Davis conducted some tests on the door and handle, which were in good working order. With the door closed, even with the handle half turned, he was unable to open it even by pushing against it as hard as he could.

Mary testified that, when Florence asked her to fetch the book, she was seated in the corner of the carriage leaning forward slightly. Mary was adamant that she only turned her back on her friend for a second or two, which was insufficient time for Florence to have risen from her seat and opened the carriage door.

The inquest jury were baffled and, although they agreed that the deceased had died from falling out of the railway carriage, there was no evidence to show how she came to fall.

19 AUGUST

1823 An inquest was held into the death of Martha Rose of Chipping Norton. On 10 August, Martha complained of feeling ill and told her fellow servants that she was going to take a 'physic'. She mixed some powders with water and offered Ann Thornton a taste. Ann took a sip and immediately spat the medicine out, saying that it burned her tongue. She offered to throw it away but Martha swallowed it in one gulp.

Five minutes later, she was writhing in agony. For the next two days she suffered terrible stomach pains and vomiting, refusing to take any of the medicine prescribed by the surgeon called to attend to her, until she finally suffered a miscarriage. Only then did she admit taking poison, adding, 'Thomas knew nothing about it.'

Thomas Gordon was a servant, with whom Martha had been having an illicit affair. Although he was aware that Martha was pregnant, the two had quarrelled, but when Martha admitted that she had taken poison, she seemed certain that she was going to recover and Thomas promised to marry her when she did.

Martha died on 16 August and it was shown at her inquest that a man named Richard Willis had brought white arsenic and oxalic acid on her behalf, pretending to be a shepherd, who would have a legitimate use for them. According to Willis, Martha swore him to secrecy and he didn't ask what she intended to do with the poison but simply told her to be careful with it.

The inquest jury found Willis's conduct reprehensible and regretted having no power to punish him. In returning a verdict of *felo de se* on Martha – an archaic term for suicide meaning literally 'murder of oneself' – they exonerated Thomas Gordon of all blame, although they added that he had been somewhat cruel in seducing her and then threatening to leave her in her unfortunate condition.

Coroner Mr R.D. Gough ordered that Martha should be buried in the churchyard between nine o'clock at night and midnight, without any funeral rites, as was customary for suicides.

20 AUGUST

1935 An inquest was held on the death of sixty-four-year-old Revd Edward Grenville Norris, the Rector of Bucknell, who was found dead in a field in the village, his pony grazing nearby.

The inquest heard that Norris was wrongly convinced that he was suffering from high blood pressure and believed that strict dieting was the only way to relieve it. Norris's brother told the inquest that both of his parents had died from apoplexy, leaving Edward terrified that he was destined to follow suit. He became obsessed with lowering his blood pressure, starving himself to the extent that his heart was permanently weakened.

Miss Hawkins, who served as the Reverend's housekeeper, told the inquest that she frequently had to grab him by the sleeve to prevent him from falling over and Dr G.H. Jones related that he had urged Norris to take a 'more liberal' diet. Jones gave the cause of Norris's death as 'cardiac syncope caused by starvation' and the inquest jury returned a verdict of 'death from natural causes'.

21 AUGUST

1937 William Gibbons and his wife of Oxford went to visit friends, leaving their daughters Mona Blanche (10) and Molly (7) in the care of their lodger, Gilbert Henry Dobson, who they described as 'a trusted personal friend.'

A neighbour heard Dobson shouting that there was a fire. Charles Hewson rushed to assist him and the two men placed a ladder up against the window of the girls' bedroom. Dobson tried everything that he could to get to the children but was unsuccessful and Hewson would later describe him as 'demented', adding that he was tearing at the wall with his fingernails. Eventually, Hewson actually knocked the ladder over to prevent Dobson from going into the bedroom, an act that, according to Hewson, would have been tantamount to committing suicide.

Both girls perished in the fire, which was found to have originated in the cupboard beneath the stairs where the gas and electric meters were sited.

At a later inquest, the jury heard that Dobson was asleep when he was woken by the children screaming and, as soon as he opened his bedroom door, he realised the house was on fire. Unable to get downstairs, he was afraid to throw the children out of the window in case he hurt them. He jumped out of his own bedroom window, raced to a phone box and telephoned the fire brigade then went back to try and rescue the girls, but, by that time, the heat and smoke in their bedroom was too intense and he was prevented from climbing into the room by Hewson.

The inquest jury returned verdicts of 'accidental death by suffocation' on Mona and Molly, adding that the cause of the fire was unknown. They went on to record a verdict of suicide while the balance of his mind was disturbed on Dobson, who was so distraught that he threw himself into the canal.

22 AUGUST

1855 Coroner William Brunner held an inquest into the death of Henry Gibbs. On 20 August, carter Joseph Cooper was sent from Witney to collect a load of stone from a demolished barn at Tackley. Told that there would be someone there to help him, Cooper could find nobody and eventually loaded the cart himself.

When he returned for a second load later that afternoon, there was still no sign of anybody to assist him. Cooper wandered round the farmyard and shouted but nobody responded and he resigned himself to having to load the stone without assistance. He had almost filled the cart when he lifted a stone and uncovered a head. Cooper ran for help then joined neighbours in clearing the rubble that had completely buried Henry Gibbs, who was employed to demolish the barn.

Gibbs was dead when he was extricated and the inquest concluded that he died from suffocation, due to being buried by a falling wall. Finding his death to be accidental, the jury theorised that Gibbs had tried to flee the falling masonry but his escape was impeded by a stack of straw about 10ft from the barn. Gibbs left a widow, who was heavily pregnant with the couple's second child.

23 AUGUST

1892   At a farm near Abingdon, twelve-year-old Herbert Hayes was left in charge of two horses transporting cartloads of grain from the fields. Along with his friends John and Alfred Collins, aged six and eight respectively, Herbert had already returned several loads to the homestead when the leading horse took fright and both horses set off at a brisk trot. Herbert, who was loading grain at the time, was dragged under the cart and the wheels passed over his neck, killing him instantly. The Collins brothers were thrown out of the cart and John was kicked in the head and face by both horses, while Alfred sustained several cuts as he fell. He was well enough to be taken home but John was sent to the Cottage Hospital, where his injuries were described as 'serious'.

Although John is believed to have survived, the contemporary local newspaper informed their readers that his parents had recently lost their twenty-one-year-old daughter, Minnie, who was lying dead in their house when the accident occurred.

24 AUGUST

1922   Thirty-one-year-old labourer George Franklin, who lived with his widowed mother at Wroxton, suddenly went berserk, leaping out of bed and drinking a whole bottle of medicine, before seizing a carving knife and two razors.

His mother fought to try and take the weapons away from him but was stabbed twice in the chest and was eventually forced to give up the struggle and run to a nearby house for help. Mrs Franklin's neighbour bravely returned to her house, finding George dead in a pool of blood, his throat cut and an open razor clutched tightly in his right hand.

An inquest was opened that afternoon but adjourned for seven days in the hope that Mrs Franklin would be able to give evidence. Although she was said to be 'in a serious condition', she is believed to have survived the attack by her son, who was deemed to have committed suicide while temporarily insane.

25 AUGUST

1893 James Gurden of St Aldate's appeared before magistrates in Oxford charged with assaulting his wife, Elizabeth, on 12 August and other days within the past six months. Elizabeth told the Bench that her husband struck her for no reason, giving her two black eyes. A week later, he hit her in the face and threw her out, threatening to kick her if she came back again. He had also thrown a heavy candlestick at her and she went in fear that he would do her some terrible injury, since his ill-treatment had been going on for weeks and he was 'sly and vicious in his ways'.

James challenged his wife's recollection, asking her if she hadn't threatened to stab him through the heart or bitten his arm. He told magistrates that he had given Elizabeth 2s 6d for food but, instead of buying groceries, she went to the pub and returned home drunk. In fact, she had been mad drunk for the past fortnight and had blackened her own eyes falling down the stairs. She had threatened to hit him with a poker and had actually split someone's head open with a hatchet. James stated that he had three witnesses to speak for him, but, when they were called, they hadn't turned up at court.

Magistrates bound him over for the sum of £5 to keep the peace and added a sum of 8s 6d for costs, with fourteen days' hard labour in default. Gurden asked for time to pay but was refused – the magistrates reasoned that since this was his seventh conviction, he should be well aware of the penalty.

26 AUGUST

1885 Coroner Mr C. Duffell Faulkner held an inquest at Bucknell into the death of Frederick Reading, who was run over by a wagon on the previous day.

Fifteen-year-old Frederick was walking with a team of horses when something startled them. Frederick tried to hold on to the front horse and although people shouted at him to let go, he didn't seem to hear them. Eventually, the boy fell over and the horses bolted, dragging the wheels of the wagon over Frederick as he lay on the road. His hip bone was completely crushed and the lower part of his belly very bruised and he died within minutes from shock and internal bleeding.

The inquest jury returned a verdict of 'accidental death'.

27 AUGUST

1874 Thomas Radband and Ann Faulkner courted for five years and were engaged until Ann grew tired of Thomas's drinking and dumped him, becoming engaged to her cousin. A jealous man, Thomas didn't take this lightly and stalked Ann, continually trying to persuade her to take him back.

Ann was making her way to her brother's house in Brize Norton, where she slept every night, when Radband approached and put his arms around her neck. 'What are you up to?' he asked and when Ann replied that she was going indoors Radband told her, 'You are not going indoors any more alive.'

Through the window, Ann's brother, John, saw his sister talking to Radband then heard her scream. He ran outside and found Ann lying on the ground, covered in blood. Radband fled as John and his wife carried her indoors and sent for a doctor, who found a four-and-a-half-inch long cut on Ann's throat, which fortunately failed to damage any major blood vessels. There were several smaller cuts on her face and chin, including a deep cut on her left cheek, along with two small cuts on her right breast and defence wounds on her hands and arms.

When Radband was apprehended, he produced a sharpened table knife from his pocket and told the police, 'That's what I done it with.' He added, 'I don't care a bugger as long as she's dead, if they hang me tomorrow or they may hang me tonight.'

In the event, Ann survived Thomas's attack and, when he was tried at the Oxford Assizes on 27 February 1875, the charge against him was wounding with intent to do grievous bodily injury. Radband pleaded guilty and was sentenced to eighteen months' imprisonment, with hard labour.

28 AUGUST

1835 Twelve-year-old Ann Thorncroft lived with her aunt and uncle in Banbury. During August, she was suspected of stealing some money and was given a telling-off by her governess, who instructed her to learn a chapter from the Bible as punishment.

Instead of taking her punishment, Ann stole another 2d, which she wrapped in a piece of paper on which she had written the words 'two pennyworth of arsenic.' She took the note and money to a doctor, who astonishingly gave her the poison when she told him that it was for her aunt.

On her way home, Ann called on a couple named Mr and Mrs Boxhold and asked for a cup of water, telling them that she needed to dissolve some medicine. Although she told Mrs Boxhold that the arsenic was magnesia and cream of tartar, Mrs Boxhold was suspicious and told her to throw it away. Ann took the cup outside, supposedly to dispose of the 'medicine', but instead drank its contents.

Although every effort was made to save her, Ann died five days later and an inquest jury returned a verdict of *felo de se.*

29 AUGUST

1893 Elizabeth Collingridge, described as 'a well-dressed lady of about fifty years of age', appeared at Oxford Police Court charged with being a rogue and a vagabond and 'unlawfully using certain subtle craft, to wit by palmistry to deceive and impose on certain of Her Majesty's subjects.'

The court heard that Elizabeth first made her presence in Oxford known by handing a card to the clerk at the *Oxford Chronicle*, which she asked him to pass around his friends. When George Mauder asked if she wanted to advertise in the newspaper, she told him no, since someone had recently been prosecuted at Margate for practicing palmistry. Mauder sent a copy of the card to the police, to act on if they wished to do so.

Detective Sergeant Prior concealed himself in St John's College gardens on 26 August, where he had a clear view of Elizabeth practising her 'dark art' with the local young women, charging them a shilling and advising them to expect an imminent change in their lives or telling them that they would marry at twenty-five and have three husbands.

Although there were no complaints from Elizabeth's victims, the police took a dim view of her activities, as did the magistrates, who fined her 10s plus 7s 6d costs, or fourteen days' imprisonment in default. 'Be sure we do not hear of you again,' warned the Mayor as she left court.

30 AUGUST

1885 Keen to spend the afternoon shooting, twenty-two-year-old Frederick Charles Walton of Upper Heyford concealed his gun in a hedgerow while he attended church. When he came to retrieve it, he caught hold of the muzzle and pulled the gun towards him. The hammer caught on a stile behind the hedge and the gun discharged.

Walton caught the full force of the shot in his head and neck, dying instantly. At an inquest held by coroner Mr C. Duffell Faulkner at The Barley Mow public house, the jury returned a verdict of 'death from shotgun wound in the neck and base of brain accidentally inflicted by himself'.

31 AUGUST

1833 The twelve-year-old stepson of the landlady of The White Hart Inn, Wantage, went downstairs in the morning to find the pub in darkness. As he crossed the kitchen, he tripped and it was only when he opened the shutters that he realised that what he had stumbled over was his stepmother Anne Pullen's severed head, which had been hacked from her body with a sharp instrument, such as a machete.

Police were told about a young man who was behaving very strangely on the night of 30 August and went to interview labourer George King, at work in the bean fields. He gave a number of conflicting statements and was eventually arrested, when a search of his pockets revealed a purse similar to one that Anne was known to carry and several silver coins, including a crooked sixpence like the one Anne kept as a lucky charm.

Brought before the coroner, King insisted that he knew the killer's identity, naming a man called Ned Grant. However, although the police searched for Grant, it was obvious that he was a figment of King's

Newbury Street, Wantage, location of the White Hart Inn. (© R. Sly)

imagination and the inquest eventually recorded a verdict of wilful murder against King.

Tried at the Reading Assizes, he was found guilty and sentenced to death, the hanging taking place on 3 March 1834, his nineteenth birthday. He made a full confession before his execution and, when a death mask was made of his face, it was discovered that he had a five-inch skull fracture, the legacy of a fall from a hay loft some years earlier.

Note: An alternative account of the murder places the scene of the crime at another Wantage pub, The Red Lion. In this version, Anne is a barmaid who was too busy to serve King immediately and, in his annoyance, he flung his money on the ground and decapitated her when she bent to pick it up.

SEPTEMBER

A village funeral. (Author's collection)

1 SEPTEMBER **1852** William Penn's loaded gun had been standing in a corner for some time when he decided that it would be safer to discharge it. He took it into the garden of his cottage in Blackthorn but the cartridge was damp and swollen and the gun wouldn't fire. Penn returned the gun to its corner and, moments later, there was a tremendous bang.

The gun discharged straight into the ceiling, making a four-inch diameter hole immediately below where Penn's children were asleep in bed. Hearing four-year-old Richard scream, Penn raced upstairs to find the room full of smoke and floating fragments of burned chaff from the child's mattress.

When the smoke cleared, Penn found that a huge chunk of flesh had been blown from his son's left hip. (Fortunately, Richard's younger brother, Fred, got up in the middle of the night and climbed into his mother's bed.) Records suggest that Richard survived under the treatment of surgeon Mr Woodward from Bicester.

2 SEPTEMBER **1930** After twelve years of unhappy marriage, Eleanor Kimber of Headington applied to magistrates for a separation from her husband on the grounds of his persistent cruelty. The application was adjourned for a fortnight and, in the meantime, Arthur John Kimber was prohibited from molesting his wife and ordered to move out of the marital home into the Oxford Church Army Home.

On 13 September, Kimber returned to Headington and, discussing the separation with a neighbour, stated, 'It will mean murder. I cannot live without her.' He then left, saying that he was going to have a dink before 'finishing it.' Thirty minutes later, he returned and approached his wife as she stood with the couple's three children outside their house, talking to a neighbour.

He followed her as she walked down the passage at the side of the house and continued to follow her as she left the house again. A neighbour saw Kimber seize both sides of his wife's head and shake her, then, moments

Church Street, Headington. (Author's collection)

later, Mrs Kimber ran to a neighbour, blood pumping from her neck. In the confusion, Kimber walked off, later handing himself in to the police.

Mrs Kimber died five days later and her husband was charged with wilful murder and tried at the Oxford Assizes in October 1930. His defence was one of insanity and it was revealed that a fractured skull in 1919 had left him very excitable and liable to suddenly lose control of his actions.

Although there was some disagreement between the medical witnesses about Kimber's mental state at the time of the offence, the jury found him 'guilty but insane' and he was ordered to be detained during His Majesty's pleasure.

3 SEPTEMBER

1898 Farmer William Gosling Rowles of Campsfield, near Woodstock, arrived home from Oxford market drunk. After drinking two cups of tea with whisky, he went to bed with his wife and, as soon as they reached the bedroom, he seized her by the throat and asked her, 'Will you ever kiss your brother-in-law again?'

Rowles's wife was used to his violent ways and instantly agreed that she would not in order to keep the peace. However, this seemed to anger her husband even more and he hit her seven or eight times in the face before fetching out his penknife and threatening to cut off her head.

Mrs Rowles pleaded with her husband to spare her for the sake of their four young children, so he decided that he would cut off his wife's hair instead of her head. For more than an hour, Rowles sawed at his wife's long hair with a blunt penknife, apparently deaf to her screams of pain and appeals for him to stop. When she was all but bald, he told her, 'Now, my dear, you do look smart. Give me a kiss,' grabbing her chin and forcing her to kiss him when she refused to do so voluntarily.

Rowles appeared before magistrates at Woodstock charged with aggravated assault. The couple's servant corroborated Mrs Rowles's account and also testified about other acts of brutality that she had witnessed. The magistrates were appalled and sentenced Rowles to six months' imprisonment with hard labour, complaining that this was the maximum sentence that they were permitted to award. They bound him over to keep the peace for six months after the completion of his sentence and awarded Mrs Rowles a separation order and £2 per week maintenance for herself and the children.

4 SEPTEMBER

1922 The jury at an inquest at Abingdon returned a verdict of accidental death through suffocation on Sir Francis Gore-Browne KC.

Sixty-two-year-old Gore-Browne was said to be in perfect health when he drank a glass of milk and went to bed on the night of 1 September. However, the next morning, when his manservant took him a cup of tea in bed, Sir Francis was dead, lying on his left side with one hand against his face.

Dr Woodward gave the cause of death as suffocation, stating that Gore-Browne's hand partially covered his mouth and nostrils and had obstructed his breathing as he slept.

5 SEPTEMBER

1900 An inquest was opened at Standlake into the death of three-month-old Bertie Rose. It concluded the following day with a verdict of manslaughter against Bertie's parents, William and Rachel.

Bertie was born in June 1900 and was a healthy baby. However, within weeks of his birth, his mother began to suffer from epileptic fits. She was incapable of caring for Bertie and, although William did his best for his son, he worked long hours. Bertie spent much of his time sitting on a heap of soiled, wet rags in a perambulator. He was always dirty, always hungry and gradually grew more and more emaciated until he died from atrophy and exhaustion, caused by want of food and general neglect. Inspector Rushton of the National Society for the Prevention of Cruelty to Children saw Bertie on 29 August and gave Rachel Rose 9*d* to get him some proper food, but by then Bertie was too weak to suck from a bottle and, at his death, he weighed only 6lbs – half the normal weight for a child of his age.

When the Roses appeared at the Oxford Assizes in November 1900, the Grand Jury ignored the bills for manslaughter by the coroner's jury and by the Witney magistrates, settling instead for the lesser offence of wilful neglect.

William Rose earned a reasonable wage and was described as a kind, sober man but also as 'partly imbecile'. Whenever he was not working, he endeavoured to feed his son, although he seemed pretty clueless and tried to give the baby bread sops. The trial jury acquitted William and, although they found Rachel guilty, they made a strong recommendation for leniency since they were unanimously of the opinion that she was incapable of caring for her baby due to ill-health.

Describing Rachel as 'weak-minded', the presiding judge blamed the couple's neighbours for not intervening to protect Bertie and passed a nominal sentence of one day's imprisonment.

6 SEPTEMBER

1851 An excursion train returning from London approached Bicester Station, where the station staff expected it to stop. However, neither the engine driver nor the guard had instructions to halt at Bicester and so the train approached the station at a fast pace, the driver expecting to continue to Oxford. Yet the station staff had altered the points in anticipation of the train stopping and, as a result, the engine became detached from its carriages, almost ploughing into the stationmaster's house, while the first three carriages overturned. Luckily, among the 200 passengers were a surgeon, Mr Aston (or Acton) and a medical student, Mr Wyatt, who immediately began to give what first aid they could to the injured, while waiting for reinforcements from Bicester and Oxford.

Six people lost their lives in the crash – Corporal Thomas Noon, Mrs Sheldon and her infant daughter, Elizabeth Easley, fourteen-year-old William Carrier and James Luckett. An inquest was opened and adjourned by coroner Mr W. Brunner, finally concluding on 16 September with verdicts of 'accidental death' on all six victims. However, the jury made a number of observations, among which were suggesting that the single line should be made a double and that, until it was, every train should stop at Bicester Station. They requested that the confusion about where the excursion trains did and did not stop should be addressed and, although they did not believe that the railway company had been negligent, they reminded the representatives at the inquest that the lives of passengers 'should not be jeopardised at the shrine of interest and dividends.'

7 SEPTEMBER   **1892**   A steam roundabout was set up for the enjoyment of those attending St Giles Fair in Oxford and, as it reached full speed, fifty-two-year-old Annie Breakspear fell off, landing heavily on the back of her head. A child also fell at the same time but landed on Annie's leg and so escaped injury.

St Giles Fair, Oxford. (Author's collection)

Annie was riding one of the outer horses and, according to witness Frederick Palmer, she just let go of the pole and fell around 9ft to the ground. Palmer rushed to help Annie, who was unconscious. He raised her slightly, noticing that the back of her head was bleeding and, as he did, blood flowed from her mouth, ears and nose.

An ambulance took Annie to the Radcliffe Infirmary, where she died from a fractured skull thirty-four hours later, without regaining consciousness. Coroner Mr E.L. Hussey held an inquest on 10 September, at which the jury were told that the roundabout was in perfect order and had no defects that might have caused Annie to fall. The child who fell was Annie's neighbour's child and it was surmised that, in trying to stop the child from falling, Annie lost her own seat with fatal consequences.

8 SEPTEMBER   **1875**   Thomas Beck of Wardington went to work, leaving his wife Mary Ann Elizabeth and their six-week-old son, William, sleeping. Thomas returned twelve hours later to find that his supper wasn't ready. Mary

Wardington, near Banbury. (Author's collection)

Ann sat near the pantry reading her Bible and when Thomas asked her where the baby was, she replied that he was upstairs.

Thomas went to dig potatoes, which he did until it got dark. When he returned, he went into the pantry to wash his hands, noticing that Mary Ann rushed in before him and stood in the corner talking to him as he did so.

Before eating his supper, Thomas went to the farm to fetch milk for his son, boiled it and put it into a feeding bottle to cool. Having eaten his supper and drunk some tea, he took the bottle upstairs to feed William but the baby wasn't there.

Thomas rushed downstairs to ask his wife where William was.

'It is in the pantry,' replied Mary Ann.

'You have not killed it?' Thomas asked horrified. Mary Ann clung to his arm to try and prevent him from going into the pantry, tearfully admitting 'I have' and begging her husband, 'Don't tell anybody.'

William was dead in a tub of water in the pantry and, according to Mary Ann, she drowned him about an hour after her husband left for work, then spent the rest of the day praying and reading the Bible. An inquest returned a verdict of wilful murder against her, although the jury informed the coroner that they believed that she was not responsible for her actions, on account of 'unskilful treatment since her confinement.'

It was not for the coroner to make judgements about Mary Ann's mental state at the time of the murder and she was committed for trial at the next Oxford Assizes on 6 March 1876, where she was acquitted due to insanity.

9 SEPTEMBER 1944 A Halifax bomber plane carrying a full load of bombs caught fire over Wallingford. Realising that the plane was in trouble, Flying Officer John A. Wilding ordered his crew to bail out while he and flight engineer

The Market Place, Wallingford, 1950s. (Author's collection)

Military funeral of aeroplane heroes, Oxford, 13 September 1912. (Author's collection)

Sergeant Frank Andrew of the 426 Squadron Canadian Air Force guided the crippled aircraft away from the town towards fields at Crowmarsh.

The plane crashed and exploded, killing Wilding and Andrew instantly. To commemorate their ultimate sacrifice, roads in the town of Wallingford have since been named after them and an obelisk bearing a plaque has been erected at the junction of the two streets.

10 SEPTEMBER   1912   Pilot Second Lieutenant Edward Hotchkiss and observer Lieutenant Claude A. Bettington of the Special Reserve Royal Flying Corps were killed when their monoplane crashed at Wolvercote.

There were several witnesses to the crash, including a doctor who watched the incident through his window and called an ambulance, before going to see if he could help the crew. They saw the plane cross the River Thames with the apparent aim of landing on Port Meadow but as the machine began to turn, there was a loud bang, followed by a series of cracking noises. The left wing of the plane crumpled and the aircraft dropped out of the air. Pieces of canvas and wood fell from the aircraft and some onlookers were convinced that a person also fell.

Both men had multiple injuries but both died instantly from a fractured skull. The aeroplane was so fragmented that it proved impossible to determine the precise cause of the crash. The logbook was recovered and the detailed entries in Bettington's handwriting ended, 'Struck rain at 8.13 over Oxford; very w . . . ' (It was thought that he was writing the word windy, although some accounts suggest he wrote 'very h . . .', meaning hazy.) Experts could only theorise that a strap around the plane's wings caught in a tree, tearing the canvas off the wing and causing the plane to crash.

An inquest was held the following day by coroner Mr A.H. Franklin The inquest jury returned a verdict that the two men were accidentally killed by falling as the result of some injury to the monoplane, although they were unable to specify what injury. In the interests of the public, the jury recommended that there should be an official government inquiry held on all plane crashes.

11 SEPTEMBER **1847** An inquest was held at The Brazen Nose public house, Cropredy, into the death of eighteen-year-old Stephen Cooknell. On 30 August, Cooknell was employed in an orchard near Banbury to shake plums from the trees so that they could be gathered more easily. He jumped down from a tree but stumbled as he landed, pitching forwards onto a stick supporting a nearby raspberry cane.

The stake penetrated Cooknell's stomach and he was carried home in severe pain. A couple of days later, Cooknell was well enough to return to work but suffered a relapse and died from peritonitis on 9 September.

The inquest jury returned a verdict of 'accidental death'.

Red Lion Street, Cropredy, 1962. (Author's collection)

12 SEPTEMBER **1874** *Jackson's Oxford Journal* reported that Mayor Mr J. Ward and the magistrates of Chipping Norton had recently sentenced Benjamin Radband to two days' imprisonment. Benjamin was charged with damaging a lock, valued at 6*d*, and, when he was found guilty, was ordered to pay 10*s* 6*d* in costs and damages. When he was unable to pay, he was sent to prison in default. Benjamin was just seven years old.

13 SEPTEMBER **1843** An inquest was held at the Radcliffe Infirmary into the death of widow Catherine Corby. In the early hours of the morning, people living in Worcester Terrace were awakened by shouts of fire from Mrs Corby's bedroom. Mrs Corby's bed was completely enveloped in flames and she died from severe burns in hospital later that morning.

The jury at her inquest returned a verdict of 'accidental burning', having determined that the fire that killed her was caused by a lighted candle having been left too close to her bed curtains.

14 SEPTEMBER **1857** William Merifeed Ashford married Eliza Salt at Wantage but sadly neglected to tell his bride that he was already married.

Eliza was a servant, who was paid £8 a year. When she married Ashford, she had managed to save £4 10*s* and, after her husband had spent it all, he deserted her. Eliza saw nothing more of him until May 1862, when she happened to spot him in Oxford and handed him in to the police for desertion.

Police enquiries revealed that Ashford married Rosetta Ryland at Bath on 23 July 1845 – he later deserted her, leaving her with one child. On 2 August 1853, he married Elizabeth Perryer at Bath followed by a Miss Jordan a couple of years later. In 1856, he married Ann Nalder, although he called himself William Norman for that ceremony. Eliza Salt was next, after which Ashford married his sixth wife, Elizabeth Dunn, in Oxford in 1862. When Eliza spotted him in Oxford, he was already considering marrying two more women named Miss Russell and Miss Hall.

Tried at the Oxford Assizes for 'feloniously marrying Elizabeth Perryer at Bath, his former wife being then alive', he was found guilty and given the maximum penalty allowed for his offence – a sentence of seven years' penal servitude.

15 SEPTEMBER **1874** Coroner Mr W. Brunner held an inquest at the Radcliffe Infirmary into the death of twenty-one-year-old John Bayliss. The deceased worked as a fireman for the London and North Western Railway and it was his job to stoke the fires that ultimately produced the steam that ran the train.

As the train neared Launton Station, travelling at 50mph, it was rocking and, as Bayliss stepped forward with a shovel full of coal, his feet slipped and he fell out of the back of the engine. The driver immediately braked but it took 900 yards for the train to stop and, once they walked back to where Bayliss lay on the line, they found that both of his legs had been run over. He was taken to hospital but his legs were so badly crushed that there was no hope of his recovery and he died within forty-eight hours.

The inquest heard that it was raining on the night of the accident. Bayliss was wearing new boots and had simply slipped on the wet metal footplate, leading the jury to return a verdict of 'accidental death'. By coincidence, Bayliss's father died four years earlier in an almost identical accident.

16 SEPTEMBER

1899 Fifteen-year-old Albert Cook died at Burford Cottage Hospital following an injury received on 8 September.

Several farm labourers were working in the fields at Signett Hill near Burford, Thomas James ploughing with a pair of horses, while Albert was driving a team of horses for carter William Day. At around midday, Day sent Albert to fetch something and, as he walked past Thomas, he jokingly remarked, 'Mind out, you silly beggar.' 'You mind out,' Thomas replied, waving his hoe at Albert. To Thomas's horror, the iron blade flew off the handle, travelled about 30ft and hit Albert on the head.

Cook shouted 'Mother!' and dropped to the ground. Calling for Day, James rushed to his friend and tried to lift him to his feet but Albert was bleeding heavily from his head and was unable to stand. It took Thomas and Day together to carry him to a nearby cottage, where they bathed and bandaged his head before taking him to a doctor.

Surgeon Herbert Frederick Lane found that Albert had a three-inch wound on the left side of his forehead, beneath which his skull was fractured. Albert remained conscious almost until death and insisted that the injury was done by accident. The jury at his inquest accepted that he and James were larking about and returned a verdict that Cook 'died in consequence of injuries to his head accidentally received.'

17 SEPTEMBER

1880 Ten-year-old Frances Nellie Jones was run over by a horse-drawn fly. Both wheels passed over her body and, although she was rushed to the Radcliffe Infirmary, she was suffering from convulsions and internal bleeding and died shortly after arriving.

Coroner Mr E.L. Hussey held an inquest at the hospital on the following day. Numerous people witnessed the accident – including the coroner himself – and all saw Frances run out into the road, directly into the path of the vehicle, trying to escape a small, white terrier dog, which was jumping up at her and tugging at the bottom of her dress.

Frances's sister informed the inquest that her sister was terrified of dogs and Mr Hussey told the jury that they must decide whether the dog was simply being playful or whether it was fierce. If the former, the dog's owner was not criminally responsible but, if it were vicious, the owner could be brought to justice for failing to exercise proper control over the animal.

The surgeon who attended to Frances on her admission to hospital testified that she had no bites or scratches on her legs and since nobody had been able to locate the dog or its owner, the inquest jury returned a verdict of 'accidental death'.

18 SEPTEMBER

1889 Jesse Hunt and his son, Jesse junior, headed home to Leafield after a day spent thrashing grain. Jesse junior stopped off to visit a married sister, returning home twenty minutes after his parents, who were sitting talking to their oldest son and his wife. Jesse junior immediately demanded to know what his parents and brother were saying about him, using such foul language that his mother asked him, 'Jesse, have you had a drop of beer?' With that, young Jesse flew at his father, ramming his pipe so far into his mouth that it knocked one of his teeth out.

Although Jesse's father tried to hold his son at arm's length, the youth continued to bite him until he was finally strong-armed out of the cottage and the door slammed behind him. Furious at being excluded, Jesse began to batter the door with a hatchet, breaking three panes of glass and damaging the door before he was disarmed.

Mr Hunt took his son before magistrates charged with assault. He insisted that he would have been willing to forget his son's violence towards him, putting it down to a drop of beer, but the following morning young Jesse attacked him afresh when he was sober.

Called to explain his actions, Jesse junior told a different story. He stated that his father had struck the first blow – which Mr Hunt admitted – adding that his father behaved dreadfully towards him, withholding his wages and beating him regularly and, with winter approaching, was now threatening to turn him out of the house.

Jesse's two married sisters asked to make statements in support of their brother but the magistrates would not allow them to speak. Their father stated that both women had abused him in connection with the case and one of them particularly was unfit to live among other people.

Magistrates found Jesse Hunt junior guilty of assaulting his father, fining him 10*s* and binding him over in the sum of 10*s* to keep the peace for six months. One of Jesse's sisters immediately paid his fine.

19 SEPTEMBER

1861 John Hall and Edward Bowell were spreading dung at Spelsbury and Hall pulled a pipe out of his pocket, lit it and began smoking.

Bowell told him to put it out and sent him to rake up the straw around some recently thatched ricks, while he went off to collect more dung. When Bowell returned, Hall was lying by the roadside. The dung was quickly unloaded and, as Bowell drove the cart towards the village, he looked back and noticed that the ricks were on fire. He immediately ran to try and extinguish the flames but there was a high wind and a pea rick, hay rick and straw rick were all destroyed.

Suspicion fell on John Hall who was asked if he smoked or if he was carrying matches. Hall answered no to both questions but since Bowell had seen him smoking, he was searched. His pipe was found in his pocket but he had no matches with which to light it.

Hall gave a number of conflicting statements. He said that he hadn't set the ricks on fire then admitted that he had, offering to pay farmer George Hirons 2*s* a week compensation from his wages if he didn't prosecute him. Hall stated that he had set the fire deliberately by lighting some pea straw and placing it beneath the rick, then contradicted himself, saying that Bowell had asked him to burn the loose straw around the ricks and the fire had accidentally spread.

Hall was charged with arson and committed for trial at the Oxford Assizes, shocking the court by pleading guilty. The presiding judge insisted that he revised his plea to not guilty and went on to try the case. It was pointed out that Hall was waiting by the side of the road when Bowell arrived back with the dung and that the two unloaded the cart and drove some distance before noticing the fire. To the judge, this seemed to indicate that Hall could not have started the blaze deliberately by placing lighted straw under the rick, since he reasoned that the fire would have taken hold more quickly.

According to the judge, the evidence pointed to Hall having started the blaze accidentally by lighting his pipe. The jury concurred, finding Hall not guilty and he was discharged from the court in tears – he was just eleven years old.

20 SEPTEMBER **1894** Farmer Arthur Machen and his wife returned to Oxford from Bewdley, where Machen signed an agreement to take the tenancy of a farm. On their return, Mrs Machen asked her husband if he would fetch her some water from the kitchen and, within seconds, he called out, 'I have done something.' When Mrs Machen went to him, her husband could only gasp, 'Carbolic acid. Run and get someone.'

Mrs Machen fetched neighbour Edmund Bannister, who laid Machen on the sofa and gave him something to induce him to vomit. Machen told Bannister that he had drunk poison by mistake and asked for something sweet, before lapsing into unconsciousness and dying.

At an inquest held by coroner Mr W.W. Robinson, the jury heard that Machen suffered from insomnia, for which he was taking medicine. Both Machen's medicine and a ribbed bottle of carbolic acid were kept on the mantelpiece in the kitchen and, when Machen went for water, he took no lamp but struck a match to see by. The inquest jury returned a verdict of 'death from misadventure', believing that Machen confused the two bottles in the poor light.

21 SEPTEMBER **1847** Charles Spencer of Caversham was sent to Buckingham for a load of coal. He spent much of the day drinking and, as he was returning home, he fell from the shafts of his waggon near Bicester, breaking his left leg.

Surgeon Mr Woodward his son, also a surgeon, set the compound fracture but four days later it was evident that gangrene was setting in.

Woodward consulted with a surgeon from the Radcliffe Infirmary, then another from St Bartholomew's Hospital in London, both of whom agreed that the leg should be amputated. However, before the operation could be organised, the gangrene had extended too far for there to be any hope of saving Spencer's life. He was to have been married the day before his death on 28 September.

Coroner Mr J.H. Cowley held an inquest at Bicester at which a verdict of 'accidental death' was recorded. The coroner hoped that the tragedy would serve as a warning to all carters who ignored the danger and persisted on riding on the shafts of their wagons.

22 SEPTEMBER 1895 Three-year-old Annie Griffin of Stonesfield died at the Radcliffe Infirmary from the effects of falling into boiling water.

On 20 September, Annie and a younger child were in the living room. Annie's mother took a pot of hot water off the fire and stood it on the kitchen floor while she went to the adjoining pantry for the wash tub. Hearing screams from the kitchen, she rushed back to find that Annie had fallen into the boiling water.

Neighbour Ada Howse also heard Annie's screams and came running to see what the matter was. Ada and Annie's mother stripped the little girl's clothes off and found that she was severely scalded. After applying 'sweet oil' to the scalds, they wrapped Annie in a blanket and took her to Dr Caudwell at Woodstock, who sent her to the infirmary.

It was not the first time that Annie had been to the hospital as, six months earlier, she fell on the fire and was badly burned. On this occasion, she died from shock to the system the day after being admitted.

23 SEPTEMBER 1899 *Jackson's Oxford Journal* printed the tragic details of the suicide at Milton-under-Wychwood of twenty-eight-year-old Emily Townsend.

After receiving a letter from the man to whom she was promised in marriage, Emily seemed distraught. She threw the letter on the fire and, later that night, slipped out of the house while her family slept and drowned in the mill pond, which was only 3ft deep. It was suggested at her inquest that Emily may have believed that she was pregnant, since she had recently been suffering from stomach pain, but a post-mortem examination showed that she wasn't.

The inquest jury returned an open verdict of 'found drowned', saying that there was no evidence to show how Emily got into the water. However, what was particularly remarkable was the testimony of the village constable, PC John Walker.

Walker testified that, on the night of Emily's death, he was on duty about a mile away when he heard the voice of a person apparently in deep distress coming from the direction of Milton. The noise continued at intervals for about half an hour, yet Walker made no attempt to investigate, since he was aware that an eccentric woman lived in that area.

'Why could not PC John Walker have taken the trouble to go and see what it was all about?' questioned the newspaper, concluding, 'What is the use of a constable on the road in the middle of the night who frames excuses for doing nothing? He might as well have been a signpost.'

24 SEPTEMBER 1839 Five-year-old William Burden was playing with other children at his home in Witney when he screamed. His mother ran to see what the matter was and found him choking and barely able to speak.

She sent for a surgeon, who used a probang to clear the child's throat. That seemed to resolve whatever ailed William, who quickly resumed

Witney, 1940. (Author's collection)

playing and showed no further symptoms until 3 October, when he suddenly collapsed. This time, the surgeon was unable to save him.

A post-mortem examination revealed a broad bean lodged about three inches down in William's windpipe, which had swollen, blocking William's airway and causing suffocation.

An inquest held by coroner Mr J. Westell recorded a verdict of 'accidental death'.

25 SEPTEMBER 1840 As John Davey was walking across his garden at Dorchester, he heard a bang and felt something hit him hard on the chest. Davey ran indoors, finding that although the skin wasn't broken, it was already showing signs of bruising.

Davey surmised that someone had shot him and his brother, Thomas, made a quick search of the garden, asking their neighbours if they had seen anything. Learning that a young man had been hanging around earlier that night, the Daveys recognised the description as resembling their nephew, William Davey.

Twenty-three-year-old William inherited a considerable fortune on attaining his majority, which he rapidly squandered on loose living. He had recently visited his uncle asking for money and John gave him £40, with a stern warning that there would be no more. Although they apparently parted on friendly terms, as William was John's heir, the Davey brothers suspected that he might have tried to shoot John for his inheritance.

Thinking that William would return to London, Thomas rushed to Reading Station and arrived in time to see his nephew entering a first-class carriage on the London-bound train. Thomas boarded the train and, when it reached Paddington, asked a railway policeman to apprehend William, who was carrying two pistols, one of which had recently been fired.

He was charged with 'shooting with intent to kill' and tried at the Oxford Assizes on 27 February 1841, where he exhibited the utmost indifference to his fate as he was found guilty and sentenced to fifteen years' transportation. Had the pistol ball not struck a metal button on his uncle's waistcoat, he might well have been executed for murder.

26 SEPTEMBER

1932 An inquest at Oxford investigated the death of a forty-two-year-old pub landlord from Farnham Royal. Walter Ludgate was enjoying a day at Thame Fair and, according to witnesses, was 'somewhat merry' when he went to watch the wall of death.

The wall of death is a wooden cylindrical structure some 30ft tall, around which motorcycles race at high speeds. Spectators stand on gantries at the top of the structure looking down into the wooden 'drum'. As Ludgate stood watching, he tried to walk along the gantry, stumbled and rolled through the canvas barrier, falling 30ft to the ground.

The inquest jury returned a verdict of accidental death, adding a rider that urgent steps should be taken to prevent similar accidents occurring in future.

27 SEPTEMBER

1884 John Rose of Witney had recently taken to drinking to excess. A jealous man, he started an argument with his wife, during which he hit her several times and threatened to cut her throat and throw her down the stairs. When he grabbed Hannah Rose around the throat, she screamed, 'Murder!' 'Oh, he's murdering mother,' shouted her daughter, Charlotte, at which her brother, John William Rose, came out of his own bedroom and shot his father.

Surgeon Edward Hyde was called and found Rose unconscious, a single bullet embedded in his brain, having entered his eye. When he died, his son was charged with wilful murder.

'I know I shot him,' John junior told the police. 'He was murdering mother. I shot once at the side to frighten him; he would not leave go, so I shot him.' However, the police could find no trace of the warning shot and determined that Rose was less than 4ft from his father when he shot him.

At his trial at the Oxon and Berks Assizes, Mr Justice Lopes instructed the jury that John Rose's death would be excusable homicide if his son acted without deliberation, without vindictive feelings towards his father and in the belief that his mother's life was in imminent peril.

John's mother and siblings – Charlotte, Mary and Frederick – all testified to the fact that John senior was behaving violently towards his wife and that they all believed that he would kill her. It took the jury less than five minutes to find twenty-two-year-old Rose not guilty of patricide and he was discharged to spontaneous applause from the court.

28 SEPTEMBER

1884 Thirteen-year-old John Henry Everett was one of four youths out for a stroll along the canal at Oxford. They came to Rowland's Bridge – a drawbridge – which was chained down on the opposite side of the canal from which they were walking.

As Everett tried to cross the bridge it suddenly descended, crushing the teenager's chest. The bridge deck then rebounded and the boy slid towards the canal before the bridge dropped again, catching him across the mouth and jamming him into the bank. His companions rushed to lift the bridge off him and he was taken to the Radcliffe Infirmary but was beyond medical help and died from internal injuries.

At a later inquest, it was shown that the boys had pulled themselves onto the bridge, causing a staple fastening the chain to give way. The inquest jury returned a verdict of 'accidental death'.

29 SEPTEMBER

1899   John Maurice Roberts of Piddington was charged with neglecting and ill-treating his children. The case was remarkable as, until recently, Roberts had been the village schoolmaster but his employment was terminated after he was convicted of ill-treating his pupils.

Roberts stated that things had gone wrong for him since he arrived in the village. His wife died in childbirth on 31 December 1898, having given birth to twins. One baby died but when Inspector Alcock of the Oxford and County Society for the Prevention of Cruelty to Children visited the house on 28 September, he found nine-month-old Mary (Mariam) and eighteen-month-old Douglas in soiled clothes, both suffering from inflamed and infected nappy rash. Two more children, Ernest and Gladys, claimed to be hungry and said that they were fed almost exclusively on bread and treacle or bread and butter, while their father ate beef steaks and sausages. The older children said that their father often turned them out on the streets and that they lived in fear of his drunken habits.

Magistrates believed that Roberts had 'given way to drunkenness' and 'put himself in a most awkward position' because of doing so. They sentenced him to two months' imprisonment with hard labour.

Official records suggest that Roberts remarried in 1900, to a woman who already had at least three children of her own.

30 SEPTEMBER

1895   Ten-year-old Frank Harris and his friend Douglas Edwards were collecting conkers in a meadow in the St Clement's area of Oxford. Frank climbed a tree overhanging the River Cherwell and was shaking the branches so that the conkers fell to the ground, where his friend picked them up. Suddenly, Douglas heard Frank cry out, 'Oh, save me.' He looked up and saw Frank falling from the tree into the river, hitting his head hard against the bottom.

Douglas ran to fetch Frank's sixteen-year-old brother, George, who then pulled his brother out of the water. Frank was unconscious and, although George did his best to revive him, he was unsuccessful. Taken to the Radcliffe Infirmary, he died on 1 October without regaining consciousness and a post-mortem examination showed that the cause of death was a small fracture at the base of the skull and concussion of the brain.

Coroner Henry F. Galpin held an inquest at the hospital and the jury returned a verdict of 'death from concussion of the brain caused by an accidental fall from a tree.'

OCTOBER

Old Woodstock market and cross. (Author's collection)

1 OCTOBER

1886 Coroner Mr C. Duffell Faulkner held an inquest at Deddington into the death of fourteen-year-old Jesse Kilby, who died the previous day as a result of an accident eight days earlier.

The deceased was carting dung and, in the early afternoon, led the two horses pulling his cart through a gate. Just as Jesse passed, a fierce gust of wind blew the gate shut, trapping him between the gate and the side of the cart. The impact crushed the youth's body and his bowels and bladder were perforated. Jesse lingered for eight days before succumbing to peritonitis.

The inquest jury returned a verdict of 'accidental death'.

Market Square, Deddington. (Author's collection)

2 OCTOBER

1880 An inquest was held at the Horton Infirmary, Banbury, into the death of labourer Samuel Coleman, who died there the previous day.

Coleman and two other labourers were employed to build a shed adjacent to the railway track and when Coleman went to speak to his colleagues, he left a plank of wood on the line.

A train approached and the driver fortunately noticed the obstruction ahead, shutting off the steam and applying the brake. However, with the train just feet away, Coleman made a snap decision to try and remove the wood. The engine caught his shoulder, knocking him into the path of a coal train.

Although thirty waggons passed directly over him, Coleman survived for several hours, his body dreadfully mutilated. An inquest jury later recorded a verdict of 'accidental death'.

3 OCTOBER

1832 An inquest was held at Woodstock into the death of eighteen-month-old Harriet Hitchman.

Harriet climbed on some iron railings at the front of a house and, as she climbed down, a spike on the top of the railings pierced the fabric at the front of her nankeen bonnet. The bonnet was tied with a ribbon beneath Harriet's chin and, suspended from the spike by her bonnet, Harriet slowly strangled to death.

Woodstock. (Author's collection)

Her elder sister, who was with her at the time, was unable to free her and ran to fetch their mother. However, by the time she arrived, Harriet was dead. The inquest jury determined that she had died an 'accidental death'.

4 OCTOBER

1878 An inquest was held into the death of twenty-two-year-old William Cowell Castle, who met his death while working as a guard for the Great Western Railway Company.

On 30 September, he was aboard the train from Wolverhampton and, when it stopped at Banbury, another guard helped him load some lamps onto the train. Then, near Kirtlington, somebody pulled the communications cord, having seen Castle hanging out through door of the guard's van apparently unconscious.

At Kirtlington Station, Castle was lifted from the train and conveyed to the Radcliffe Infirmary. He had a massive head wound and died in hospital, the bones of his fractured skull driven deep into his brain.

Railway Inspector Derrick examined the carriage in which Castle was travelling and found large quantities of blood on the step, beneath which was vomit. Derrick walked back along the line, following a trail of blood past Somerton, Ayhno and King's Sutton Stations, finding blood on each platform. A porter's cap was found just past Banbury Station.

At the inquest, it was theorised that Castle felt unwell and leaned out of the train window to vomit, his head hitting a bridge as he did so. The jury returned a verdict of 'accidental death', adding that by what means the deceased came by his injuries there was no evidence to show.

5 OCTOBER

1762 At Crawley, near Witney, a gypsy persuaded a person to part with more than eleven guineas on the promise that 200 guineas, a watch, a gold ring and some silver buckles and shirt buttons would be placed under his pillow in return. The windfall was supposed to be brought by three white doves on the night after the payment had been made to the gypsy.

Needless to say, no such bounty was forthcoming and by that time, the gypsy had long since flown with the money.

'Frauds of a similar kind have been so often practised heretofore that we might have reasonably hoped no person would, at this time of day, have suffered himself to be imposed upon under such ridiculous pretences,' commented the *Oxford Journal*.

6 OCTOBER

1825   Mr Muloch, a fanatical evangelist, preached the gospel of a new cult, according to which it was an offence against God for men to marry and have families. Amazingly, several previously happily married men left their wives, forcing them to turn to the parish for support.

On 6 October, a meeting of the members of Muloch's cult was held at the home of apothecary Mr Hunt in St Thomas's, Oxford. The deserted wives got wind of the gathering and barged their way in, smashing windows, ripping the men's clothes and pelting them with dirt and filth.

Muloch later argued that his preaching had been misinterpreted and that his call for men to leave their wives had been aimed only at certain men amongst his congregation, including one whose wife was, according to Muloch, 'a wicked person; a manifest reprobate concerning the faith and an irretrievable apostate from the living and true God,' and another whose wife refused to allow him to donate any of their money to support Muloch's religion.

7 OCTOBER

1839   One of the grooms at The Bird in Hand at Burford was walking to the stables at five o'clock in the morning when he was attacked by a rat. The animal flew at Thomas Cook's leg, biting him several times and, although he kicked it off, it kept coming back until he ran for a pitchfork with which to defend himself against the ferocious rodent.

The animal fled, running across the road and attacking Henry Watts as he left his cottage to go to work. Watts threw his greatcoat onto the animal, then he and Cook together stamped it to death.

8 OCTOBER

1850   Ann Edmunds of Alverscott, a devout Primitive Methodist, was singing hymns with her friends at home when her husband strode into the room, snatched her hymnbook from her hands and threw it into the fire. Ann ran out of the room and went upstairs, followed by her husband who, according to Ann, threw her down the stairs and threatened to 'beat out her brains.'

Ann had been married to William James Edmunds for just two months and, when William was brought before magistrates at Bampton charged with 'assaulting or threatening to assault his wife and to do her some grievous bodily harm', she was described as 'a disappointed woman.'

It was rumoured that William resented Ann using his money and taking food from the house for religious gatherings and that he had engaged the town crier to warn shopkeepers not to give his wife credit on his account. In his defence before the magistrates, William gave a completely different account of the events of 8 October. According to William, he was in bed that morning when his wife crept into the bedroom and, thinking him asleep, proceeded to pick the pocket of his 'inexpressibles', taking £2 10s, along with his purse. His threats towards her were attempts to get her to return the money. William's allegation against his wife was the start of a prolonged battle of words between the couple, which was eventually terminated by the magistrates.

They ruled that threats had been used and Ann obviously felt that she was in danger. Therefore, they released William on bail, charging him to keep the peace with his wife for the next six months.

9 OCTOBER

1904 An inquest jury at Tackley returned a verdict of 'wilful murder by person or persons unknown' on the death of Frank Ernest Allwood.

Twenty-nine-year-old Allwood was a carpenter, who left his Birmingham home in September 1904 looking for work. When he left, he was known to have £7 on him but when his body was found he had only a few coppers in his pocket.

Allwood was discovered in a barn in Tackley, his body concealed by straw and rubbish and his head beaten in. At the inquest, a cyclist from Oxford came forward to say that he had seen Allwood being closely followed by two tramps. Their behaviour was so suspicious that the cyclist actually dismounted to get a better look at them. However, even though he was able to give a good description of the men, the police were unable to trace them. Two tramps were later arrested at Faringdon but were released without charge, as was a man who was arrested in London in September 1905.

Allwood was known as a compassionate and generous man and his family believed that someone had approached him for alms, which he would have gladly given. He was probably attacked when his killer realised that he was carrying money.

10 OCTOBER

1901 A group of women were returning to Benson after a shopping trip to Wallingford. Nineteen-year-old Edith Marcham was walking a little ahead of the main group, pushing a perambulator in which two young children were riding.

Benson Lock. (Author's collection)

In the darkness, Edith strayed off the path and fell into the River Thames with the pram. The other women tried to rescue her and one toppled into the river as she tried to reach the pram but was hauled out by one of her companions.

People came rushing to help in response to the women's screams and two local youths, Ernest Letter and Harry Humphries, dived again and again, eventually recovering Edith and her charges from the river but, although artificial respiration was attempted, all three were drowned.

The names of the two infants were given in the contemporary newspapers as Payne and Boston, who were said to be aged thirteen and five months respectively. The first is William George Payne (or Paine), whose family lodged with the Marchams, whereas the second is most probably Ivy Elizabeth Barton.

11 OCTOBER

1841   William Broomhead was a commercial traveller for his family firm of sickle makers and, on 29 September, he stayed overnight at The Rose and Crown at Brill. He left there the next morning to walk to Bicester and was never seen alive again.

On 11 October, William Penn went to farmer John Cross at Arncott and reported finding a dead body in the nearby stream. Penn and Ezekiel Savage had managed to pull the body halfway up the bank and Cross helped to remove it and transport it to The Plough at Arncott. There the body was searched and £9 4s 1½d was removed from the dead man's pockets, as well as some account books belonging to William Broomhead.

Broomhead's brother was summoned to identify the body and insisted that his brother should have been carrying almost £300 in cash, a figure supported by the account books and corroborated by those who had settled their accounts.

Penn and Savage were seen bending over something on the bank before they went to Cross and, in the months following Broomhead's death, both spent money freely, seeming to have an endless supply of banknotes.

The two were charged with having feloniously stolen from Broomhead's body and appeared at the Oxford Assizes. However, a material witness was ill and the trial was postponed until July 1843, when Savage and Penn were found guilty of stealing Broomhead's money and were given prison sentences, two years for Savage and one for Penn. Since Savage appears to have bragged about murdering Broomhead by hitting him over the head, they were extremely fortunate not to have been charged with a capital crime.

12 OCTOBER

1806   *Jackson's Oxford Journal* recalled a celebrated murder in Oxford, for which Jonathan Bradford was executed in 1736.

Bradford kept an inn on the London Road, Oxford, and one night a man named Hayes asked for a room. Before retiring to bed, Hayes enjoyed a few drinks in the bar and unwisely mentioned that he was carrying a large sum of money.

Later that night, the other guests at the inn were aroused by groaning from Hayes's bedchamber and found Hayes dying in a pool of blood, with Bradford bending over him, a lamp in one hand and a knife in the other.

Bradford was arrested and kept in custody to await the next Oxford Assizes, where he strongly protested his innocence. According to Bradford, he was awakened by the sounds of a scuffle and picked up a lamp and a knife, with which to defend himself. When he reached Hayes's bedroom, he drew back the covers to find that Hayes had been stabbed and, at that minute, the two guests burst into the room and caught him bending over Hayes with a knife.

Later newspapers give differing accounts of the trial. Some report that the two guests swore that there was no blood on Bradford's knife, while others state that Bradford was so shocked at his grim discovery that he dropped his knife into Hayes's blood. Either way, Bradford was found guilty of wilful murder and swiftly executed.

Eighteen months later, Hayes's footman fell ill and, on his deathbed, confessed to having committed the murder for which Bradford was executed. The servant stated that he crept into his master's room with the intention of robbing him but, when Hayes awoke, he stabbed him in the throat, before grabbing his money and valuables and fleeing just seconds before Bradford entered the room.

Although the servant's confession exonerated Bradford from the murder, the *Journal* article argues that, in going to Hayes's room with a knife, Bradford intended to commit murder and was thus still guilty. The fact that, like the two hotel guests, Bradford could have been innocently investigating a disturbance is not considered, although the newspaper states that, before his execution, Bradford confessed to a priest that he had planned to rob and murder Hayes and was thus morally guilty.

13 OCTOBER

1873 As James Bannard and his sister picked blackberries near Grimsbury they found the body of a baby girl lying in a ditch. The infant was wrapped in a cloth and had a piece of bandage tied tightly around her neck. James sent his sister to fetch a policeman but, while he awaited PC Preston's arrival, tailor William Iley came along and took it upon himself to cut the bandage to see if the baby's throat had been slashed.

At the inquest, coroner Mr A. Weston unleashed his wrath on Iley for meddling. Given that the bandage around the child's neck had been cut, doctors struggled to determine whether or not it had been tight enough to strangle her and eventually concluded that the cause of death was suffocation resulting from pressure on the throat by fingers. The medical witnesses had no doubt that the baby was born alive and lived for anything between half an hour and a day before being murdered.

With no clue as to the identity of the baby or her mother, the coroner suggested adjourning the inquest for one week to allow the police to investigate further. When the inquest reopened seven days later, Inspector Bottrill told the coroner that the police were no closer to identifying the child, her mother or her killer(s) and the jury were forced to return a verdict of 'wilful murder by person or persons unknown'.

14 OCTOBER   **1869**   Coroner William Simmons held an inquest at The Row Barge public house, Henley-on-Thames, into the death of fifty-eight-year-old John Barry.

Barry was a former soldier, who had served in India. Having injured his knee, he had recently been in hospital but was discharged on the morning of 13 October with a prescription for medicine and lotion for the troublesome knee injury.

High Street, Henley-on-Thames, 1919. (Author's collection)

Barry took a room at The Row Barge and borrowed money from the landlady to get his prescription made up. The following morning, he was found dead in his bed at the inn, the empty bottles of medicine and lotion on his bedside table. Surgeon Mr Jeston concluded that Barry had died from an overdose of laudanum, having drunk the bottle of lotion intended for external application to his knee. Since death had occurred several hours previously, the surgeon suspected that Barry had taken the lotion in a state of semi-consciousness while half asleep. The inquest jury returned a verdict of 'accidental death'.

15 OCTOBER   **1900**   On 14 October, Arthur Andrew Robert Hastings started a new job as a driver with mail contractor John Porter and, the next morning, one of his first tasks was to fetch the mail van from the yard at the back of Porter's premises. To do so meant travelling along a passage underneath some suspended workshops.

The top of the mail van was within five or six inches of the massive beams supporting the workshops and foreman William George Berry was horrified to see Hastings start to drive the van through the passage. Berry rushed across the yard and stopped the two horses, telling Hastings that if he drove through, his head would hit the beams. Berry told Hastings that he should always dismount and lead the horses through the passage but suggested that, on this occasion, Hastings should duck down in his seat and Berry would lead the horses for him.

The van got part of the way through the passage before the horses stopped abruptly and Berry looked up to find Hastings jammed tight between the top of the van and a beam. Berry called for help and, with assistance, backed the horses and got Hastings down from the top of the van. He was taken by ambulance to the Radcliffe Infirmary, where he lingered until 18 October before dying from a dislocation of the upper part of his spine.

Coroner Mr Galpin held an inquest at the hospital on the following day, at which the jury returned a verdict of 'accidental death'. They suggested that Porter placed a notice where everybody could see it, forbidding people from driving under the beams.

16 OCTOBER

1894   Coroner Mr Galpin held an inquest at the Radcliffe Infirmary into the death of forty-five-year-old Thomas Glanville, aka Shaney.

Glanville was employed by Mrs Henrietta Wilson of Derbyshire, who ran a 'galloping horses' fairground carousel. On 14 October, Mrs Wilson's show arrived in Oxford on several vans, drawn by a traction engine. The trucks were too tall to pass beneath the railway bridge so had to cross the line instead.

The traction engine climbed the slope at the corner of Mill Street but struggled to cross the railway line. Manager William Wilson, Glanville and the other labourers uncoupled the trucks and got the engine over alone. They then took a length of stout chain and coupled two of the vans to the traction engine to pull them over separately.

Once the vans were across the line, Wilson applied the brakes to stop them from running backwards down the slope. However, one of the vans slewed round and, although they tried to straighten it, it continued sliding, dragging the other van with it. Glanville was between the first van and the traction engine and suddenly shouted, 'Whoa!' The engine driver immediately shut off steam but, whereas the engine stopped, the van continued and Glanville was crushed between them.

An ambulance was summoned and Glanville was sent to hospital, although William Wilson later said at the inquest that he believed that Glanville died even before the ambulance arrived. A post-mortem examination showed that his chest was crushed and he had numerous broken ribs, which had punctured his lungs.

The inquest jury returned a verdict of 'accidental death'.

17 OCTOBER

1866   Twelve-year-old Harriett Jane Mitchell appeared at the Oxford Quarter Sessions charged with unlawfully administering poison to Philip Henry Cox at Newnham Murren so as to endanger his life.

Harriett was engaged as a nursemaid by Philip's parents and, on 10 August, after only two days in her new job, baby Philip was heard to scream. Mrs Cox rushed to see what the matter was and Harriett claimed to have dropped him on the fire grate. A surgeon was called to examine the infant and discovered that Philip had been fed a corrosive substance, most probably nitric acid. Harriett seemed distraught but her main concern seemed to be whether she would still be needed as a nursemaid if the baby died.

There was a bottle of nitric acid on a shelf in the kitchen and marks in the dust showed that it had been moved. Confronted with this evidence, Harriett said that she was dusting the shelf while holding the baby in her arms and the bottle fell between them. She tried to stop the contents going in the baby's mouth but the bottle had a broken cork and she failed.

When surgeon Mr Marshall was called, baby Philip seemed lifeless and had no discernible pulse. The lining of his throat had been destroyed by some corrosive substance and, for the next two weeks, there was blood in the baby's bowel movements. Philip then seemed to make a full recovery, although Marshall estimated that he had consumed at least a tablespoonful of the acid and that the bottle must have been held directly to his mouth, since there were few marks on his clothes.

In spite of what seemed to be overwhelming evidence against her, the jury acquitted Harriett, possibly because Philip's mother unwittingly confirmed her story that the bottle of nitric acid had a broken cork but more probably because of her youth.

18 OCTOBER   **1940**   Twenty-year-old John William Dalgarno from Aberdeen, who was serving with the Royal Artillery, appeared at the Oxfordshire Assizes charged with robbery with violence. The court heard that as Mrs Marjorie Carter was walking home from a dance, Dalgarno pounced on her without warning. He knocked her down and, having hit her several times in the face and chest, he snatched her handbag containing 1s 6d and ran away. When the jury pronounced Dalgarno guilty, Mr Justice Charles sentenced him to six months' hard labour, with six strokes of the cat-o-nine-tails.

19 OCTOBER   **1948**   At Iffley Lock, the only way from the River Thames to the road was through a toll gate belonging to Lincoln College. Folklore stated that, if ever a corpse was taken through the gate it would immediately be freed from toll and, on 19 October, the gatekeeper was taking no chances.

Iffley Lock. (Author's collection)

When the body of forty-four-year-old Frederick Dudley Penfold of Oxford was recovered from the river, the gatekeeper refused to allow the police through the gate with the body, forcing them to lift it over a wall. A spokesperson for the college verified that the superstition did exist but could not say whether it was founded in law, although he confirmed that the keeper had not been officially instructed to prevent the passage of corpses.

20 OCTOBER

1836 After several days spent drinking, sixty-six-year-old asthmatic William Parker Bryan of Oxford was found dead in bed. An inquest was opened on his death and, as was customary at the time, the jury were compelled to view his body.

To the coroner's amazement, when they inspected Bryan's corpse, the jury declared that he was not dead. They based their conclusion on the fact that the body was unusually warm, even though Bryan had supposedly died some hours earlier.

The coroner sent for a surgeon, who examined Bryan and pronounced him well and truly dead. However, the jury were unwilling to accept his opinion until they heard from the dead man's relatives that a dog had been lying on the corpse's chest until immediately before the jury arrived to inspect the body. Once the reason for the warmth was explained, the jury determined that Bryan 'died by the visitation of God.'

21 OCTOBER

1940 Twenty-nine-year-old Royal Army Service Corps driver George Beesley appeared before Mr Justice Charles at the Oxford Assizes charged with the wilful murder of domestic servant Irene Sherry.

The jury heard that Irene was found dead at her lodgings in Richmond Road, Oxford. She was sitting upright in a chair and had a single wound, made by a bullet fired from a service rifle.

According to the prosecution, Beesley and Sherry were courting but when Beesley visited his girlfriend at her lodgings, he found romantic and intimate letters from another soldier. He challenged her about the letters and, finding her explanations unsatisfactory, jealously shot her once through the heart.

Beesley was found not guilty of murder but guilty of manslaughter, for which he was sentenced to ten years' penal servitude.

Mr Justice Charles. (Author's collection)

22 OCTOBER

1892   Coroner Mr W.W. Robinson held an inquest at The George Hotel, Dorchester-on-Thames into the death of twenty-three-year-old Andrew Jeffries.

The deceased was employed as a flagman for a traction engine and it was his duty to walk in front of the engine and warn other road users of its approach. As George Wise drove between Shillingford and Clifton Hampden on 21 October, Jeffries was walking about 20 yards in front of the engine. Wise told the inquest that he briefly took his eye off the road in front of him to make up the fire, when the steersman suddenly cried out. As he steered the engine into a gateway to allow two ladies in a trap to pass, William Cozens saw Jeffries falling backwards under the front wheel of the engine. Although Wise stopped as soon as he heard Cozens shout, Jeffries was run over and disembowelled.

Jeffries, who was Cozens's nephew, was a steady young man, who had drunk only one pint of beer at lunchtime before the accident and was therefore sober. On occasions, he had been reprimanded for riding on the driving bar of the engine and on this occasion, a passer-by stated that he believed that Jeffries was not walking in front of the engine but was either getting off it or was just in front of it when he fell. The inquest jury could not explain how Jeffries came to fall under the engine and returned a verdict of 'accidental death'.

The George Hotel, where the inquest was held. (Author's collection)

23 OCTOBER

1887   A verdict of accidental death was returned at an inquest held by coroner Mr W.W. Robinson.

On 19 October, nineteen-year-old Richard James Biggs was at a farm in Woodstock, where he was thrashing barley in a barn with seven or eight other labourers. Edward Osborne was using a two-pronged pitchfork when Biggs unexpectedly walked in front of him and his pitchfork struck Biggs in the right ear, a prong becoming embedded in his brain.

Biggs was carried home and attended by surgeon Mr Welsford, but inflammation of the brain set in and he died. Conscious and sensible almost to the last, he insisted that the injury was accidental and that Osborne was not to blame.

24 OCTOBER

1763 When a manservant at Wolvercote complained of feeling a little off colour, servant Jane Parlett offered to make him some gruel. However, it tasted so foul that after the first spoonful he immediately accused Jane of trying to poison him.

Indignantly, Jane offered to eat some of the gruel herself to prove that it was all right. Within a short time, both she and the manservant were suffering from symptoms of arsenic poisoning. Although the man recovered, Jane died and it was found that, unbeknown to her, the oatmeal she used in preparing the gruel had been doctored with poison for the purpose of killing rats.

The jury at the inquest returned a verdict of 'accidental death', calling for more restraints on the sale of poison.

25 OCTOBER

1884 Francis William Evans appeared before Mr Justice Lopes at the Oxford Assizes charged with the manslaughter of James Whiting.

On 6 August, several people were drinking in The Rose and Crown at Shilton, near Burford, when a trivial argument broke out between Evans and Whiting. The discussion grew heated and the landlord told both men to 'take it outside', where Whiting punched Evans hard. Evans retaliated and before long Whiting was beaten almost senseless, blood dripping from his nose and mouth. Although he was knocked down three times, the spectators didn't call a halt to the fight as they didn't think it was serious. When Whiting was unable to continue fighting, Evans moved him to the side of the road and went home.

Whiting was found some time later by a policeman, who heard him groaning in pain. He was taken home but died from his injuries soon afterwards, when an inquest returned a verdict of manslaughter against Evans.

At the trial, it was shown that Evans had been most reluctant to fight and had been goaded into doing so by Whiting. Furthermore, Evans was a steady, sober, hard-working and peaceable man, whereas his alleged victim was known to be a heavy drinker and a pugnacious and quarrelsome drunk.

Mr Justice Lopes came to the conclusion that, since Whiting had done everything in his power to avoid fighting, there were extenuating circumstances. He ordered the jury to find Whiting guilty of manslaughter, which they did, adding a recommendation for mercy. Lopes then sentenced Evans to one week's imprisonment, without hard labour.

26 OCTOBER

1886 Hiram Bowell of St Clements appeared at the Oxford Assizes charged with two counts of attempted murder. Bowell had long held suspicions that his wife, Jane, was unfaithful and, on 1 July, he was at work when someone mentioned that they had just seen a man named Simmons (or Simmonds) at his house. Bowell immediately downed tools and went home. Finding Charles Simmons there, he snatched up a bread knife and plunged it into his throat.

Simmons was badly injured, although fortunately, the handle came off the knife and ended Bowell's ferocious attack. Bowell then moved to his wife, cutting her throat with his penknife and leaving her for dead.

When Bowell left the house, Simmons followed and handed him over to a policeman, to whom Bowell remarked that he had cut his wife's throat and he hoped that she was dead, adding that Simmons would also have died, had the knife not broken.

At Bowell's trial, it was established that he once worked for Simmons and had known him for many years. There was nothing to suggest any intimacy between Jane Bowell and Simmons, who had actually been invited into the house by Jane's sister and was sitting talking to her in the kitchen when Bowell arrived home and attacked him.

Bowell's defence counsel tried to persuade the jury that Bowell was provoked into attacking his wife and Simmons and that, in his own mind, he was simply dispensing justice for his wife's infidelity.

In his summary of the case for the jury, the judge intimated that Jane Bowell should have considered how her conduct might have affected her husband, who she knew to be a jealous man. Bowell did what might be expected from a frenzied man, stated the judge, adding that it was evident that Bowell intended to do grievous bodily harm but not that he planned to murder his wife and Mr Simmons.

Believing that Bowell had acted in the heat of passion, the jury found him guilty of two counts of wounding with intent to do grievous bodily harm and he was sentenced to twelve months' imprisonment with hard labour.

27 OCTOBER

1894 The presence of scaffolding outside the chapel at Brasenose College proved too much of a temptation for several of the college undergraduates, who delighted in climbing it.

One was twenty-four-year-old William Heaton Rhodes, who had apparently climbed the scaffold on several occasions. However, on 27 October, he fell 15ft and landed on the stone paving below.

He was carried unconscious to his bed and doctors were called to attend him. They found that he had a massive swelling at the back of his head and a fractured skull, through which his brain was oozing out. Rhodes was beyond medical assistance and died shortly after his fall.

The inquest held by coroner Mr F.P. Morrell heard that Rhodes was perfectly sober at the time of the accident and that he was just 'larking about'. The scaffolding was in excellent order and, in the coroner's opinion, no blame could be attributed to the contractor, who erected the scaffolding to carry out repairs to the chapel and had taken all reasonable safety precautions. The jury agreed, ruling that Rhodes died an accidental death, for which there was no one to blame but himself.

28 OCTOBER

1855 An inquest was held by coroner Mr G.V. Cox at The Isis Tavern, Iffley, into the death of John Tremenheere Johns of Crowan, Cornwall.

Johns was a student at Pembroke College and, on 26 October, he and some friends hired canoes, intending to paddle to Iffley. On the way, they began deliberately bumping into each other and Johns' canoe overturned. He sank in about 15ft of water and although his friends waited for him to surface, sadly he never did.

The alarm was raised and within five minutes people were dragging the river for Johns' body, although it was over an hour before it was located roughly 20 yards from where his canoe originally capsized.

Pembroke College. (Author's collection)

The inquest jury returned a verdict that Johns 'met with death by the accidental upsetting of a boat', making several suggestions to improve safety on the water. Johns had only been at Oxford for two weeks and his father, who brought him up from Cornwall, remained with him for several days to ensure that he was settled.

29 OCTOBER

1808 Perturbed by the number of people in Abingdon being bitten by mad dogs, the Mayor published a handbill advising people that all dogs were to be locked up for the next twenty-one days. 'We have seldom heard of such repeated instances of mad dogs at any one period,' commented the local newspaper, detailing several attacks on dogs and people.

Sadly, the Mayor's handbill was largely ignored, compelling him to issue a second on 3 November stating that from then on, 'proper persons would parade the streets to destroy all dogs that may be found therein.'

30 OCTOBER

1900 George Green and Amelia Stanley of St Ebbe's appeared at the Oxford City Court charged with neglecting Rose Green, who was George's daughter.

Eleven-year-old Rose and her father lived with Amelia and her son, Bertie Braithwaite, and Bertie was the favoured child. Bertie had a proper bed, whereas Rose slept on a pile of old rags and was usually kept awake by mice running over her all night. Rose was dirty, verminous and neglected and was often turned out of the house to fend for herself. Both Green and Amelia Stanley drank and there was rarely enough money in the house for food – however, whatever food there was, it was given to Bertie.

Rose's married sister took her in on occasions when their father wasn't working and several neighbours had taken pity on Rose, giving her shelter and food. However, magistrates decided that it was time that Green assumed responsibility for his own child and sentenced him and Mrs Stanley to one month's imprisonment with hard labour.

31 OCTOBER

1893 Thomas Cave of Oxford was constipated and reached for a packet of Epsom salts, which he dissolved in water to ease his symptoms. Within minutes of drinking the solution, he began vomiting and suffered from crippling stomach pains and diarrhoea.

Thomas's fifteen-year-old son, Thomas Spencer Cave, went for the doctor and was given a prescription for medicine, which Mr Cave took. He didn't vomit again but when the doctor called to see him that evening, he was barely conscious and died later that night.

It occurred to both father and son that there were some vermin-killing powders in the house and that Cave might have taken one by mistake. However, Thomas junior was positive that he had seen his father throw an empty packet marked Epsom S... onto the fire.

Samples of vomit and diarrhoea were sent to County Analyst Mr Fisher, along with a packet of crystals labelled 'Epsom Salts' and the sweepings from the cupboard in which Cave stored his medicines. The vomit and diarrhoea both contained large amounts of arsenic, whereas the salts and the sweepings contained none.

Cave had recently been in trouble with the police for allowing betting to take place on his premises and had served a few days in prison. He was deeply ashamed and, at the inquest into his death held by coroner Mr E.L. Hussey, questions were asked about whether he might have committed suicide. Thomas junior put an end to such speculation, saying that his father thought all suicide foolish.

It was pointed out that the room in which the Epsom salts were kept was quite dark and as a consequence it would have been easy for Cave to have picked up the wrong sachet by mistake. Yet, by law, arsenic had to be coloured red, blue or black and there was no trace of colouring in the samples, which Cave had dissolved in water and noticed no signs of colour.

The inquest jury eventually concluded that death was caused by white arsenic taken by Mr Cave himself, accidentally and by mistake.

NOVEMBER

Aerial view of Henley-on-Thames. (Author's collection)

1 NOVEMBER

1888 Herbert, William, James and Henry Louch of Enstone habitually played with a very old, rusty double-barrelled shotgun and were exploding toy caps on the gun's nipple. As Herbert took his turn, there was a very loud bang, followed by a child's scream. The boys' father rushed in from outside to see what had happened and, to his horror, William Louch found that part of Henry's face had been shot completely off.

There was so much blood that it was impossible to gauge the full extent of the child's injuries. Louch raced to the nearby Post Office and telegraphed for a surgeon, who found the eight-year-old suffering from broken upper and lower jaws, along with severe injuries to his mouth, lips and the right-hand side of his face. In spite of the surgeon's efforts, Henry succumbed to his injuries early the next morning.

A close examination of the gun showed that the left nipple was missing. It was supposed that a charge of powder in the left-hand barrel of the gun had probably been forgotten for many years and that, by chance, Herbert used the left nipple when it was his turn to explode a toy cap.

At the inquest held at The Harrow Inn by coroner Mr Duffell Faulkner the jury returned a verdict of 'accidental death'.

2 NOVEMBER

1899 Although he was only twenty-one years old, Frederick Lacy had worked at Osney Mill for a year, and at other mills before that. Thus it seemed inconceivable that, when a belt came off the workings, Lacy would try to replace it while the mill was in motion. However, that was precisely what he tried to do, with the result that he became entangled in the machinery.

Lacy's foreman was alerted to the catastrophe by an unusual noise and, when he went to investigate, he found the young man suspended from a shaft by the belt. In spite of the fact that one of Lacy's legs had been completely severed, he was still fully conscious and able to explain precisely how the accident happened.

He was taken to the Radcliffe Infirmary, where he died later that day, and, at the inquest, the jury were amazed that there were no guards in place to stop the belts coming off. Foreman Thomas Scroggs explained that it was Lacy's job to ensure that all the belts and straps were in the proper working order once the mill was set in motion. Any sensible man would have stopped the machinery before replacing the belt, said Scroggs, but, 'with contempt for danger which grew from familiarity', Lacy tried to cut corners. The mill owners felt very strongly that the fatal accident was the deceased's own fault and, although they welcomed any suggestions to make the mill safer, they took no responsibility for his demise.

The jury returned a verdict of 'accidental death', recommending the installation of guards on the machinery to prevent any future accidents.

3 NOVEMBER

1868 Widow Mary Anne Russell was the landlady of The Flowing Spring public house at Eye and Dunsden on the Oxfordshire side of the Thames and, on 3 November, she attended a dance at The Crown Inn at Sonning, on the Berkshire side of the river. She was accompanied by her fiancé, George Holloway.

During the dance, a group of drunken men were behaving in a very disorderly manner. Holloway took issue with them and the group were thrown out of the pub. When Holloway and Mrs Russell left, accompanied by a friend, William Wheeler, the angry men followed them across the river.

Mrs Russell was walking between Holloway and Wheeler, her arms linked with theirs. When the rowdy group of men seized Wheeler and pulled him away, Mrs Russell fled in fear, running home and slamming the door behind her and, minutes later, Holloway arrived very much out of breath. As soon as Mrs Russell let him into the pub, the men attacked the door and Holloway grabbed a poker to defend himself and his fiancée. He rushed out into the melee brandishing the poker and immediately dropped to the ground mortally wounded, his skull fractured by a large stone the size of a baby's head.

Joseph Bennett, George Matthews, James Dansels, John Hooke, Edward Little, George Banks, William Hayes and John Morris were charged with feloniously killing and slaying Holloway, appearing at the Oxfordshire Lent Assizes in 1869. At their trial, Mr Justice Keating ruled that there was little to connect Bennett and Morris with the attack and ordered the jury to acquit them. Keating explained that, although only one man could have thrown the fatal stone, in the eyes of the law, all were equally guilty.

The jury heard conflicting evidence from witnesses, who all seemed to have seen and heard completely different incidents. However, the deciding factor for the jury was the possibility that Holloway had accidentally fallen on the stone. This raised sufficient doubt in their minds to return verdicts of not guilty for all of the defendants.

4 NOVEMBER

1929 Edgar Skuce was piloting a Gypsy Moth aircraft on a return journey from Port Meadow in Oxford to Reading Aerodrome. As he took off from Port Meadow, a small piece of metal fell from the bottom of the cockpit and Skuce decided to land to retrieve it. However, as he prepared to land, a large crowd of people gathered and Skuce had seconds to choose between crashing into them and landing on swampy ground. He chose the latter option.

Skuce's passenger, Mr S. Buckle, jumped clear of the plane as it neared the ground, escaping with minor cuts and bruises. As it touched down, the aeroplane turned a complete somersault and Skuce was trapped beneath it. Once freed, he was rushed to the Radcliffe Infirmary with a fractured skull and other injuries.

He is believed to have survived the accident.

5 NOVEMBER

1871 Shortly after daybreak, the body of a woman was found in a field on the Botley road, just outside Oxford. Her throat had been slashed and a piece cut from her cheek.

The body was found about 15 yards into the field and, a further 15 yards from the body there was a large bloodstain. It looked as though the woman's throat had been cut there and she had managed to walk towards the gate before fainting from loss of blood. The body was found only yards from the Botley Turnpike Gate, yet the gatekeeper had heard no sounds of a struggle and no screams.

The body was identified as that of Betsy Richards (aka Hopkins) who suffered from fits and was described as being 'of weak intellect'. There was no doubt in anybody's mind that she had been murdered, although nobody could think of any motive for killing her.

The police searched the area but found no knife or any other weapon and, although they followed up numerous leads, the identity of Betsy's murderer(s) remained a mystery. The Secretary of State offered a reward of £100 for information, which prompted a labourer to contact the police.

Soon after the murder, he found a knife on the road from Oxford to Eynsham. It was described as a household knife, which had been ground down to resemble a shoemaker's leather knife. The handle appeared to have been recently scraped and the blade ground, possibly to obliterate any traces of blood.

The police theorised that an itinerant shoemaker went into the field with Betsy for an immoral purpose and that he probably tried to rob her. Having killed Betsy, he then went 'on the tramp', discarding the knife as he went. Perhaps unsurprisingly, the identity of Betsy's killer remains a mystery to this day.

6 NOVEMBER

1909 An inquest was held at Kidlington into the deaths of twenty-six-year-old Emily Hall and her children, two-year-old Rosetta and eight-month-old Percy, who were found floating in the canal on 5 November.

The inquest heard from Mr Boyd, who stated that at half-past twelve in the afternoon, he heard a child scream. He rushed to the canal bridge and saw Mrs Hall's body in the water. Boyd and a passing boatman removed the three bodies from the water but although artificial respiration was attempted, it proved hopeless.

Mrs Hall's mother told the inquest that she was helping her daughter with her laundry when Emily announced at midday that she was going

Moor Street, Kidlington. (Author's collection)

to meet the children from school. With nothing to suggest how they came to be in the water, the inquest jury returned open verdicts of 'found drowned' on all three victims.

7 NOVEMBER

1900 In response to a message received from Revd G.C. Bowring, Inspector Andrew Walsh of the National Society for the Prevention of Cruelty to Children visited Ann Beesley at her home in St Ebbe's, Oxford. Two days earlier, Bowring found ten-year-old Arthur Beesley barefoot on the streets at 9.45 p.m. Bowring took Arthur home and was greeted with a torrent of abuse by the boy's mother, who was drunk.

Bowring was no stranger to the Beesley family. He had often seen Ann drunk and was once called in by her husband to try and reason with her about her dissolute behaviour. Now, fearing for the safety of Arthur and his nine-year-old sister, Emily, Bowring reported their plight to the NSPCC.

Walsh found the Beesley's house dirty but not excessively so. Ann Beesley denied neglecting her children, who were well fed, if dirty, so Walsh left but called back later that evening, this time finding Ann 'mad drunk'.

She was brought before magistrates charged with neglecting and cruelly ill-treating her two children, by which time her husband William had taken them out of the house, having witnessed her throwing a cup of hot tea at them while drunk. William told the court that he gave Ann £1 a week, which she spent on drink. She regularly pawned household items and the children's clothes and Arthur's schoolmaster told the magistrates that the boy was often sent home because he was dirty.

In spite of a rambling statement of denial to the magistrates, Ann was found guilty and sentenced to fourteen days' imprisonment with hard labour.

8 NOVEMBER

1891 William Simms worked as a head carter at Steeple Aston and his horses were his pride and joy. He frequently made up extra bran mashes for them and, when he was found dead in the hog-tub house, it was assumed that this is what he was doing.

The hog-tub was where slaughtered pigs were soaked in boiling water so that their bristles could be scraped off. The hog-tub at Steeple Aston contained about eighteen inches of water mixed with pig offal and Simms had fallen face first into it, his mouth wide open.

Deputy coroner Mr G. Coggins held an inquest at The Red Lion Inn, at which the jury deduced that Simms suffered a seizure while making the mash and pitched forward, landing face down in the tub. They returned a verdict of 'accidental death from suffocation while in a fit'.

9 NOVEMBER

1610 Blessed George Napier (aka Nappe or Napper) was hanged, drawn and quartered at Oxford Castle for his Catholic faith.

Born in Holywell Manor, Oxford, in 1550, Napier entered Corpus Christi College as an undergraduate but was expelled for Catholicism in 1568. He studied in France, returning to England as a missionary in 1603 with the aim of helping to re-establish the Roman Catholic Church.

On 19 July 1610, Napier was arrested in Kirtlington and found to be carrying priestly paraphernalia. Tried for being a priest, he was found guilty and sentenced to death, although later reprieved. However, his trial took place only five years after the Gunpowder Plot – a failed attempt by Catholics to destroy the House of Lords and kill King James I – and since Napier refused to swear an oath of allegiance to the King, he was executed as an example. He was beatified in 1929.

10 NOVEMBER

1894 Forty-six-year-old labourer James Robinson of Adderbury appeared at the Oxford Assizes charged with committing a criminal offence against his fifteen-year-old daughter, Florence Emily Robinson, on 24 June.

The prosecution explained that Robinson lived alone with Florence and a younger daughter, Anne, in a one-bedroomed cottage. The offence with which he was charged took place repeatedly for many years and was compounded by the fact that Robinson had tried to trick Florence into signing a piece of paper, on which he had persuaded her younger sister to write words to the effect that the allegations against him were all untrue.

Robinson denied the offence and stated in court that he very much hoped that the jury would let him off as he would like to go home. However, having listened to testimony from Florence and Anne, as well as from a doctor, the jury found Robinson guilty. In passing sentence, the judge bemoaned the fact that the law did not provide a specific punishment for men who had criminal intercourse with their own children. Instead, Robinson was seen in law as a stranger to the girl, rather than a man who ought to have been ready to lay down his life to save her from any such horror as this. Accordingly, the judge sentenced Robinson to the maximum punishment allowed by law, which was two years' imprisonment with hard labour.

11 NOVEMBER

1867 It was the proud boast of Isaac Grubb, the former Mayor of Oxford, that he had never conducted any business with the Universities. However, in 1867, it was discovered that Grubb, a baker, was supplying the Universities with bread at between 6*d* and 6½*d* a loaf, while the people of Oxford were paying between 8*d* and 9*d*.

On Saturday 9 November, riots occurred in the city as the people demonstrated their anger at what they saw as the injustice of bread prices. It was expected that the riots would resume on 11 November and between 300 and 400 special constables were sworn in to deal with the uprising. Since it was anticipated that corn stores at the Great Western Railway would be targeted, all of the station porters were sworn in as specials and the Berkshire Police were drafted in to assist. At the request of the Mayor, the Home Secretary sent two companies of the Grenadier Guards by special train.

As darkness fell, tradesmen closed their shops and a large crowd of people assembled from Oxford and the surrounding villages. The rioting was centred on Isaac Grubb's shop in Queen Street, where an angry mob smashed windows with stones and tried to gain admittance. Thwarted by the special constables, the rioters went to Grubb's private residence, where once again a large body of men had been stationed in anticipation of trouble.

The mob went back to Oxford, breaking gas lamps on their way, as well as windows in colleges and private houses. Meanwhile, Grubb's second shop in the suburbs was under attack and every pane of glass on the premises was shattered. The doors had been barricaded from the inside with sacks of corn and flour, which successfully prevented the crowd from breaking in.

Several arrests were made and, at about ten o'clock in the evening, the focus of the riot moved to the police station, which was pelted with stones. The mayor read the Riot Act and, after a concerted effort by the special constables, the streets were cleared. Order was restored to the city when the prices of bread were lowered in line with those paid by the Universities.

12 NOVEMBER

1845 Robert Hall of Chipping Norton realised that there was a quantity of chaff missing from his premises. William Slatter stabled his horse adjacent to Hall's stable and, suspecting Slatter of stealing his chaff, Hall went to confront him. Slatter denied the theft but Hall could see chaff in his stable, which he believed belonged to him.

Eventually, Hall sent for the police. Inspector Charles Knott asked Hall if the chaff in Slatter's stable was his and Hall answered yes and began to put it into a bag. Slatter objected and eventually Knott told him, 'I'll see if I can't have the chaff,' and, pulling his truncheon from his pocket, hit Slatter hard on his head. He was about to strike Slatter again, when Hall and others intervened to prevent him from doing so.

Slatter was handcuffed and marched to the local gaol. PC James Mayhew checked on him soon afterwards and found him well but the next morning Slatter was dead and a post-mortem examination determined that he had a fractured skull, undoubtedly caused by Knott's blow. The inquest returned a verdict of manslaughter against Knott, who was committed for trial at the next assizes.

At Knott's trial, the medical witnesses agreed that Knott had caused Slatter's death by hitting him with his truncheon. However, both doctors told the court that Slatter had an unusually thin skull and, quite by chance, Knott's blow landed on an area of bone that was especially thin.

Hearing that Slatter was well known to the police in Chipping Norton and that Knott was highly respected for his excellent character, good conduct and humanity, the jury found him not guilty. The verdict was greeted with spontaneous applause.

Note: Knott's rank is variously given as constable and inspector in different accounts of the incident.

13 NOVEMBER

1890 Catherine (or Katherine / Catherina) Theresa Riordan appeared at the Oxford Assizes charged with attempting to murder Dr James Franck Bright, the Master of University College.

The court heard that on 6 November, Riordan called at Bright's residence and asked to see junior dean John Thomas Augustine Haines. She was told that she could not see him, so asked to see Bright's daughter. Again, she was told that this would not be possible but eventually Haines agreed to speak to her. When Dr Bright interrupted the discussion between them she left, although she returned to Bright's residence shortly afterwards and asked if she might see Bright for just a moment. She then shot him in the stomach and fled.

Catherine and Haines had a long-standing intimate relationship dating from 1888, during which Haines had given her several large gifts of money. The last such gift was £50 at the end of 1889 but, according to Haines, both he and Catherine accepted that there would be no more gifts. However, Catherine believed that Haines had promised to marry her and became almost deranged when he announced his engagement to Dr Bright's daughter. She threatened to shoot herself and also threatened to kill every single member of Miss Bright's family. Haines had letters written by Catherine, in which she threatened, 'I am nearer to you every day than you think and, By God, I will be a murderess.'

When Catherine was arrested in London, she denied having been anywhere near Oxford at the time of the shooting. Nevertheless, she was committed for trial at the assizes, where the jury found her guilty of the lesser offence of wounding with intent to do grievous bodily harm. Remarking that the jury had been very lenient, Mr Justice Mayhew sentenced her to six years' penal servitude, which she appears to have served at Knaphill Female Convict Prison in Woking.

14 NOVEMBER

1874 An inquest was held into the death of forty-two-year-old Richard Breathwitt, a clerk of the works engaged in the construction of Keble College Chapel.

A steam derrick was used to lift materials to the highest parts of the job, the bricks, stones and mortar being loaded into a wheelbarrow,

Keble College Chapel. (Author's collection)

which was raised by three chains, one attached to the wheel and the others to the two handles. Sometimes, the labourers chose to ride in the wheelbarrow, although this practice was very much frowned upon.

On 13 November, Breathwitt hitched a lift in the wheelbarrow, which already contained forty bricks. As it reached the required height, labourer Henry Coppock reached out to pull the barrow towards the unloading platform and Breathwitt stepped out, missing his footing and falling backwards 70ft to the ground. Coppock touched his hair as he fell but was unable to grab Breathwitt without being pulled after him.

Breathwitt fell on his back on a large block of stone, bouncing off to land face down on the floor. He died instantly, both of his legs broken and his skull fractured.

Coroner Mr W. Brunner passed an opinion that Breathwitt's demise was nobody's fault but his own, adding that he saw no more danger in hoisting the men up to their workstations in the wheelbarrow than in the way that men were raised and lowered in collieries.

15 NOVEMBER   **1884**   The *St James's Gazette* printed the cautionary tale of a woman who went to visit a female patient at Littlemore Lunatic Asylum.

The woman told the porter that she was there 'to visit a female patient' and was handed over to the care of a nurse, who apparently caught only the last words of the porter's introduction. Believing that the woman was 'a female patient', the nurse shut her in an empty room. Minutes later, more nurses arrived and stripped the woman naked. She was given a bath and put to bed, her frantic protests and desperate struggles serving only to reinforce the mistaken belief that she was indeed a mad woman.

The helpless visitor was confined to bed for several hours before the mistake was realised and she was liberated.

16 NOVEMBER   **1835**   Servant Thomas Nash appeared at Oxford City Court charged with assaulting Harriet Whitlock.

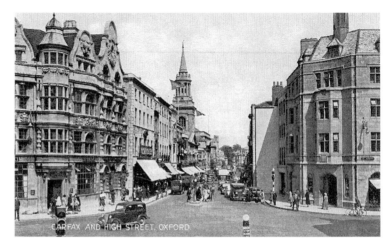

Carfax and High Street, Oxford, 1950s. (Author's collection)

Harriet attended a service at Carfax Church the previous evening, seating herself in a pew belonging to Mr Midwinter. Nash arrived at the church and told Miss Whitlock to leave the pew as she was in his place. Miss Whitlock argued with Nash and he eventually barged past the others sitting in the pew and seizing her wrists, pulled her bodily out of the pew.

Miss Whitlock complained to the 'pew opener' who confronted Nash and told him that he had no right to stop her sitting in that particular pew. Nash reluctantly made room for her but spent the whole service digging her with his elbows and treading on her feet, hurting her so much that she almost fainted with pain.

She summoned Nash for assault, her story corroborated by a gentleman who was sitting near her in church. In his defence, Nash stated that he thought the pew concerned was his master's pew and that Miss Whitlock had no right to be there. Magistrates fined him 20s plus costs.

17 NOVEMBER

1825 The inhabitants of Henley-on-Thames were thrown into a state of panic by the appearance of a mad dog in the market place. The dog bit the nose off a pig and also bit several other dogs as it rampaged through the streets for more than an hour before it was finally killed. Fortunately, no people were bitten.

Magistrates distributed handbills ordering all dogs to be tied up and, throughout the course of the day any dog that appeared to have been bitten was destroyed. In all, almost twenty were killed.

18 NOVEMBER

1831 An inquest was held by coroner Mr Cecil at the Radcliffe Infirmary into the death of six-year-old Jesse Weaver, who died after being run over by a cart pulled by two horses.

The inquest heard that Mr Church, the owner of the cart, had entrusted it to a ten-year-old boy. The child was away from the cart, cutting himself a stick from the hedgerow, when the horses suddenly moved off, knocking Jesse under the cart to be killed by the wheels passing over his body and crushing him.

Although the jury censured Church for his foolhardiness, they didn't believe him criminally negligent and returned a verdict of 'accidental death'.

19 NOVEMBER

1928 An inquest on three victims of a car accident near Benson concluded that their deaths were a pure accident.

As chauffeur James Smith Foster was driving Mrs Mabel Frances Williams (66) and her friend Mrs Jane Ethel DeLap (61), they came to a crossroads on the road between Benson and Henley. Another car was approaching and both Foster and the other driver politely slowed down at the same time, to allow the other right of way. Unfortunately, both drivers then simultaneously accelerated, each assuming that the other car was going to remain stationery. The two vehicles collided and the saloon car driven by Foster was cut in half. Foster and his two passengers suffered fractured skulls and died at the scene of the accident, while the driver of the other vehicle was severely shocked but otherwise unhurt.

20 NOVEMBER

1893 Coroner Mr Coggins held an inquest into the death of nine-year-old Rosetta Mary Judge, who was killed by a falling tree at North Aston.

On 18 November, there was a tremendous gale and Rosetta's brother Hubert saw it as a chance to get some free firewood. He and his two sisters went out collecting sticks near North Aston Hall and, as they did, Hubert happened to glance at a massive elm tree and realised that it was about to fall.

His warning shout to Rosetta was lost in the high winds as the top part of the tree crashed into her, knocking her over. She sustained a fractured skull and her throat was lacerated from her windpipe to her ear, severing all of the main blood vessels. A doctor arrived about an hour after the accident and stitched Rosetta's wounds but she died soon afterwards.

In returning a verdict of 'accidental death', the jury censured Hubert for allowing his sisters to be out in such dangerous conditions. One of the members of the jury was a carpenter at the North Aston Hall estate and pointed out that he was the only person with the authority to clear away the fallen wood and that Hubert had no right whatsoever to take it.

21 NOVEMBER

1835 Coroner Mr Cecil held an inquest at Oxford Gaol into the death of shoemaker John Paine.

There was a warrant for Paine's arrest on a charge of assault and, on 15 November, he was taken into custody by William Gardiner, the Marshall for the City of Oxford, and constable John Billing. Paine resisted and he and Billing fell to the ground.

Gardiner testified at the inquest that he chose that moment to fetch something from his house, which was only a few yards away. He returned in half a minute, by which time Billing and Paine were standing up. Paine began swearing at Gardiner, threatening to fight him, but was eventually subdued and taken to the City Gaol, where he was handed over to gaoler Thomas Gardner, to whom Paine seemed very drunk. He was placed in a cell, where he immediately fell asleep. Gardner checked him overnight, stating that Paine wished him 'Goodnight Tom' on the last occasion.

The following morning, Paine jokingly asked for a pint of beer. The gaoler suggested that Paine got up and dressed but Paine asked for an extra thirty minutes sleep, at the end of which he claimed to be unable to move. A doctor was summoned and, although everyone believed that Paine's illness was caused by drink, he was moved to a cell with a fire. However, in spite of the care of the gaol surgeon and his assistant, Paine weakened, dying on 19 November. A post-mortem examination revealed a large skull fracture, as well as an extraversion of blood on the brain, which surgeon Mr Wingfield believed resulted from Paine falling heavily and banging his head on the floor.

The main task for the inquest jury was to determine whether or not Billing and Gardiner were to blame for Paine's death. More than one witness stated that Billing was bragging in the pub that he had kicked Paine in the head and beaten his head against a wall but, after much deliberation, the jury finally ruled that Paine's death was accidental, although they censured Billing and Gardiner for their violence towards him. At a subsequent meeting of the City Magistrates, a resolution was passed unanimously that Billing and Gardiner's conduct was so reprehensible and improper that they should be dismissed from their positions immediately.

22 NOVEMBER   **1877**   George Stroudley, who worked as a maltster, appeared at the Henley-on-Thames Petty Sessions charged under the Aggravated Assaults (Women's) Act (1853) with ill-using his wife. The Act allowed stiffer penalties for those accused of beating their wives, enabling magistrates to sentence men to up to six months' imprisonment. Even so, George seemed surprised when he was awarded six months' hard labour for brutally assaulting his wife after arriving home to find that his meal wasn't quite ready.

Stroudley begged magistrates to substitute a fine for imprisonment so that he could work to 'support his dear little children'. Having heard that Stroudley had continuously abused his wife for their entire seven-year marriage, the Bench declined to revise the sentence.

23 NOVEMBER   **1830**   A riotous mob of several hundred people visited the villages of Benson, Crowmarsh and Ewelme among others, where they destroyed several threshing machines. Another machine was burned at Steeple Barton and, over the next few days, there were more attacks at Chipping Norton, Heythrop Park, Neithrop and Banbury, which the yeomanry were called upon to quell. At Henley market on 25 November, the King's Proclamation respecting 'outrages and incendiarism' was distributed and the Oxfordshire County Fire Office announced a £500 reward for the apprehension of arsonists who had fired ricks and farm buildings.

Although the protestors were widely dismissed as 'idle, ill-disposed fellows bent on mischief', their grievance was that the mechanisation of agriculture was preventing them from working and that their wages were below subsidence level. In early December 1830, several of the national newspapers published a letter from Banbury, which stated:

> The average wages (hay time and harvest excepted) of a farming labourer who has a wife and family have, for the last two years, been 9s a week. Allow the family three meals a day – breakfast, dinner and supper: allow one penny per head for each meal. At the end of the sixth day the whole wages will have been spent and not a single farthing left for the seventh day, for fuel, for clothing, for the other little articles absolutely necessary to keep a family in cleanliness. Observe I say average wages; if there are instances of 10s, there are others of only 8s. The wages of a stout single man have, in winter, been only 3s, sometimes 3s 6d, very rarely 4s a week.

24 NOVEMBER   **1845**   Maid Fanny Gosling, who was in service in Oxford, took a train to visit friends at Clifton Hampden. She alighted at the station and, as her train departed, she walked across the line behind it. Unfortunately, she did not notice the Oxford express train travelling at between 30 and 40mph, which ploughed into her, carrying her body for almost 50 yards before the driver could bring the train to a halt. She died instantly, the lower half of her body much mutilated.

An inquest was held by coroner W. Brunner that evening at The Railway Hotel and the jury heard that, although the train driver tried his hardest to stop the train, Miss Gosling stepped out only 5 yards in front of him and he had absolutely no chance of avoiding her. The jury returned a verdict of 'accidental death'.

25 NOVEMBER

1929 An inquest on the death of Philip Millman Lapthorn was concluded at Oxford.

Lapthorn, a chef at Balliol College, complained of feeling unwell while at work and, according to greengrocer's assistant Edwin Thomas Clifford, appeared to be in pain. After going to the sink and drinking a glass of water, Lapthorn collapsed and was rushed to the Radcliffe Infirmary, where he subsequently died.

A post-mortem examination showed that his death was caused by corrosive poisoning, following the ingestion of hydrochloric acid. Lapthorn was fully conscious almost to his death and was desperately keen to recover, which seemed to rule out suicide. Pathologist Dr A.G. Gibson thought it impossible for the acid to have been maliciously administered by anybody without Lapthorn's knowledge, thus the ingestion of the corrosive fluid seemed to be accidental.

Since nobody could fathom how Lapthorn could have ingested hydrochloric acid accidentally without remembering doing so, the jury returned an open verdict on his death.

Balliol College and Martyr's Memorial. (Author's collection)

26 NOVEMBER

1852 Severe flooding in Oxfordshire caused delays to several trains and the down-train from Oxford pulled into Heyford Station about an hour later than expected. Unfortunately, it collided with the up-train, which had been shunted into a siding while a horsebox was coupled to it and was protruding onto the main line by 2 or 3ft.

George Thompson, the driver of the down-train, realised at the last minute that a collision was inevitable and jumped clear. The other crew and passengers on both trains escaped with minor injuries but Thompson landed on a trackside points lever, severely injuring his head and sustaining a compound fracture of his right leg. He died almost instantly.

An inquest into his death held by coroner Mr Churchill concluded that Thompson had failed to notice that the danger signals were displayed as he approached the station. The accident resulted in the dismissal of the stationmaster at Heyford, who the jury believed had acted with want of judgement and gross neglect.

27 NOVEMBER

1908   An inquest at Kidlington investigated the sudden death of eighteen-year-old Margaret Olive Mary Turney.

Margaret's sister was diagnosed with diphtheria and her doctor recommended that asthmatic Margaret should be given diphtheria antitoxin to guard against her catching the disease. Within seconds of receiving the injection, Margaret complained of smarting pains and told her doctor that she was suffocating – minutes later, she fell from the surgery chair dead.

A post-mortem examination suggested that Margaret suffered a severe asthma attack triggered by the injection of antitoxin. The antitoxin was used daily in every part of the country and, over the past ten years, hundreds of thousands of people had been injected. This was the first ever recorded incident of its kind and in the opinion of several eminent doctors nobody could have anticipated such a reaction to the injection.

The inquest jury returned a verdict in accordance with the medical evidence, adding that the injection had been administered with proper care.

28 NOVEMBER

1895:   Angelina Lee was one of a group of gypsies who were camping close to the gravel pits in the parish of Benson. Her nephew, Joseph Smith, went to collect firewood, leaving eighty-four-year-old Angelina inside the tent peeling potatoes, but, when Smith returned after a few minutes, the tent was on fire. Helped by a labourer who was working nearby, Smith put out the flames before turning his attention to his aunt, whose skirts were burning from her stays down.

Angelina was taken to the Workhouse infirmary, where she was found to be badly burned on her right-hand side. She was unable to explain how she came to be on fire and, when she died on 8 December from a combination of burns and shock, the jury at a subsequent inquest returned a verdict of 'accidental death'.

29 NOVEMBER

1943   Thirty-eight-year-old Private John H. Waters from Illinois was found guilty at a US Army court-martial of murder, self-maiming and absence from a guard post without leave.

In February 1943, Waters was based at Henley-on-Thames, where he began courting local woman Doris Staples. However, by July, thirty-five-year-old Doris had tired of the relationship and was gradually trying to distance herself from Waters. When he heard rumours that Doris had been seeing other American soldiers, Waters went to the draper's shop where she worked and shot her several times.

Passers-by heard the shots and called the police but by the time they arrived, Waters was barricaded in a toilet at the rear of the shop. The police and fire brigade used tear gas and water cannons to get into the shop, at which Waters placed his pistol to his head and pulled the trigger.

Although badly injured, he survived to face his court-martial, where he was sentenced to death. Appeals for clemency from the other soldiers in his unit and from the townspeople of Henley came to nothing and he was executed at Shepton Mallet Prison on 10 February 1944.

30 NOVEMBER

1899 Nineteen-year-old Frederick Watsen was a fireman on a steam engine, employed by the Great Western Railway. As his driver Richard Spry Wilcox was shunting trucks at Oxford Station, Watsen happened to notice that the engine was losing steam from the external piston glands and told Wilcox that he would go and tighten the seals.

It should have taken him no more than four minutes to do the job but Wilcox was given the signal to move his train backwards. He called to Watsen, 'Look out, Fred,' and Fred raised his hand and replied, 'All right.' However, as Wilcox was manoeuvring his engine, another driver, Joseph Lewis, suddenly put up his hands and shouted, 'Whoa!'

Wilcox applied the brakes and, to his horror, saw Watsen lying under one of the trucks. He had a few marks on his knees and right shoulder but the fatal injury was a four-inch cut on his head, with corresponding skull fractures and lacerations to the brain. According to the surgeon who conducted Watsen's post-mortem examination, he had not been run over but appeared to have fallen and hit his head on something, such as the edge of the rail, or received a sharp blow, possibly from the engine.

Nobody had witnessed Watsen's accident and there were no marks on the train to suggest how it occurred. Wilcox insisted that he would never have moved the train if Watsen hadn't said, 'All right.' He believed that, when Watsen signalled that he was clear to move, he was standing on the ground but, with hindsight, suggested that he may possibly have been standing on the front of the train adjusting the seals. However, this was all conjecture and coroner Mr H.F. Galpin's inquest jury eventually returned a verdict of 'accidental death', without claiming to understand how the accident occurred.

DECEMBER

The Green, Cassington. (Author's collection)

1 DECEMBER

1852 Local and national newspapers wrote of the alarming floods affecting much of the county of Oxfordshire. 'The Cherwell and Isis are more like seas than rivers, for the width of each could be measured by miles instead of yards,' stated the *Morning Post*.

The flood waters were tainted with the carcases of sheep, pigs and horses and there were several human fatalities. One woman was overtaken by a sudden rush of water and was too elderly and infirm to escape. The coroner who conducted her inquest had already dealt with three people who had drowned and had another three awaiting inquests. Another victim of the inundations was the driver of a waggon, who was jerked from his seat and killed outright when his horse fell into a deep pool.

'It is feared there has been a fearful destruction of property and loss of life which has not yet come to light,' concluded the *Morning Post* article.

2 DECEMBER

1859 Miss Cypher went to the end of the garden at her aunt's house in Childrey to use the outside lavatory. She had not been there long, when, without any warning, a huge pollard elm tree fell onto the lavatory, crushing it completely.

The tree was at least 100 years old and had a massive trunk, so it was some time before seventeen-year-old Miss Cypher could be extricated. Not surprisingly, she was dead and it was believed that she died instantly when the tree flattened the toilet.

At an inquest into her death, the jury surmised that melting snow had washed away soil from the bank on which the tree stood, loosening the tree's roots and making it unstable. In returning a verdict of 'accidentally killed by the falling of a tree', they advised the owners of neighbouring properties to check the safety of any trees in their own gardens.

3 DECEMBER

1831 *Jackson's Oxford Journal* reported on an outrage against public decency that took place in front of thousands of people. A market was

Banbury market place, 1952. (Author's collection)

held every Thursday at Banbury and, according to the newspaper report, on 24 November, a man sold his wife.

The couple came from a neighbouring village and the newspaper stated that a willing purchaser had been found who was happy to pay 10s for the woman. 'This is the first offence of the kind against common decency we remember to have taken place in Banbury,' the report concluded.

4 DECEMBER

1939   An inquest was held at Oxford by coroner Mr H.F. Galpin into the death of nineteen-year-old Kathleen Read.

With Great Britain at war, Kathleen was undergoing training at Kidlington to become an Air Raid Precautions Warden. Part of the test procedure was for recruits to perform a gas test, where trainees would sniff gases from different phials to help them identify different poisonous gases by smell.

Kathleen collapsed and died almost immediately after her gas test but a post-mortem examination confirmed that the cause of her death was cerebral haemorrhage, which could have occurred at any time. The inquest heard that there were almost 8,000 gas testing kits nationwide and that there had never been a fatality reported in connection with their use and, in returning a verdict of 'death from natural causes', the jury accepted that Kathleen's death was not connected with the poisonous gas.

5 DECEMBER

1866   Coroner William Brunner held an inquest into the deaths of Martha Smith, Walter Scott, Amelia Wetherby and Ellen Mary Lucas.

The deceased were babies aged around eight months old, who died while in the care of the Home of Compassion, a foundling hospital near Oxford with the facilities to care for fifty illegitimate children. The home opened in 1864 and during the past year, seventeen children had died there. The deaths of the subjects of the inquest, all of whom died within a week, had fuelled rumours of ill-treatment by the Sisters of Mercy, who ran the home.

Surgeons found that each of the babies was suffering from inherent disease or from emaciation caused by neglect – none of the four was larger than a normal one-month-old infant. It was demonstrated that the mortality rate for the home was around 40 per cent, which compared favourably with the general rate of mortality in foundling hospitals of between 60 and 80 per cent.

The church wardens of Cowley, who initiated the inquiry, pronounced themselves satisfied with the jury's verdicts of 'death from natural causes', with the rider that, in the jury's opinion, the running of the home was conducted in a satisfactory manner and the Sisters of Mercy showed every care and compassion for the foundlings in their care.

6 DECEMBER

1833   Thirty-five-year-old John Archer had been out shooting and went for a drink at The Barge public house at Cassington Wharf, where he bumped into Thomas Wild.

Wild had an appointment to keep and Archer agreed to accompany him. The two men drank two pints of beer together then, as the time for Wild's appointment neared, he urged Archer to hurry up and finish his drink.

Archer picked up his gun from where he had left it in the corner of the room and tucked it under his left arm while he drank his beer. As he passed the jug to Wild, the gun slipped out from under Archer's arm and hit the floor.

There was a loud bang and Archer turned to his friend and said calmly, 'Oh, Tom. I have shot my poor arm off.' Although Archer was rushed to hospital, he died from his injuries six days later, leaving a wife and three children to mourn his passing. The inquest jury subsequently returned a verdict of 'accidental death'.

7 DECEMBER

1763 Coroner Mr Way held an inquest at Fulbrook into the death of William Dutton, who fell from a horse near Swinbrook.

A drunken man was having difficulty in controlling two horses and asked Dutton to ride one for him. Dutton was given a leg-up but before he was properly seated on the horse, its owner set off at a gallop. Dutton's horse followed and he fell, but his foot caught in the stirrup and he was dragged at full speed for almost two miles.

'He was mangled in a most dreadful manner,' wrote the *Oxford Journal*. 'His flesh was so torn from his body that there scarce appeared anything of human form; his head was almost dashed to pieces; his legs and arms all broke and almost torn from his body and upon the whole he was rendered a most frightful spectacle.'

8 DECEMBER

1893 Miss Kate Laura Dungey was housekeeper at Lambridge House near Henley-on-Thames, although she was usually there alone since the owner and his family lived in London during the week.

On 8 December, two brothers who worked on the farm and slept in the house were unable to get in. The doors were locked and nobody responded to their knocking, so at just before ten o'clock at night, the tired boys walked to their home at Assendon.

The boys' father went to farm manager George Dawson and all four walked back to Lambridge. After walking round for some time, they noticed an open window and, on gaining admittance to the house, they found bloodstains in the kitchen. There was no sign of Miss Dungey, whose body was later discovered in a wood about 30 yards from the house, where she had evidently died as she ran for her life. A post-mortem examination suggested that she had been both beaten with a blunt object and stabbed.

Initially, Dawson was a strong suspect but the police were also interested in Walter Rathall, who was Dawson's wife's brother. Rathall was staying at The Red Lion Hotel in Henley with his wife and baby for around eight weeks before the murder but suddenly fled before police could speak to him, owing money and leaving no forwarding address.

Rathall was arrested in Daventry and brought back to Henley for questioning. No blood was ever found on his clothes and the soles of his boots had a particularly distinctive pattern, which did not match the boot prints at the scene of the murder. In fact, there was nothing whatsoever to connect him with Miss Dungey's death and police were forced to release him without charge.

The Red Lion Hotel, Henley-on-Thames. (Authors collection)

Numerous suggestions were put forward regarding the identity of Miss Dungey's killer(s) but the police believed that she interrupted burglars at the house and strongly suspected Dawson and Rathall. Yet there was insufficient evidence to convict them or anybody else and, in spite of a £100 reward offered by Miss Dungey's employer, her murder was never solved.

9 DECEMBER

1833 Seven-year-old Thomas Whiting lived with his aunt, Elizabeth Evans, at Temple Cowley and, as Elizabeth walked through her living room on the way to the garden, she noticed Thomas standing innocently by the fire. Mrs Evans had progressed about 10 yards into the garden when she heard two loud explosions.

She rushed back indoors but the house was filled with smoke and she was unable to locate Thomas in the gloom. Mrs Evans ran for her neighbours and, by the time they arrived, the smoke had cleared somewhat and she was able to find Thomas and drag him outside, having first extinguished his burning clothes. Sadly, the little boy did not survive.

Coroner Mr Cecil held an inquest at which it emerged that lodger Peter Baclari had left his gun in the parlour, along with a bag of shot and a tin of gunpowder. It was surmised that Thomas had placed some of the gunpowder in a tobacco pipe, which he then lit in the fire.

The inquest jury returned a verdict of 'accidental death' and the coroner scolded Baclari for leaving the gunpowder so close to the fire, in a place where it was so easily accessible to a young child.

10 DECEMBER

1931 The trial of twenty-one-year-old James Alun Davies opened at the Old Bailey. Davies, a student at Lincoln College, was charged with the manslaughter of PC Alfred Needle, who was run down by a car on 14 October at the corner of Magdalen Road and Cowley Road, Oxford.

Twenty-three-year-old Needle was hit by a sports car, which was said by witnesses to have been travelling at a terrific speed and which failed to stop after the accident. Davies claimed that there were dark spots and

Lincoln College. (Author's collection)

shadows on his windscreen and he put his head round the edge of the screen to get an uninterrupted view of the road and an oncoming cyclist. Having determined that the cyclist had sufficient room, he continued driving and didn't realise that he had hit the policeman, thinking that he had merely bumped the kerb until his passenger told him otherwise. According to Davies, he panicked and fled the scene of the accident.

The prosecution contended that Davies was driving in a reckless and dangerous manner, whereas the defence insisted that the policeman's death was a terrible tragedy but not a crime. The jury seemed swayed by the fact that Davies admitted that he had peered round the windscreen to ensure that a cyclist had enough room – if he showed such consideration, they did not believe that he was driving recklessly, with disregard for life. It seemed most probable that he just hadn't seen Needle and the trial jury found him not guilty of manslaughter.

Mr Justice Charles told Davies that, while he agreed with the jury's verdict, he strongly advised him not to drive a car again, since, in the judge's opinion, he was not fit to drive.

11 DECEMBER

1827 The Mayor of Oxford, John Hickman, announced a reward of £100 for information leading to the discovery and conviction of the murderer of Ann Crotchley (aka Crutchley, Priest, Price or Preece).

Ann was found slumped in a doorway on 6 December, apparently very drunk. Her presence was reported to the city watchmen, who showed a distinct lack of interest for several hours, until they checked back on Ann and found her lying in a huge pool of blood. She was placed in a wheelbarrow and taken to an apothecary, who recommended that she should go straight to hospital but, instead, Ann was taken to her lodgings, where her landlady left her to sleep off her excesses, until she noticed that Ann was bleeding heavily from her 'women's parts'.

Ann told her landlady that she had been ill-used by a man and, although a doctor was called, she died from loss of blood on 8 December. A post-mortem examination showed her to be heavily bruised and suggested that a sharp instrument had been violently thrust into her vagina, causing two deep lacerations, from which she had bled to death.

The investigations into her murder focused on John Williams, a passer-by who had tried to help get Ann back to her lodgings. Williams spent a considerable amount of time alone with Ann while people tried to borrow a barrow or handcart, but there was absolutely no evidence that he was her killer and, although he was brought to trial, the Grand Jury found insufficient evidence against him to proceed.

Blue Boar Street, Oxford, where Ann Crotchley was found. (© N. Sly)

The reward was unclaimed and the murder of Ann Crotchley remains unsolved.

12 DECEMBER

1869 At about eight o'clock in the morning, labourer James Betteridge saw a horse and cart in front of his house. Its owner, Richard Green, had left The Old Bell public house at Shillingford the previous evening. His horse knew the way home and it was Green's custom to sleep in the bottom of his cart and let the animal find its own way so, when his cart was seen two hours later, nobody thought it unusual that Green wasn't driving.

Shillingford bridge. (Author's collection)

Betteridge checked the cart and saw Green curled up apparently asleep. Betteridge tried to wake him but a closer inspection revealed that Green had been brutally murdered, having serious head injuries. His stick was broken into several pieces, suggesting that he tried to defend himself but, strangely, his money and watch had not been stolen.

A post-mortem examination indicated that, of the seven wounds on Green's head, six were potentially fatal. Many had corresponding skull fractures and were thought to have been caused by blows from a blunt instrument. In addition, Green had a broken jaw and injuries to his right hand.

An inquest returned a verdict of 'wilful murder against some person or persons unknown' and in spite of exhaustive police enquiries, the murder was apparently never solved.

13 DECEMBER

1869 Coroner Mr A.D. Bartlett held an inquest into the death of Mary Ann Clarke, who lived at South Stoke, on the Oxfordshire side of the Thames. Mary Ann crossed the river by ferry to visit her sister-in-law, the landlady of The Beetle and Wedge at Moulsford and, that evening, she took the ferry home, accompanied by her son, son-in-law and an unnamed little girl.

When the ferry landed, the party disembarked onto a wooden jetty, which was about a foot above ground level. In the dark, Mary Ann either slipped or lost her bearings and walked off the edge of the platform and, with the little girl in her arms, she fell into the river.

The water was only inches deep and Mary Ann and the child were rescued within two minutes. Yet, while the child was none the worse for her unexpected ducking, Mary Ann appeared lifeless when she was dragged onto the boat and, although every effort was made to revive her, she died.

Since there was no clear reason for her demise, it was supposed that she must have been suffering from a weak heart and that the sudden shock of the cold water caused her death. With no conclusive evidence, the inquest jury returned a verdict of 'accidental death'.

The Beetle and Wedge, Moulsford, 1920. (Author's collection)

14 DECEMBER

1650 Twenty-two-year-old Anne Greene was hanged at Oxford Castle, having been found guilty of the wilful murder of her illegitimate child. Her body was delivered to the anatomy school for dissection, where surgeons noticed that it was unexpectedly warm and that her chest was moving slightly. Somebody stamped hard on her chest but, rather than putting Anne out of her misery as intended, it had the opposite effect, bringing her corpse back to life.

Anne was severely bruised and was unable to talk for several days. When she did recover the power of speech, she had absolutely no memory of having been hanged. Although she never recalled any details of her judicial hanging, she went on to marry and produce a legitimate family, living for fifteen years after her brush with death.

15 DECEMBER

1899 Coroner Mr Galpin held an inquest into the death of forty-four-year-old James Leach, who left a wife and six young children.

Leach had worked for the Great Western Railway for thirty years and, as a foreman platelayer, it was his duty to inspect the line from Radley Junction to Abingdon every morning. As he did this on 14 December, he was hit by a train.

Neither the train driver nor the fireman was aware of having hit anybody and it wasn't until they reached Abingdon Station that the train guard informed them that an accident had occurred. They immediately retraced their journey, finding Leach lying at the side of the track. He was conscious and asked to sit up but seemed unable to understand how he came to be injured.

Taken to the Radcliffe Infirmary, he was found to be suffering from a fractured jaw and ribs, and cuts to his left hip, buttock and leg. He was unable to speak when he arrived at the hospital, although he did make a special effort for his wife when she visited him, saying, 'I hope you will . . .' Sadly, Mrs Leach never did find out what her husband hoped, since he died without finishing his sentence.

The inquest heard that driver Joseph Richard Partridge was not yet fully qualified, although he had passed exams and was nearing the end of his training. There was never any suggestion that his driving was at fault and it was surmised that Leach suffered a moment's careless inattention and failed to get out of the way of the approaching train. The inquest jury returned a verdict of 'accidental death' and donated their fees to his widow.

16 DECEMBER

1830 Joseph Bates of Summertown, Oxford, heard a rustling sound coming from a heap of straw on the floor of his cart-house. 'Who's there?' he shouted and the straw parted, revealing a naked woman.

When Bates recovered from the shock, he asked the woman where her clothes were and she replied that she had been forced to sell them to buy food for her twelve-year-old daughter. The child had gone to buy bread and her mother, who gave her name as Mary Johnson, told Bates that her feet were sore and her bones ached so badly that she was glad of a rest.

When her daughter returned, Bates was anxious that they should leave his premises and the child – also named Mary Johnson – promised that if they could sleep in the outbuilding, they would leave first thing in the morning. Sadly, young Mary's promise was not kept, since her mother died during the night.

At the inquest into her mother's death, Mary revealed that her father had died two years earlier and that her mother supported them by taking in washing. However, after falling ill, she could no longer work and for the past six months, she and her mother had been tramping from London to her mother's family home in Worcester.

On arriving in Oxford, Mary senior applied for parish relief and was given two loaves and told to consult an apothecary, who provided her with some powders and later a bottle of medicine for her illness. She was also given two payments of 1s 6d but was unable to afford proper food for herself and her daughter and had only 1d left when they arrived at Bates's house and asked his wife if they might sleep in his outbuilding.

A post-mortem examination showed that Mary Johnson died from liver disease, accelerated by the lack of proper nourishment. The inquest jury returned a verdict that Mary 'died by visitation of God but death was accelerated by the want of proper food and necessities'. The fate of her orphaned daughter is not recorded.

17 DECEMBER

1874 As labourer George Brown was walking home from Yarnton to Wootton, his attention was attracted by a flock of crows, which seemed to be pecking something on the ground. Curiosity compelled him to investigate and, at first glance, the object looked like a dead rabbit. However, when Brown looked closer, he realised that it was the naked body of a baby.

There was snow all around but none had fallen on the body, suggesting that it had been placed there recently. A post-mortem examination suggested that the baby girl was born alive but may have been slightly premature. Surgeon Mr Perry estimated that the child had been born between ten and fourteen days earlier and had never been fed – he believed that she had bled to death for want of attention to the umbilical cord at birth. There were no obvious marks of violence but the face and back were disfigured, having been pecked by birds.

The police made extensive enquiries to try and establish the child's parentage but were apparently unsuccessful and, when coroner Mr W. Brunner held an inquest at The Red Lion Inn, Yarnton, the jury returned an open verdict of 'found dead'.

18 DECEMBER

1933 An inquest at Oxford returned a verdict of 'death from coal gas poisoning while of unsound mind' in respect of fourteen-year-old Marion Elinor Mattock.

After being served with a summons to appear at the Juvenile Police Court relating to the theft of 3d from a bus conductor, Marion was insistent that she hadn't taken anything, even though the bus conductor positively identified her. According to James Richard Higgin, he had missed almost 35s in coppers altogether and that the money always disappeared when Marion was a passenger on his bus.

Marion placed her head in the gas oven just days after receiving the summons. She left a note reading: 'Good-bye mammy, daddy and all. I am sorry to do this but I cannot stand being accused of doing what I did not do.'

19 DECEMBER

1912 William Hall, an elderly tramp and pedlar, was sleeping in a shed at Ipsden when some men burst in and told him to get out. Faced with three angry young men, Hall was quick to comply with their request but when he left the barn, the men followed him. They beat and kicked him, stuffing his cap into his mouth to prevent him from crying out for help. The contents of his basket were tipped onto the ground and trampled on, before he was knocked into a ditch and left to die in the cold weather.

Fortunately for Hall, a patrolling policeman found him and he was taken to Wallingford Infirmary, where he was found to have a broken rib and two severe cuts on his face, as well as numerous other superficial injuries.

Farmhands George Cook, James Cook and Alfred Greenaway were arrested and appeared before magistrates at Caversham on 11 January 1913. Their attack on Hall was described by magistrates as 'most brutal and unprovoked' and each man was fined £4 for his part in the vicious assault, with two months' hard labour in default.

20 DECEMBER

1861 Gamekeepers Thomas Curtis and Stephen Moulder were in Shear's Copse, looking for poachers. Hearing some birds flapping, they made their way towards the noise and spotted two men.

The gamekeepers silently followed the pair through the wood until a sound alerted the poachers to the fact that they were being followed and one suddenly turned and, without warning, fired his gun. The shot hit Moulder and he instantly dropped to the ground, groaning just once before dying.

The shooter fled, leaving his startled companion to face the music. John Tuckey seemed shocked by the shooting and didn't resist as Curtis grabbed him and frogmarched him to a nearby cottage, where he emptied his pockets, showing that he was unarmed.

Tuckey insisted that he knew nothing about his companion, other than that he was called Jack and had once been a soldier. He described Jack's clothes as breeches or trousers with gaiters and a velveteen jacket and cap. The description matched John 'Jack' Hall, who was quickly apprehended and, although he denied shooting Moulder, he was carrying a powder flask, a bag of shot, percussion caps and some pheasant wires.

Anxious to save his own skin, Tuckey's memory improved dramatically and he made a statement saying that he was several yards in front of Hall when Hall suddenly fired his gun. Claiming to be very deaf, Tuckey stated that he had not even realised that the gamekeepers were following them.

A post-mortem examination found sixty-two pieces of lead shot in Moulder's body, which had seventy-two entrance wounds made by pellets. Eighteen lodged in his heart, while the remainder were extracted from his kidneys, intestines, liver, and arms. An inquest jury returned a verdict of wilful murder against John Hall, who was committed for trial at the next Oxford Assizes.

Finding Hall guilty of wilful murder, the trial jury strongly recommended mercy, since they believed that the shooting was 'a momentary act', intended to disable rather than kill Moulder. Although Hall was sentenced to death, his sentence was later commuted to transportation for life and he sailed for Western Australia on board *Clara* on 28 January 1864.

21 DECEMBER

1877 An inquest into the death of Mary Hannah Allen of Cassington held by coroner Mr W.W. Robinson returned a verdict of 'wilful murder' against her former suitor, Henry 'Harry' Rowles.

Rowles was a strong-willed, somewhat unstable young man with a fearsome temper and a fondness for drink. Mary's grandfather begged her to find a more appropriate beau and in July 1977, Mary dropped Rowles in favour of a young man from Bladon. However, Rowles was most unhappy and devoted a lot of time and energy trying to win back Mary's affections.

On 14 December 1877, he spent the day in a pub in Islip before walking to Cassington to see Mary. He so upset her that her grandfather went to a local magistrate the following day to ask for protection against him.

Meanwhile, Rowles visited a pub in Yarnton before walking to Cassington again, where he continued drinking in The Red Lion. He sent a message to
Mary, who refused to see to him, but he went to her home regardless and shot her dead. A neighbour heard the sound of gunshots and bravely walked Rowles to the police station at Eynsham, where Rowles surrendered his gun and handed himself in.

Rowles appeared at the Oxford Assizes on 13 March 1878 and, since he was caught holding the proverbial smoking gun, the main consideration for the jury was the question of his sanity at the time of the shooting. Although numerous people testified that he had behaved oddly since childhood, that he seemed completely mad in the aftermath of the murder, that he had apparently suffered an epileptic fit in the police station after his arrest, and that he was delusional, the jury found

The Red Lion, Cassington. (© N. Sly)

Above: The church at Cassington where Mary Allen is buried. (Author's collection)

Right: Mary Allen's grave, Cassington churchyard. (Author's collection)

him guilty with no rider on insanity, although they did recommend mercy on the grounds of provocation suffered by Rowles at the hands of his errant fiancée. Their recommendation was ignored and Rowles was executed on 1 April by William Marwood.

22 DECEMBER **1876** Coroner Mr W. Brunner held an inquest at the Headington Union Workhouse into the death of forty-six-year-old Elizabeth Bull. The inquest heard that, while working at a public house in the area, Elizabeth had

Headington. (Author's collection)

occasion to visit the stables where she found a dead camel that someone had disembowelled! The smell arising from the remains was so obnoxious that it made her vomit and caused her to suffer from persistent diarrhoea.

When Elizabeth died suddenly on 21 December, the coroner asked for a post-mortem examination and surgeon Mr Hitchings found that she suffered from ulceration of the lower intestine and a burst abscess in her pelvis. Although the abscess was the primary cause of death, leading to a verdict of 'death from natural causes' from the jury, Hitchings reasoned that the offensive smell may well have accelerated Elizabeth's death.

23 DECEMBER

1882 Fifteen-year-old Albert Powers of Bloxham appeared at the Banbury Quarter Sessions charged with obtaining a quantity of cigars and fuses under false pretences. He pleaded guilty and was sentenced to a month's imprisonment.

As he was taken to the cells, his mother, Ann, went to follow him down the stairs and either tripped, fainted or suffered from an epileptic fit, falling from top to bottom of the steps. She was unconscious and bleeding heavily from a wound on her forehead as her husband picked her up and carried her to the guard room.

Dr Griffin was in court and, having examined Mrs Powers, he pronounced her dead. Fortunately, he was somewhat premature as Mrs Powers gradually came round and was eventually well enough to be taken home in a cab. She is believed to have survived her near-death experience.

Little Bridge Road, Bloxham. (Author's collection)

24 DECEMBER

1874 The train from London to Oxford, Birmingham and the North was packed with people going to spend Christmas with their families.

As the train neared Shipton-on-Cherwell, a metal tire on a third-class carriage broke, causing it to leave the rails. It skidded along for some 300 yards before swerving left down a 20ft embankment.

The carriage was 'smashed to atoms' and the following carriages plunged after it. 'The crimsoned snow on the brink of the embankment told terribly what was to be expected of an inspection of the carriage . . . blood and brains were bespattered all over the interior, interspersed with portions of human hair and on the floor, amid the wreck of wood and torn cushions, the broken glass lay stiffly frozen in blood,' reported a contemporary newspaper.

Local people pitched in to help the wounded and the dead were taken to nearby Hampton Gay Paper Mill to await identification. When the rescue operation was complete, there were thirty-four fatalities, with a further sixty-nine people injured.

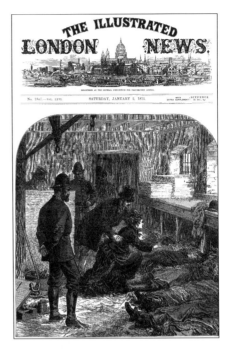

Identifying the dead at Hampton Gay Paper Mill following the railway accident at Shipton-on-Cherwell.

An inquiry into the accident discovered that, once the driver was alerted to the presence of the broken tire by a passenger, he applied the brakes and reversed the engine. Unfortunately, the carriages did not slow down and the third-class carriage was crushed by the weight of those behind, which then jumped off the rails in consequence. Had the driver shut off the steam and applied the brakes gradually, it was believed that the accident could have been avoided.

25 DECEMBER

1844 Two young men walking along the banks of the River Cherwell at Grimsbury noticed a hole in the ice, with a boy's cap floating on the water. The men raised the alarm and before long the bodies of brothers Job and George Eaglestone, aged twelve and fourteen, were pulled from the water.

The two boys had been sent to deliver a gig to Banbury and were returning on foot. They were accompanied by seventeen-year-old John Green, who lived next door to their home in Wardington and, since Green was missing, locals began dragging the river, continuing until nightfall. Green's body was recovered when the dragging recommenced at first light the next day.

An inquest heard that the three boys had been seen sliding on the ice near Grimsbury Mill by a little boy, who tried to join them. However, one of the Eaglestone boys had shouted at him, calling him 'mutton head' and he had decided not to play after all. The inquest jury returned a verdict of 'accidentally drowned' on all three victims, the coroner remarking that it was extremely fortunate that there hadn't been a fourth.

Note: There are some discrepancies between various accounts of the tragedy in respect of the names of the Eaglestone brothers. They are variously referred to as Jacob, Job, Joshua, John and George. Official records indicate that their correct names were Job and George.

26 DECEMBER

1890 Seventy-five-year-old James Shouler died at Littlemore Asylum, where he was a patient.

On Christmas Day, he was dozing comfortably by the fire when he was called to the tea table. Shouler, who was a rather irritable man, rudely indicated with a profanity that he was quite happy where he was and had no intention of moving. Attendant Frederick Bradbury went to 'persuade' Shouler to have his tea but Shouler picked up two large spoons and threw them at Bradbury. As he picked up a third, Bradbury tried to take it from him and the two men wrestled, falling onto the floor. Eventually, Shouler was physically carried to the table, where he ate his tea without further protest.

After Shouler's death, a post-mortem examination revealed that he had two dislocated ribs and an 'extraversion of blood' in his chest. However, the actual cause of his death was peritonitis, resulting from a very small hole in his intestines.

Coroner Mr Robinson held an inquest on Shouler's death, at which Bradbury downplayed the amount of physical force used in getting Shouler to the tea table. Inmate John Luckett, who assisted Bradbury to carry Shouler, stated that the warder knelt on Shouler and banged his head on the floor, prompting Shouler to protest, 'Why do you use an old fellow like me in this manner?' According to Luckett, Bradbury also boxed Shouler's ears.

The Asylum chaplain suggested that Luckett had been coached by another inmate and consequently his evidence was not reliable. The inquest jury returned an open verdict of 'death from peritonitis' and although they stopped short of blaming Bradbury, they recommended that he should be cautioned against using more force than necessary in dealing with his charges.

27 DECEMBER

1874 An inquest was held into the death of butcher's boy Andrew Alfred East, who was sent out to deliver meat around Barrington and Windrush on 26 December, with his employer's seven-year-old son for company. Near Burford, Andrew's pony and trap passed labourer Edwin Moss and soon afterwards, Moss heard a child crying for help.

Moss ran towards the sound and found an overturned trap. Andrew East lay dead, the wheel of the vehicle crushing his chest, while his young companion sat bawling in a snowdrift some distance away, fortunately unhurt.

East was a steady, reliable young man and the pony he was driving was normally very quiet. At the inquest, his employer's son stated that the pony had shied at something and one of the wheels of the trap went up onto a snowdrift at the side of the road, upsetting the vehicle, which then fell over. Andrew was crushed beneath it, while his young passenger was thrown clear, landing in a snowdrift, which cushioned his fall. The inquest jury returned a verdict of 'accidental death'.

28 DECEMBER   **1942**   A Wellington bomber flew fast and low across the village of Bodicote, before crashing into an elm tree in a valley near the church, killing all six occupants.

The plane – a training craft – was piloted by twenty-two-year-old Flying Officer John Gordon Byrne and records suggest that the purpose of the flight was to test his fitness to fly. Also on board were Flight Sergeant William McMillan (26), Canadian Flight Sergeant Jack Thompson McDonald (26), Leading Aircraftman Leslie Hamilton Nicholson and Aircraftmen 2nd Class John Ernest George Beaumont (19), and Granville Broadhurst (19), all of whom died instantly.

There were various theories about the cause of the crash, although none proved definitive. Witnesses who saw the plane immediately prior to the accident believed that one engine was smoking, although this could have been an exhaust trail. The weather was bad and there was no wireless operator on board, leading to suggestions that the pilot dipped below the low cloud because he wasn't sure where he was and wanted to get his bearings. Yet the plane was flying on a direct route to an airbase, suggesting that the pilot was well aware of his position.

It has also been suggested that the pilot experienced difficulties while trying to land the plane and deliberately chose to crash in the countryside in order to spare the lives of the villagers of Bodicote.

Vickers Wellington bombers. (Author's collection)

29 DECEMBER   **1873**   Keziah Morrey gave birth to a baby boy at Neithrop. Throughout her pregnancy, Keziah lived with coal heaver John Evans but the couple made no preparation whatsoever for their child's birth and Keziah refused to go into the Workhouse for her confinement. When she went into labour, Evans waited eight hours before calling a midwife.

The baby was born dead and an inquest held by coroner Mr C. Duffell Faulkner heard that there was no food in the house and not a stick of furniture, apart from an old mattress on the floor on which Keziah gave birth.

Surgeon Mr Hudson was of the opinion that the baby's life could have been saved if it had received the proper treatment at birth. The inquest jury returned a verdict of 'stillborn' and, after berating Evans for his manner of living, the coroner bemoaned the fact that there did not appear to be any offence with which Evans or Morrey could be charged, adding that it was lamentable that such gross conduct and inhuman treatment was not punishable by law.

30 DECEMBER

1868   PC Thomas Hawtin was on patrol on the road between Thame and Towersey when he came across uncle and nephew Robert and Frederick Cox. Hawtin stopped the two men and found that Robert was carrying a bag containing poaching nets.

As soon as the nets were discovered, Robert Cox bolted, pursued by his nephew and the constable. The chase finally ended in some allotments at Thame but, when he tried to arrest Robert, Hawtin was knocked down and pinned to the floor.

'Frederick Cox, I call upon you in the name of the Queen to aid and assist in apprehending Robert Cox for an assault,' Hawtin called to Frederick, who was standing about 20 yards distant. However, Frederick made no effort to come to Hawtin's aid and it was eventually left to a member of the public to help.

The pursuit had attracted a number of spectators and, when Frederick Cox appeared at the Oxfordshire Lent Assizes in 1869 charged with refusing to aid and assist a police constable, all of the witnesses denied as one having heard Hawtin ask for help. The jury found Cox not guilty and he was discharged without penalty.

31 DECEMBER

1899   As fifteen-year-old farm servant Alice Hine was out walking at Chacombe, twenty-six-year-old labourer John Scarsbrook suddenly leaped out of some bushes and knocked her over. Scarsbrook then flung himself on top of Alice and fumbled about under her clothing, leaping to his feet when her terrified screams brought two railway labourers running to her assistance.

Charged with indecent assault, Scarsbrook appeared at the Oxford Assizes in February 1900 claiming that his attack on Alice was meant as a joke and that he never intended to do her any harm. He begged the judge to treat him mercifully, since he had a wife and four children to support.

When the jury found Scarsbrook guilty the judge announced that, in view of his previous good character, he intended to deal lightly with him. Scarsbrook was sentenced to two months' hard labour, the judge apparently giving no consideration to the likely consequences for Alice but for the fortuitous presence of the two labourers.

BIBLIOGRAPHY

Books

Brindley, Giles, *Oxford: Crime, Death and Debauchery*, Stroud, Sutton Publishing (2006)

Jerome, Jerome K., *Three Men in a Boat*, Bristol, J.W. Arrowsmith (1909)

Newspapers

Banbury Guardian

Illustrated Police News

Jackson's Oxford Journal

London Evening Post

Morning Post

Oxford Chronicle

Oxford Mail

Oxford Times

Reading Evening Post

St James's Gazette

The Guardian / Manchester Guardian

The Times

INDEX